Sensibility and Creation

STUDIES IN TWENTIETH-CENTURY FRENCH POETRY

EDITED BY ROGER CARDINAL

CROOM HELM LONDON

BARNES & NOBLE BOOKS · NEW YORK
(a division of Harper & Row Publishers, Inc.)

© 1977 Roger Cardinal

Croom Helm Ltd
2-10 St John's Road, London, SW11

ISBN 0–85664–339–4

Published in the U.S.A. 1977 by
Harper & Row Publishers, Inc.
Barnes & Noble Import Division

ISBN 0–06–490957–3

LC 76–40876

Printed and bound in Great Britain by
REDWOOD BURN LIMITED
Trowbridge & Esher

CONTENTS

ACKNOWLEDGEMENTS

We wish to express our thanks to Çaroline Bailey, Dave Kelley and Linden Stafford for contributing to our discussions; to Jill Godfrey, whose unpublished dissertation on Jacques Dupin was most helpful; to Madame Follain for allowing access to certain unpublished material; and to Mrs Alys Jones, Dora Musi, Mrs Lisbeth Owens, Priscilla Sheringham and Mrs M. H. Windle for their valuable assistance with correspondence and the typing of scripts.

INTRODUCTION

The poet moves in a world drawn into meaningful focus by the workings of his sensibility and his imagination. The subjectivity receives certain incoming signals which in large part orientate the creative impulse: the written poem emerges as the record of a series of responses which define the relation of self to world, and will constitute, within the alternative space of literature, a register of the meanings which external reality from time to time yields to the patient pursuer. Approaching phenomena with his senses on the alert, the poet attends to things to which apparently he does not belong, and attains to an intimacy, an affinity, whence he is able to deduce a sense.

This kind of conception of the poetic sensibility was first given decisive definition by Baudelaire, who envisaged sensations as so many tokens of an underlying meaningfulness, the external world being a 'magasin d'images et de signes auxquels l'imagination donnera une place et une valeur relative' — reality being seen, that is, as the bounteous provider of raw materials which the poet selects and arranges according to his own motives and preferences. In Baudelaire's model of the poetic consciousness, external data are not simply ordered by the creative mind but are at the same time distilled, in such a way that their original range of appeal, the purely sense-bound, is amplified so as to promote a succession of spiritual resonances within the poet's deeper being. Thus a perfume may be not just the instigator of a specifically physical response, an animation of the olfactory nerves, but equally the carrier of a whole wealth of possible meanings perceptible to what we might think of as an extension of the nervous system into the psychic domain: as though the scent, after passing up the narrow olfactory pathway, came upon a disproportionately vast area of dilation within the percipient's mind. The process is most dramatically depicted in the prose poem 'Un Hémisphère dans une chevelure', where the poet's responses to the scent of his mistress's hair proliferate immeasurably — smell becoming synaesthetically allied with parallel agitations of sight, taste and hearing, as well as giving rise to extraordinary flights of fantasy and spiritual euphoria. The scent is an invitation to a reverie so expansive that this oderiferous hair may be said to encompass a whole dream universe of colour, warmth and pervasive languor.

Laisse-moi respirer longtemps, longtemps, l'odeur de tes cheveux,
y plonger tout mon visage (. . .) . Si tu pouvais savoir tout ce que
je vois! tout ce que je sens! tout ce que j'entends dans tes cheveux!
Mon âme voyage sur le parfum comme l'âme des autres hommes
sur la musique.

Tes cheveux contiennent tout un rêve, plein de voilures et de
mâtures; ils contiennent de grandes mers dont les moussons me
portent vers de charmants climats, où l'espace est plus bleu et plus
profond, où l'atmosphère est parfumée par les fruits, par les
feuilles et par la peau humaine.

The process of transmutation whereby the physical stimulus acts as the
point of departure for an ecstatic voyage of the mind operates so
smoothly as to make undeniably immediate and real to the reader's
own sensibility the connections posited between the sense datum, its
'horizontal' extension across other orders of sensation, and its 'vertical'
extension into the sphere of spiritual connotations. In establishing the
credibility of a *correspondance*, or analogical affinity, between these
different categories of experience, Baudelaire was able to orchestrate
the different themes issuing from perception, emotion and imagination
and create a polyphony so subtle, so seductive that in the end the
separate melodic lines merge into a perfect harmonic continuum.

The resonances of Baudelaire's evocations of 'les transports de
l'esprit et des sens' echo through the poetry that followed. With
Rimbaud, the exploration of extreme sensations, pursued to the
point of visual hallucination and physiological disorders, prepared the
way for invented as against actual perceptual impressions, and gave
rise to a poetry fertilized concurrently, and in almost equal measure,
by sensory vividness and pure verbal energy. Of this the poet once felt
moved to boast that he had invented 'un verbe poétique accessible,
un jour ou l'autre, à tous les sens'. Mallarmé moved in another direction,
adamant in the belief that the poet's task was to construct a Great
Work to dispel the accidents of the universe and nullify the contingen-
cies which contact with phenomena entails. His citadel of pure poetry
is erected upon a foundation of denied sensation — sensation, that is,
purified to the point of negation. Thus, to take but one example
amongst many, his way of rendering a bedroom with a lace curtain at
the window is to filter off all substance and all features, 'abolishing'
the curtain and 'absentifying' the bed, so that they linger on in the
poem only as negative thoughts, not as presences.

Une dentelle s'abolit
Dans le doute du Jeu suprême
A n'entr'ouvrir comme un blasphème
Qu'absence éternelle de lit.

It was in order to escape from the Symbolist tradition of indirectness
and tenuousness, which had dominated his earlier work, that Guillaume
Apollinaire, in the first poem of the boldly innovatory *Calligrammes*,
announced a return to sensory sources:

J'écris seulement pour vous exalter
O sens ô sens chéris
Ennemis du souvenir
Ennemis du désir

Over-hasty though it is in its dismissal of the private dimensions of
memory and desire, this proclamation represents a forceful indication
of the readiness of the modern poet to refer to his actual perception
of immediate reality when he tries, in Yves Bonnefoy's phrase, to
'donner un sens à ce qui est'. While it would be an exaggeration to say
that poets since Apollinaire have all followed this call to exploit sensa-
tion as a poetic property, it is true that a climate of attentiveness to
the sensible world has become firmly established within modern French
poetry.
     A corresponding climate has been encouraged in recent years by the
work of certain French critics who, in responding to the direction taken
by modern poetry, have also laid the bases for a critical approach to
literature at large. In his book *De Baudelaire au surréalisme*, Marcel
Raymond looked on poetry as a system of applied intuitions that deals
with external phenomena in order to set out man's deeper feelings
about existence in the form of poetic imagery. He advocates a respect-
ful yet profound investigation of the nature of the poet's 'concret
psychique', that private space wherein sensation comes to fruition as
poetic form. The penetrating researches into the creative mind made by
Gaston Bachelard opened up a whole new map for literary criticism
upon which a given writer could be situated according to the arche-
typal element — fire, air, water, earth — to which his imagination was
drawn, or rather: whose nature most consistently reflected its motions.
Bachelard's phenomenology of the imagination offers a wealth of
insights to the reader of any poetry, propelled by the central idea that
reverie is not an idle retreat from life but a dynamic activity which

re-integrates man in the cosmic scheme from which abstract thought tends to alienate him. Georges Poulet brought to the critical task an urgent sense of the need to catch the moment when the shape of a work first begins to arise out of nothingness within the author's mind. The point of departure of his criticism is the establishment of the writer's primary ontological act, the *cogito* of self-apprehension whence proceeds consciousness of the world beyond the self. Finally, Jean-Pierre Richard approached literature on the assumption that this moment of becoming conscious implies a passage from a prior stage of sensory contact with the world to the stage of creative apprehension in which intelligence and imagination engage with the raw material of sensation and pre-critical reverie. His presentations of poets in books such as *Onze Etudes sur la poésie moderne* amount to a laying-out of each poet's distinctive themes and images — recurrent shapes, textures, qualities, sensations and the like — in patterns which are then available to us as models of that poet's total expressive sensibility. Each of these critics adumbrates in his own way a style of regarding poems according to which the experience of the literary work is appreciated as a function of sensibility. Criticism of this type, whether it be called *critique de la conscience*, phenomenological criticism or thematic criticism, is broadly to be understood as a mode of reading and responding to a literary text which seeks to honour the intrinsic processes, both sensory and imaginative, whence that text arose — or which that text embodies as an emblem of their vitality. It is above all an endeavour to treat poems as living organisms and to study both the circumstances of their genesis and the way they grow in meaningfulness for us.

To investigate the modern poet's favourite things or elective sensations may therefore be a convenient way to assess the overall character of his artistic sensibility and so provide the reader with a useful view of the *modus operandi* of the poetic consciousness. But if the poem is a net which filters the data of experience and reveals to us a constellation of images and impressions peculiar to a given sensibility, it is also equally a system of literary functions, a network of signifieds characterized by a particular way of handling the signifiers, the words. Thus if the successful poem is the one which convincingly affirms, in Breton's phrase, 'la persistence de ce pont qui unit le monde extérieur au monde intérieur', it is also a deployment of rhetorical figures within the field of syntax. The patterns of a poet's sensibility and the corresponding patterns of images in his work may, at a further stage of enquiry, be found to correspond to the configurations of language, contained within the strictly textual space of the poem.

The guiding principle in this collection of studies of modern French
poets is basically simple: a recognition of the poetic process as in-
volving the self's coming to terms with the world. However, it must
at once be asserted that sensation is only one 'way in' to the poetry,
and that many considerations militate against the over-simplified
view of the poem as being stylised sensation alone. The examples of a
few of the poets discussed in this book may serve to indicate the
variety of perspectives that open up for poet and critic alike when
they consider the role of sensation in the shaping of poetry.

One might expect the Symbolist sympathies of Paul Valéry to have
encouraged a motion away and above sense-perceptions in his poetry.
The man who could invent that most abstract of heroes, Monsieur
Teste, would surely see raw sensations as anarchic and suspect, and
would need to cleanse them of all corruptive association with their
origins before allowing them to function as fuel for the intellect. Can
objects irradiate at all for Valéry? Can concrete experience have any
part to play in his dramas of pure mental life? Unexpectedly perhaps,
the poet of *conscience pure* turns out also to be a poet who appreciates
the richness of the *chaos familier* of our perceptions. In his poems, it is
fascinating to witness the moment where sensation is celebrated as the
antithesis of the ideal of Symbolist purity which elsewhere obtains as
the *raison d'être* of his literary effort. Such a moment occurs in *La
Jeune Parque* at the point where the heroine of that poem, to whose
bodily existence we are scarcely asked to give much credence, stands at
the edge of a cliff wrestling with the notion of total physical and
mental extinction, at a pitch of spiritual rapture so extreme that pure
consciousness is all but transcended into sheer nothingness. At this
dizzy limit of aspiration away from all that can be felt and thought, the
girl is all at once recalled to the reality of physical existence. On her
agonizingly self-enclosed mind there intrudes the sudden realisation
that cold salt spray is being blown across her cheek from the sea, which
heaves exultantly below her feet, bearing the urgent call back to life
that is similarly voiced in 'Le Cimetière marin': 'Il faut tenter de vivre!'.
The physical lure, perhaps because it is borne on air and is so subtle an
insinuation of sensation into consciousness, creates a stunningly
sensuous aftertaste to our reading of what is otherwise an unnervingly
pure interior monologue.

> . . . Alors n'ai-je formé, vains adieux si je vis,
> Que songes? . . . Si je viens, en vêtements ravis,
> Sur ce bord, sans horreur, humer la haute écume,
> Boire des yeux l'immense et riante amertume,
> L'être contre le vent, dans le plus vif de l'air,
> Recevant au visage un appel de la mer.

Pierre Reverdy has described the dual solicitation which the modern poet has had to face: on the one hand, the challenge of Mallarmé to strive upwards to airless heights where all sensation is eclipsed, and the other that of Rimbaud to track one's way downhill into the obscure gulf of the blood, over which fleshly sensation holds full sway. It seems that Reverdy experienced the two solicitations with equal violence, and in a sense was able to draw artistic stimulation from the anguish that this conflict created in him. As a young man, he sought to maintain his distance and to allow his mind to reflect the external world only to the extent that perception might serve as a springboard to higher truth: what he calls *le réel* is perceptible to the mind alone, and is indeed determined by the poet rather than deduced from the data received from outside. In time, however, Reverdy shifted from this 'Cubist' position of being the arranger of select elements of reality within an aesthetic frame which effectively protects the poetry against the encroachments of the perceptible world, and took up a more open, perhaps less arrogant attitude. Late in his career he was moved to speak of the revealed relation between phenomena – the armature or fibre of the Real – as not simply a determination of the mind, but an actual, existing relation which it is the poet's function simply to *register*. Reverdy's recognition of the full status of sensation found expression in this poetic programme, formulated in *Le Livre de mon bord*:

> Jouir d'appliquer la plasticité de son intelligence sensible à tous
> les contours, à toutes les aspérités, à tous les creux de la
> réalité. Epouser toutes les formes jusqu'à l'identité. Les couleurs,
> la lumière, et les parfums, le soleil, les paysages, les gens dans les
> attitudes de leur destination. Remplir de son esprit et de sa
> sensibilité l'abîme vertigineux de la distance. La délicieuse
> souffrance de la séparation . . .

Here the willingness to let poetry arise out of the contact of the sensibility with the sharpest aspects of external existence is conveyed in

terms which hint at an almost mystical absorption in the being of
things. Reverdy's problem, however, is that he can never guarantee
a lasting coincidence of the self with what lies beyond the self; he
seems to take an almost masochistic pleasure in the recognition of how
wide the gulf can be that separates phenomena from the conscious-
ness that strives to merge with them.

Many writings by André Breton are devoted to an exploration of
his sensibility, and chronicle those moments where subjectivity en-
counters objectivity in an intense and meaningful way. Breton will
often note things down in the form of affective lists wherein each
item marks a point on the graph of his sensibility: the resultant curve
delineates the exact perimeter of his taste and receptivity to a particu-
lar order of experience. Examples of this occur in the poem 'Sur la
route de San Romano', where the poet several times turns from his
intellectual argument that poetry asserts itself independently, defying
all that is anti-lyrical — 'Elle a l'espace qu'il lui faut (. . .)/ Elle a tout
le temps devant elle' — to enlarge on the point by letting the space of
the poem itself swell with catalogues of favourite perceptual
experiences. Here is one of them:

> Les figures de danse exécutées en transparence au-dessus
>   des mares
> La délimitation contre un mur d'un corps de femme au lancer
>   de poignards
> Les volutes claires de la fumée
> Les boucles de tes cheveux
> La courbe de l'éponge des Philippines
> Les lacés du serpent corail
> L'entrée du lierre dans les ruines

This sequence of seven talismanic percepts suggests a general message
in that the common denominator would appear to be the sinuosity of
each shape alluded to — the looping figures of a dance (the
reference might be to dragonflies darting over a stagnant pond,
possibly even to a skater on ice), the contours of a woman's body,
spirals of smoke, the curl of a woman's hair, the curvature of a
sponge, the intertwining of a snake's coils, the convolutions of plant
tendrils. An impression of precise outlines, of a specific focus upon
these particular events suggests that they stand as a kind of corporate
metaphor for a particular facet of poetic experience for Breton: they
constitute an *argument through images*. But this argument, nurtured as

it is by sensory experience and imaginative response alike, is infinitely
more complex than any abstract statement Breton might have made.
The lines may be read as a sequence of noun-phrases in apposition,
and once one lingers over them, there is a whole proliferation of
relations and interactions to account for. The separate percepts now
seem similar, now dissimilar; now to cohere, now to conflict.
Semantic currents engender a fluent interplay of meanings that sets
the mind's eye darting from one line to another to witness the
modifications each undergoes when read in conjunction with a con-
tiguous or more distant one. For instance, the insubstantial swirl of
smoke acts upon the curls of the woman's hair, lending them a dream-
like intangibility. The references to daggers and to the snake impart
qualities of sharpness and firmness to the ivy that might not otherwise
be atttributed to it. The woman's body carefully outlined in daggers
(the knife-thrower's attentions may seem at once violent and oddly
tender) and the curling hair make it plausible to see an oblique sexual
allusion in the last line. Other ways of apprehending the sensory
qualities of the lines release other sorts of interaction. If one
considers the sense of speed, then the swift flashing of what might be
taken to be the transparent wings of dragonflies in the opening line,
along with that of the knife-thrower's daggers, work strangely against
the slowness of the smoke and the snake, and the all but motionless
hair and ivy. Either tempo may impose itself on the other, in rotation,
and subvert our perceptual habits so that we suddenly imagine the
snake and the plant jerking rapidly; or else, see the knives travel
through the air in slow motion. Again, consideration of the texture
of each item reveals a subtly disturbing correlation of the intangible
and the sleekly sensual: elusive dragonflies and smoke as against the
softness of a tropical sponge, the warm skin of a snake from the
South seas, the leaves of a clinging plant. Another flurry of imaginary
sensations is set off: smoke caressing the skin, a sponge as soft as air.
Such refined meta-sensations represent the fertile product of readings
forever oscillating between the uniform and the discrepant. Poetry of
this sort is an adventure in words, yet above all an adventure in
meanings which the reader elicits by consulting his own sensory
system: he participates in a game which shifts all the while between the
level of verbal relationships and that of perceptual relationships.

The writings of Francis Ponge are steeped in a sober affection for
objects in the external world. Delighting in the shape, texture and
substance of things like moss, pebbles, a cigarette, a lizard, a slice of
meat, he submits to the authority of the thing itself, anxious to avoid

imposing his own demands upon it. What he prizes is the self-suffi-
ciency of the object, which puts human certainties to shame. The
craggy crust of a loaf, the sticky amorphousness of mud, these
seem to send out challenges which he takes up with naive fervour,
embarking in each fresh poem on a new 'voyage dans l'épaisseur des
choses', advancing by patient degrees towards the object in its
unadulterated specificity. He will for example write tenderly of the
fragile shrimp, constructing with infinite precaution a net of words
to catch the creature without endangering its essential nature. Of
course, this is not an actual capture, for however brilliant an
evocation of sense-impressions, the poetic text will inevitably remain
at a remove from the thing itself. But it can aspire to become *like*
the thing, to be as close a verbal equivalent as possible. 'Il ne s'agit
pas de "rendre", de "représenter" le monde physique', Ponge insists,
'mais de *présenter* dans le monde verbal quelque chose d'homologue'.
The ideal text will be the one that does most homage to its object by
integrating the multiple facets of perception into a homogeneous
whole whose inner structure exactly mirrors that of its physical
counterpart. Creating verbal objects which are 'poreux à la sensibilité
et à l'esprit', Ponge is engaging in a creative compromise between the
'parti pris des choses' and the 'compte tenu des mots'. On occasion
he likes to toy with the idea that language might have a materiality all
of its own, as when he reminisces about his earliest realisation of his
vocation: 'J'ai trouvé *un autre monde*, celui des vocables, des mots
(. . .) , un monde aussi réel pour moi, aussi faisant partie du monde
extérieur, aussi *physique* pour moi que la nature (. . .) elle-même'.
For such a sensibility, the substantiality of things and the density of
words maintain a balance of distinct attractions, which means that it
would be a critical caricature to see Ponge as exclusively 'the
champion of objects' or 'the champion of language'.

The twelve studies in this book represent an enquiry into modern
French poetry in terms of the issues raised above. The poets chosen
are far from being the only poets of interest or importance in this
connection: Artaud, Claudel, Deguy, Fargue, Guillevic, Jaccottet,
Jouve, Michaux and Péret are but a few of those excluded because of
limitations of space. However, the twelve poets selected offer a
variety of significant profiles and a reasonably representative sample of
styles. Thus, however incompletely, these studies form a general
introduction to the French poetry of this century, at the same time

as they reflect the specific critical perspective on the relation of sensibility to creation.

A majority of chapters treat the sensibility of the individual poet in wide-ranging terms, developing a general argument around specific examples drawn from his work. Some studies, however, apply a finer focus by concentrating on a particular theme or aspect, as with the chapters on the image of the tree-top in Valéry, that of the sun in Apollinaire and that of night in René Char, or on the sense of sight in Reverdy. Several essays, such as those on Saint-John Perse and Ponge, examine the linguistic means adopted by the poet in order to articulate the relation of self to world; while the essay on Paul Eluard presses further in considering the semantic and syntactical dimensions that open up within a poetry where images and impressions are so dependent on the reader's creative participation. It may be hoped that the combination of different poetic views on to reality, discussed in ways which vary inasmuch as they reflect the shifts of emphasis characteristic of the poets themselves, will offer some general insights into the way modern French poets write, while giving the reader new to this poetry the incentive to get to know the individual works more closely.

The central tenets of this book are, then, that there is a continuity of preoccupation within twentieth-century French poetry: that it concerns itself with problems of Being, with the relation of the subjectivity to a world more or less resistant to human interpretation; that it deals in impressions drawn from sensory experience in a way that seeks to bridge the gap between the world directly perceived and the private space of emotion and idea; that it seeks with peculiar intensity to make these accommodations by attending to the operations of language, the medium or even the modifier of experience; that, finally, it may incline to an accommodation whereby language is allowed a certain priority over sensation — though it may be argued that even the least sense-bound poet will need to make allowance for the sensory check if his images of the real are to maintain their validity. This book's point of departure in the realm of sensation will have been justified if we feel that Bonnefoy is right to assert that 'la poésie se poursuit dans l'espace de la parole, mais chaque pas en est vérifiable dans le monde réaffirmé'.

Seen from this viewpoint, the poets in this book share a family likeness. But there would be no point in writing about them separately were they not, even more strikingly, individuals with idiosyncratic ways, writers who assert themselves as sponsors of uniquely distinctive worlds. However valid our generalisations, it will be evident that the twelve poets studied are far from being all of a piece. The tender attention that Jean Follain directs to the sound of a falling hairpin; the controlled empathy that is Valéry's response to the swaying tree-top; Breton's absorption in the shimmer on a butterfly's wing; the obstinate overtures to pebble or shell that Ponge rehearses on the seashore; the reverence with which Char regards a candle-flame in the shadows; Jacques Dupin's violent grappling with a woman's body; the wistful awe with which Bonnefoy attends to the call of a bird; the strange osmosis of external and mental space that Jules Supervielle experiences when on a walk in the country; – all these are separate and irreducible responses. Authentic poets are always spontaneously themselves, and their poetry will reflect their individuality: Reverdy's drab landscapes are worlds apart from Eluard's glowing utopia, Apollinaire's miscellaneous urban scenarios are different again from Perse's aristocratic panoramas of sea, wind and snow.

It is true that convergences occur at specific points, as when both Apollinaire and Dupin explore the image of the sun in association with decapitation; or when a significant number of poets – Char, Breton, Bonnefoy and Dupin (incidentally, all writers in the surrealist orbit) – declare their allegiance to night, with all its risks and promises. The reader may trace for himself other cross-currents of this kind, though he should bear in mind that the coincidence of two minds seizing on the same image or theme is not of itself proof of a deep affinity between them: even more telling may be the different way it is handled in either case. When for instance it rains in Perse's 'Pluies', it is not the same rain that enters Ponge's 'Pluie'. The one experience is of a splendid cosmic pageant; the other of a collection of ingenious comparisons in which the rain is likened to a curtain, a clockwork mechanism, and so on. The one experience transports us, the other intrigues or amuses us.

This is but to underline the point that the import of individual moments of poetic experience will be determined by the creative sensibility intrinsic to the poet concerned. Indeed, much of the reader's excitement can derive from his awareness of an alien system of values and responses that is processing items of experience which might not normally appeal to him at all. The poet is the man who convinces us that his perceptions are important for us too: and he does this by operating in our common idiom, language, as witness Follain describing a banal scene outside his backdoor.

sur le fourneau le fer chauffait
la lentille cuisait sombre
par la porte ouverte
la beauté du feuillage amer
et des oiseaux à gorge rouge
devant les mots humains
que gouvernait une syntaxe éprouvée
resplendissait.

For it is syntax and vocabulary that finally seal the otherwise incomplete bond between self and world, as between poet and reader. The meaning that a poet's sensibility elicits from his experience of external facts is only reliably registered in the form of words. 'C'est grâce aux mots, c'est grâce au langage, c'est grâce aux images que l'homme s'approprie le monde extérieur', writes Reverdy, whose idea of reality as a system of signs to be transliterated is not very different from Baudelaire's notion of the world as a storehouse of images that imagination puts into order. The fact that poetic language thrives upon the possibility of creating analogical relations between disparate things reflects what the surrealist poets in particular see as a progression towards full imaginative participation in the world revealed through poetry, the acceptance of the continuity of mental and sensory reality. For it is through language, through the exchange of words in all their semantic and phonic fertility, that man is reconciled to the world he strives to name and to know. In this sense it is possible to speak without fear of over-dramatisation of the existential role of language for the modern poet. What Char defines in *Partage formel* as 'la communication et la libre-disposition de la totalité des choses entre elles à travers nous' is nothing less than a total existential reconciliation of man with his universe, a certainty yielded at the angle of intersection of perceptual immediacy and the defining word.

Because the stakes are so high, most poets give painstaking attention to the choice and usage of words. Perse's poetry, for example, is equipped with a rich supply of accurate technical terms derived from botany, geology and other sciences. Ponge likewise is never loath to plunder the dictionary for rare words or rare meanings of words that may help sharpen his definitions. On the other hand, it is true that poets such as Reverdy and Bonnefoy find they can define their insights through manipulating a relatively restricted and colourless range of commonplace or general words.

Many of the poets studied here are as sensitive to the sonorous virtues of words as they are to the meanings and associations they contain. Ponge's enquiry into the nature of the *cageot* is coincidentally coloured by the discovery that the word lies midway between *cage* and *cachot*. Breton's phrase 'seins de spectre de la rose sous la rosée' is born of a willingness to permit words to form spontaneous alliterative and paranomastic (similar-sounding) pacts which, later, turn out to be the generators of unsuspected semantic chains. Eluard's *poésie ininterrompue*, his maintenance of a fluid texture made up of moments of consciousness, drifting images and fragments of memory or dream experiences, is guaranteed by the interweaving of phonic with syntactical and semantic patterns, a kind of cross-stitch that knits the strands of the poetry into an uninterrupted fabric.

Engagement of any intensity with the verbal microcosm sometimes makes the real world seem remote. The poetic evocation of sensory realities in any case presupposes that they are not immediately available — otherwise the poem would be redundant. In many modern texts there persists, explicitly or implicitly, the Mallarmean notion that things are poetically appropriate in so far as they are *in absentia*, and so allow the operation of what Dupin calls 'connaissance par défaut'. The orange in Ponge's 'L'Orange', for example, is described as a substantial and tasty fruit: and although one does not *eat* 'L'Orange', the literary artifact can assert its claim on our attention so strongly that it begins to appear as an object in its own right, with its *own* kind of substance and taste. As Reverdy once wrote: 'Toute la valeur d'une œuvre est dans la saveur singulière qu'elle inaugure dans la réalité. C'est par la qu'elle prend place, au meilleur rang, parmi les choses de la réalité. Ainsi, et comme par miracle, l'oeuvre faite devient une chose réelle . . .' What if the unique verbal artifact takes on a wholly substantial 'thereness' such that it dispenses with all support from concrete reality? There is a sense in which the bird in the poem is more valuable than the bird in the bush. Supervielle for one was well aware of the capacity of verbal fantasy to stabilise its own immanence, to the point where imaginary fictions become as powerful and solid as anything concrete. And to the extent that all phenomena are mediated through our subjective responses to them, it is not surprising that people of heightened sensibility should sometimes isolate response from stimulus and then generate new responses independently of outside stimuli, as in some private park walled off from the jungle of phenomenal immediacy. The reader who ventures into this closed area, the space of the poetic text, may find not real sensations faithfully transcribed or skilfully distilled, but what amounts to a play of 'abstract' sensations, the ghostly counterparts to real ones, whose existence is backed up only by the degree of 'substantiality' that may be attributed to language. A writer like Eluard will calmly assure us of his faith in this meta-reality. 'Je n'invente pas les mots. Mais j'invente des objets, des êtres, des événements et mes sens sont capables de les percevoir (. . .) S'il me fallait douter de cette réalité, plus rien ne me serait sûr . . .' The poet's enticing line

> Ta chevelure d'oranges dans le vide du monde

is confirmation of his ability to combine impressions of vivid colour and sensual tactility with a feeling that the rest of the sensory world is eclipsed. This hair belongs to a woman whose reality is precisely commensurate with the words in which she is conjured up.

If in the range of poets studied here, there is an oscillation between two contrary positions — on the one hand, the view that a poetic image encapsulates a sample of phenomenal experience; on the other that it embodies something akin to an idea or an abstract value — there is also a marked tendency to attempt to reconcile these extremes. Thus Char provides us with a verbal flash of lightning which is something which we should feel no reluctance about responding to as a frightening, though exhilarating *experience*, on a par with our experience of real lightning, and equally as an exhilarating *idea*, a signal of abrupt illumination and of intense insight into the obscure being of things. Bonnefoy similarly stresses the capacity of perceptual entities to act as containers of metaphorical meanings relating to metaphysical truth. His referential vocabulary is so designed as to allow for an intermingling of the concrete and the universal, the here-and-now of sensation and the transcendent meaning released through the poetic formula, such that the reader may receive the abstract term *immortel* as though it were a concrete one, and so truly savour 'dans le lierre et partout, la substantielle immortalité'.

We may conclude that the purpose of poetry is to negotiate a concord between the activities of reflecting the world perceived and projecting the world imagined. In the interval between world and self which Dupin suggests must be exploited rather than abolished, the sparks of language connect reality to mind and generate the marvellous light wherein we can perceive what he calls 'l'intégration de la nature à la substance poétique'. All of which must surely be an encouragement to the reader of the poets studied here to approach their work in a spirit of availability to a whole range of resonances, from the senses across the emotions to the intellect, and to develop that 'sympathie pénétrante' which Marcel Raymond sees as the pre-condition of true participation in the movement and meaning of poems. If, as Ponge puts it, language is man's shell, then we should not remain stubbornly with our head inside it, but emerge into the world to which language gives us access. By the same token, we should beware of remaining for too long inside the enclosure of criticism. That this collection of studies comprises a high proportion of quotations is to be taken as an invitation to the reader to venture out further into the poems themselves.

Roger Cardinal

1 VALERY AND THE IMAGE OF THE TREE-TOP

Christine M. Crow

There is a naïve view of poetry according to which the world is on one side and the poet on the other, and language is simply the instrument for expressing what the poet sees. Branches tossing at the top of a tree, for instance. What simpler, when we come to this word-picture in a poem, than to assume that somebody — the poet — has 'seen' such a phenomenon and recorded it in words?

Even brief reflection begins to reveal the inadequacy of such a view, and Valéry spent years amazing himself, one might almost say inspiring himself, with the complexity of the problem, the problem of the nature of artistic expression and thus of the relation between language, the self and the external world which poetry seems to reveal in one of its most startling and fundamental forms. Why branches at the top of a tree, for example? Already the tree in a poem reveals a privileged existence in that it has been selected from a multitude of other objects and is therefore partly the record of an act of personal choice. Meanwhile the tree in a landscape has the obvious 'advantage' over the tree in a poem in that it has a reality to the perceiver independent of the pre-structured notion of a tree triggered off by the word. What attitude will the poet adopt to the inevitably verbal nature of his creation in a poem? Will he accept the purely approximative nature of words and use them obliquely to convey or refer to an experience of tossing branches? Will he be content to let the realities of words themselves take the initiative? Or will he find some means of making his words double back on themselves, take stock of their own fragmenting role in the wholeness of experience from which they were initially derived?

Obviously it would be possible to build up a more and more complex picture along these interrogative lines, the advisability of basing any critical response to poetry on the idea of a straightforward equation between language, the self and the external world diminishing as one realizes the inevitable interdependence of these elements in the first place. Indeed, one would not have to pursue such an enquiry very much further before establishing just how misleading it might be to assume that the tree in a poem springs, even indirectly, from some one actual experience of a tree in the real world which the poet is attempting to recreate. This would surely be not only to underestimate

the inventive fertility of the creative imagination a poem makes
manifest, but also to deny the potential capacity of a poetic image
— say the image of the tree-top — to explore or embody the creative
imagination itself. Such problems are relevant to the appreciation of
all poetry to a certain degree. Rather than pursue them further as such,
I shall try to discover how far Valéry's own highly developed awareness
of their nature seems actually to affect the type of poetry he wrote.
What attitude to language or to the relation between language and the
sensation of living seems to be most frequently reflected in Valéry's
poetic use of words? What type of poetry is possible to a mind as
critically aware as his of the seductions and the inadequacies of
language itself?

To suggest possible openings to this subject, I have chosen to
concentrate on Valéry's treatment, in *La Jeune Parque* and a few of
the poems of *Charmes*, mainly 'Au Platane', of a particular theme,
motif or set of related images, centred, as already hinted, on branches
tossing against the sky at the top of a tree.

There are several reasons why this particular theme lends itself to
such an enquiry. First, the fact that it occurs in not only one, but in
several major poems, suggests that it had a particular appeal to
Valéry's imagination and thus a particularly important role in the
architecture of his poetic universe. Because it combines visual stimulus
with an intricate analogical network of ideas and emotions, the region
at the top of the tree seems to act as a centralising focus to the imagina-
tion and thus to invite an appreciation of metaphor and analogy not
simply as figures of speech external to what is being said in the poem,
but as modes of being by which the poet may suggest the creative
imagination as being operative outside words themselves. Secondly,
the recurrence of the tree-top idea makes it possible to appreciate the
way in which Valéry may vary the same basic set of word patterns
to express the shifting mental attitudes which may accompany the
same 'moment' of human experience, the way in which he constantly
varies the perceptual framework of his images themselves. So deeply
embedded is the tree/sky locus in the act of imaginative perception
with its various degrees of detachment and involvement at the heart
of Valéry's poetry, that it can hardly be called a mere theme at all,
but rather a 'source', a source of creative self-reflective imagination
renewing itself perpetually in contact with the interaction of external
reality and inner experience, the centre of what Bachelard calls 'une
activité poétique idéative et rêveuse'.[1] And with typical self-awareness
of his own imaginative 'obsessions', Valéry came — as we learn from

his notebooks — to treat the tree consciously in this way.[2]

> L'étonnant printemps rit, viole . . . On ne sait d'où
> Venu? Mais la candeur ruisselle à mots si doux
> Qu'une tendresse prend la terre à ses entrailles . . .
> Les arbres regonflés et recouverts d'écailles
> Chargés de tant de bras et de trop d'horizons,
> Meuvent sur le soleil leurs tonnantes toisons,
> Montent dans l'air amer avec toutes leurs ailes
> De feuilles par milliers qu'ils se sentent nouvelles . . .
> N'entends-tu pas frémir ces noms aériens,
> O Sourde! . . . Et dans l'espace accablé de liens,
> Vibrant de bois vivace infléchi par la cime,
> Pour et contre les dieux ramer l'arbre unanime,
> La flottante forêt de qui les rudes troncs
> Portent pieusement à leurs fantasques fronts,
> Aux déchirants départs des archipels superbes,
> Un fleuve tendre, ô Mort, et caché sous les herbes?
>
> (*La Jeune Parque*, P.I, 103)[3]

On a purely thematic level, this is a point of dilemma and transition in the Parque's inner monologue, a point where two apparently conflicting urges — the urge towards self-annihilation and the urge towards self-renewal — begin to proceed forward into a complex synthesis of instincts and attitudes. Made aware of the conflicting needs of her being through identification with the coming of spring and its effect on the trees, the Parque sets in motion the potential resolution of her dilemma by conscious appeal to herself, in the form of an address to death, to respond and listen to the movement in time she senses around her in the natural world.

Of the imagery central to this passage — the imagery of the trees bursting up into the sky with the force of the spring sap within them — Valéry has said that it was in a sense grafted on to the primary structure of the poem in order to 'soften' the work by the addition of sexuality (P.I, 1621). As he hints himself, this by no means implies, however, that the passage is less central or important. On the contrary, it is possible to suggest that by bringing in an image of such imaginative significance to himself personally, Valéry was invigorating the poem with a depth it might otherwise have lacked, using the tree image as a 'transformer' through which the fictitious development of the poem — the growth or modulation of the heroine's consciousness in the course of a night — might be deepened and extended in human range. Perhaps it was this kind of universalising subjectivity he had in mind when he referred to *La Jeune Parque* as 'une autobiographie par la forme'.

By making the whole movement of the poem with its general themes of life and death coincide with the structuring activity of an individual mind, he was writing the 'autobiography' of human consciousness: his own, the reader's, the Parque's. It's all one. From the point of view of most interest here, such a close cohabitation of formal and thematic structure implies that the various analogical devices through which the tree image is presented — in this case varying degrees of personificatory metaphor and simile — have a dynamic role to play in the overall meaning of the poem.

One of the main sources of unity in the drama of self-integration acted out in this passage is, in fact, personification, a sensitive device which enables Valéry to reflect the way in which a mental state — in this case the near-identification set up in the Parque's semi-conscious mind between her own dilemma (simultaneous acceptance and rejection of the force of her own awakening sexuality and involvement in life) and the effect of the coming of spring to the trees — fluctuates from the point of view of the degree of detachment and involvement available within the process of identification or projection itself. The Parque's mind discovers its own reaction in the object of its perception, brings to bear on the object a renewed self-awareness, and so on, the image of the trees acting in this highly charged field of inner and outer relationships as the catalyst or 'révélateur'[4] of the central thread of herself.

'L'arbre beau, grand, me semble mon propre bras dressé', Valéry once noted of what is obviously a very similar process of empathy or semi-identification between self and object; and he goes on to generalise about this vital imaginative capacity which belongs, consciously or not, to all human experience: 'L'homme est une chose qui voit un arbre, y lit son propre bras dressé, enfante un geste, une force, une colère, une victoire et de cet arbre fait un drame sur le moment' (*Cahiers* I, 334). This being so, it is obvious that we can expect the mental processes poetically embodied in the tree passage of *La Jeune Parque* to come very close to those of which as an artist Valéry was particularly conscious in himself in the presence of trees, but with the important difference — and this is, of course, one of the reasons why the work of art can never be rewardingly approached as a mere vehicle for personally preferred modes of imaginative vision — that the poem handles with critical control and impartiality on the part of the poet those very processes which in the case of the Parque are only semi-conscious and uncontrolled. In other words, it is as if the tree passage in the poem gives the reader (and Valéry himself as the reader of his own poem) the chance to look back from a standpoint of achieved serenity and order through the adventure of self-awareness by which such order is achieved, the Parque embodying an earlier stage of consciousness — the 'fate' of human consciousness in general, as her name suggests — which the artist holds within himself, but which he is always potentially beyond. Indeed, whereas to the reader the trees in the poem indicate an articulate world of shared human experience, to the Parque they are the forms towards which her consciousness surfaces from the trauma of previously disorganised experience.[5] It is her own imagination which projects them on to the dark screen of her consciousness — the symbolic night of the spatial and temporal décor of the poem — and her own power of inner organisation and endurance which enables them, dark figments of the unconscious struggling towards daylight, to shine out like real trees in real sunshine in the darkness of herself. To perceive the trees of the real world in the way he does poetically, Valéry too must have surfaced from such inner turmoil[6]; here it is as if he uses the triumphant image of real trees to explore retrospectively the inner processes from which such visions were achieved.

Closer analysis of the personificatory element in the passage reveals the presence of various closely related analogies which wind in and out of each other with a vigour and urgency which reflects in itself the Parque's state of mind and thus a unity of experience which is never disrupted despite the apparently chaotic kaleidoscopic flicker of the constantly changing relationships within it. In the first place, the foliage and branches of the trees are endowed metaphorically with human, or half human, half animal physical attributes: arms, for instance ('chargés de tant de bras'), hair or fleece ('leurs tonnantes toisons'), wings ('avec toutes leurs ailes') and foreheads ('leurs fantas-ques fronts'). Within this dense analogical framework, based more often than not on a sense of visual comparison leading in turn to the emotive or conceptual (the outstretched branches of the trees *look* like arms, for example, and suggest simultaneously the emotion or idea of loneliness and longing felt by the Parque herself in the action of perceptive comparison), are further analogies springing from an all-embracing, almost visceral identification between the Parque and the trees; and indeed the feeling of a mind not yet fully in coincidence

with its own freedom but in the process of perpetual self-discovery
in the face of nature (the poem is in a sense a demonstrated definition
of consciousness on the part of Valéry) is reinforced by the fact that
the sense of logical comparison on which all the analogies are based
is kept purely implicit, almost as if the analogies were imposing them-
selves from within. Thus throughout the passage strongly physical or
emotive words such as on the one hand 'regonflés', 'entrailles', 'recou-
verts d'écailles', 'chargés de tant de bras', and on the other 'candeur',
'tendresse', 'se sentent nouvelles', 'frémir' allow a parallelism to be
set up between the half threatening, half fascinating force of her own
bodily and sexual experience as it surfaces to the Parque's conscious-
ness, and the single regenerative force at work in the trees. Through
such a fluid handling of the tree image in terms of implicit personific-
atory analogy, Valéry can suggest the complex attitude of a human
consciousness to its own inner contradictions, the mixed feeling of fate
and autonomy experienced by the individual self as it steers its way
through time.

A second set of analogies interwoven in the passage concerns the
idea of sound, or at least of meaningful discourse on the part of the
trees. In a sense this is, of course, a fantasy — a fantasy springing
up once more, on the level of the narrative viewpoint of the poem,
from a confusion between an actual characteristic of the trees and the
'humanising' imagination projecting into nature its own dilemmas and
needs. 'N'entends-tu pas frémir ces noms aériens,/O Sourde! . . .',
says the Parque, calling on that side of herself which identifies with
death to 'hear' the 'message' of the branches, or rather the message
she appears to hear in her mind's ear at the sight of the leaves and
branches with their invisible life. At points like this, Valéry's imagery
is at its most imaginatively ambiguous and thus most thought-provoking.
Is there, for example, any actual sound on the part of the trees such as
the rustling of leaves in the wind? The word 'tonnantes' is, of course,
a sound word, but the magnification of sound in such a term suggests
mental rather than purely aural perception. Or is the Parque at the same
time hearing the 'thundering' of her own blood in her ears and blend-
ing this internally experienced sound with the trees she is 'visualising'
as an anticipation of the coming of spring? In any case — and all
imaginatively logical interpretations are of course possible with such
suggestive imagery — her injunction to herself to 'hear' or respond to
what her own mind has partly created, is a moving example of Valéry's
poetic vindication of the power of human intelligence to create as well
as to seek order in experience, to make use of 'fantasies' at the same

time as being sufficiently detached to be aware of them as such. This is
not the only case where his poetry makes us sense that all our percep-
tions of nature − not simply the anthropomorphic − are in a sense
'fantasies', but 'fantasies' which are both highly precise instruments
of involvement in the real physical universe they embody and detectors
in a flow of consciousness miraculously distinct in direction from the
randomly subjective perceptions from which it is made up. Valéry has
used analogies in such a way that, as we read them, we simultaneously
'see through' and cherish the creative potentialities of analogies them-
selves, analogies of which our own consciousness, like that of the
Parque, is built up.

The third analogy in this dense passage draws together the
movement of the branches at the top of the trees and the motion of
rowing: 'Pour et contre les dieux ramer l'arbre unanime' − and here
is a perfect example of the way in which the concrete, the metaphoric
and the symbolic in Valéry's poetry radiate one into the other, giving
the reader, at the same time as he reacts to the actual theme of the
poem, the constant feeling that behind and through the subject-matter
is the poetic celebration on the part of the poet of the range of the
creative imagination itself. Once again, the 'fanciful' nature of the
metaphor is not allowed to go beyond its basis in the visually possible:
the movement of oars straining against the sea, while the whole analogy
has been prepared in advance by the image of the tree's arms ('chargés
de tant de bras') and perhaps even by the notion of steering and self-
orientation present in the phrase 'et de trop d'horizons' with its
implications of voyage in a turbulent medium such as the sea. At the
same time, however, the imaginative logic of the image spreads far
further than the concrete visual comparison at its base. By means of
the notion of striving implicit in the rowing theme, Valéry allows the
image to 'take off' into a conceptual one, in this case into the concep-
tual image of the gods and the 'human condition'. 'L'arbre unanime' −
the single organism made up in the Parque's mind by the united move-
ment of the trees of the forest? − 'rows' in a way which suggests both
harmonious alignment with nature and defiant rebellion ('pour et
contre les dieux'). Like a form of representative, it offers a
transposition of the Parque's own position, the postion of 'pure'
consciousness in the natural world.

One of the most powerful aspects of Valéry's poetry is the way in
which the kind of analogies picked out above change or 'modulate'
one into another, welded together by a structural coherence. The
analogy between the movement of branches and of oars implies, for

instance, yet a further set of analogies introducing water and islands, these in turn giving rise to associative links with more abstract themes of departure, loss and death. Although deeply sensitive in range, and bringing the relational imagination of the reader into play 'outside' the poem, the mechanism of the imagery is still ambiguous in a precisely controlled way 'within' the poem, that is, in terms of psychological realism, within the associative field of the Parque's own mind by which the direction of the monologue is shaped. The implicit analogy between the sea and the sky introduced by the image of the rowing branches leads, for example, to the image of the forest as a floating island, 'la flottante forêt', made up in turn of collections of smaller islands, 'archipels', and connected with the theme of heart-rending human departure and loss, departure on the Baudelairean sea-voyage of death:

> La flottante forêt de qui les rudes troncs
> Portent pieusement à leaurs fantasques fronts,
> Aux déchirants départs des archipels superbes,
> Un fleuve tendre, ô Mort, et caché sous les herbes?

Once more Valéry's poetry reveals an extraordinarily close blend between the imaginative and the biologically precise, the full working of imagination in the Baudelairean sense of 'la plus scientifique des facultés'. The sap rising up from the roots of the trees is literally like a river with its estuary amongst the leaves/islands of the sea/sky above it, while the call of spring, urging the trees like the Parque herself to a process of self-renewal, is literally at the same time the call of death, the completion of the life-cycle in which individual consciousness is trapped. Even here, however, it is the emotional and intellectual resonance of these biological principles in human experience, in the mind of the Parque discovering and incorporating them, that reveals the true depth and subtlety of Valéry's poetry, its power to give shape to complex mental sensations of fleeting but piercing significance to the inner self even at the same moment as some more violent or abstract situation is perceived. The idea of death is partly threatening, for instance, but it is in the vicinity of death and its gentleness ('Un fleuve tendre, ô Mort') that the inescapable call of spring begins to appear less as an alien force. Something of the proud and grave acceptance of a force from which there is no escape, but in the acceptance of which lies the chance of a positive redirection of mental energies in individual life, is reflected perhaps in the heavily charged human epithets transferred at this point to the islands and trees: 'portent pieusement', 'archipels superbes'.

I have tried to suggest that the overall unity of a passage like this from *La Jeune Parque* is provided not by the imagery itself, but by the way in which its treatment in the context of the whole poem enables Valéry to express the movement of the mind behind the image-making itself. We as readers have 'felt' the Parque's sense of self-identity reaffirming itself in the process of comparison, selecting from the self-generated image of the tree only those points of identification necessary to its own constantly forward-moving existence. We have 'experienced' the way consciousness can strive forward through the night of the self with analogies for oars; or, as Valéry said himself, we have a knowledge of a human being which has been learnt by being felt, not simply known.

In 'Au Platane', where the tree image next occurs in a major form, two main changes in presentation have been made, and by dwelling on these as a whole, I hope to suggest how Valéry has used the same basic imagery to express a quite different perspective or 'level' of the creative imagination at work. First, the image has been extended throughout the whole poem rather than being simply a condensed fragment of the whole as it was in *La Jeune Parque*. Secondly, the narrative framework has shifted. The creative sensibility of the speaker no longer 'projects' the tree image. Instead, the process has, so to speak, been inverted, and we feel the speaker's direct reaction to the sensuous presence of a real and actual tree. The sexual content of the imagery has correspondingly changed towards the more controlled and erotic. The tree is addressed in the intimate 'tu' form ('Tu penches, grand Platane, et te proposes, nu . . .') and it is interesting to note meanwhile that where the tree image entered the Parque's consciousness at the point where she became most aware of her own awakening sexuality, the trees surrounding the plane tree suggest to the 'speaker' or narrative consciousness of this poem the image of a woman who is virtually herself a form of 'Jeune Parque' (a fantasy image of a different self or ego state seen from a different point of view?):

> Quand l'âme lentement qu'ils expirent le soir
>   Vers l'Aphrodite monte,
> La vierge doit dans l'ombre, en silence, s'asseoir,
>   Toute chaude de honte.

Elle se sent surprendre, et pâle, appartenir
    A ce tendre présage
Qu'une présente chair tourne vers l'avenir
    Par un jeune visage . . .

By making the narrating consciousness distinguish the plane tree itself
from this element of human 'fantasy' ('Mais toi, de bras plus pur que
les bras animaux'), it is as if Valéry is finding a means of conveying
the perception of mind at a different stage of intellectual power from
the Parque, testing its ability to free itself from the network of images
it has inevitably created around it. The various analogies of the poem
can perhaps best be examined with reference to this framework of
shifting intellectual power.

First, the personification of the tree in terms of the human body.
From the very first words of the poem, 'Tu penches, grand Platane,
et te proposes, nu', the plane tree is personified. 'Blanc comme un
jeune Scythe', 'candeur', 'pied', 'front', 'bras', 'personnage', 'corps
poli', 'tête superbe' and so on. As in *La Jeune Parque* certain abstract
words ('candeur', for example) have double meanings which suggest the
source of the analogy on a level of visual comparison (the whiteness of
the bark [Lt. *candida*]), at the same time as the filtering of the visual
sensation through a human mood (the idea of purity, candour and so
on). Through Valéry's handling of these images we are conscious both
of the way in which a human predicament is being transferred to the
tree by the perceiver – the theme of striving and limitation – and of
the way in which the perceiving mind remains conscious of its separate
identity even at the points when its identification with the tree is most
precise. Indeed, the final stanzas of the poem where the poet-persona
asks the tree to *become* the analogies with which his imagination has
reacted to it, and where the tree seems to refuse to do so, tossing its
head with its famous 'Non', are surely to be interpreted as a final
affirmation of the speaker's lonely freedom to create and reject
personification at will. It is he who makes the tree 'speak' to pro-
claim an existence beyond language and thought.

A second already familiar analogy to be found in 'Au platane' is
that between the moving branches of the trees – the plane-tree's
companions – and the human action of rowing:

Le tremble pur, le charme, et ce hêtre formé
    De quatre jeunes femmes,
Ne cessent point de battre un ciel toujours fermé,

Vêtus en vain de rames.

Once more the image is visually logical – the branches beat against the sky as oars beat against water (in this case the analogy has been discreetly condensed into the form of word-play set up between 'rame' [oar] and 'ramure' [branch]), and once more the visually logical is closely linked with the conceptual: 'un ciel toujours fermé', 'vêtus en vain de rames'. In *La Jeune Parque* the conceptual aspect of this same rowing image concerned the ambivalent nature of movement ('pour et contre les dieux'). Here it concerns the limitation of movement itself. The trees are supplied with 'oars' in vain, oars that beat but get nowhere, trapped in restless immobility, while the image of the closed sky acquires the wider connotation of a metaphysical impasse shared by man and the trees. Yet whereas the Parque suffered from a sense of individual limitation proportionate to the overwhelming force she felt in nature, the speaker in 'Au Platane' might be said to experience his own imaginative freedom, its potential exhilaration and its potential loneliness, in proportion as he takes stock of the limitations imposed by the biological world. Limited like the tree, the branches of his imagination may none the less move where those of the tree cannot.

Despite the presence of the rowing image, water imagery is not used in 'Au Platane' as it was in *La Jeune Parque*, the main theme of the poem being the tree's living immobility or growth within limits, rather than its participation in the flux or river of time symbolised by the coming of spring. Instead, stressing the theme of continuity between limitation and freedom, stability and movement which he saw as the most important aspect of man's mental and physical being, as indeed of any living organism, Valéry draws on the resources of the tree as an 'objective correlative' – an image in its own right – of relational continuity: continuity between roots and leaves, darkness and light, earth and sky. The luminous regions at the top of the tree, where the branches move against the light, are contemplated metaphorically on two levels of human comparison. For example, in the lines

Ce front n'aura d'accès qu'aux degrés lumineux
    Où la sève l'exalte,

Valéry is playing on the theme of growth within limits which the human mind shares with the biological organism: the plane tree is becoming more and more like a vast mind the more the mind of the

speaker contemplates it and finds it activates within him his own
growth processes. In the lines

> Toi qui formes au jour le fantôme des maux
>   Que le sommeil fait songes,

— the second level of the comparison — the imagination of the be-
holder has 'climbed' still further into the process of human identifica-
tion, allowing the plane tree temporarily to bear the weight of human
emotions and his own perceiving mind to stretch into its own most
intimate feelings as his eye stretches to follow the tree's visible growth.
From purely visual notation to the intellectual and emotional fantasies
of vision, it is as if Valéry is expressing in this poem the ascending
stages of the creative imagination, that kind of 'imagination of move-
ment' associated with trees by Bachelard in *L'Air et les Songes*:
'. . . l'arbre, être statique par excellence, reçoit de notre imagination
une vie dynamique merveilleuse. Sourde, lente, invincible poussée!
Conquête de légèreté, fabrication de choses volantes, de feuilles
aériennes et frémissantes'.[7]
    A final tree analogy in 'Au Platane', and one already seen at work
in a more minor way in *La Jeune Parque*, is that between the sound of
the wind in the leaves and the notion of articulate sound or language.
The tree's presence, imitatively borne in on the reader's mind through-
out the poem by the rocking rhythm of the verse with its alternation
of long and short lines and its carefully interwoven patterns of vowels
and consonants, is very much a 'sounding' one, the inner effect of the
branches on the perceiving ear and eye stimulating the response of the
beholder whose mind is the fictional source of the 'tree/poem' itself.

Looking back at *La Jeune Parque* and 'Au Platane', in the light which
such comparative analysis of the tree theme might throw on his poetic
universe, it seems possible to suggest that Valéry is concerned in both
poems with evoking the inner space in which relationships between
language, the self and the external world are constantly formed and re-
formed in the human mind. From the extensive analysis carried out
in the *Cahiers* we know that he considered that only part of our
experience is purely verbal, whether or not we are thinking to our-
selves in words or actually speaking aloud. He writes, for instance:
'L'Un et le Seul se distingue — *La Personne qui parle* n'est pas *ce* qui
n'est pas personne, et qui *Sent* et qui ne sait *Parler.*' (XVII, 742.)

This being so, it is not surprising to find him laying such stress through-
out his writing on the unificatory function of poetry, on its importance
as an attempt by the whole mind to make articulate and to communi-
cate, by exploiting to the full the evocative, organisational and
metaphorical power of words ('un langage dans le langage'), the quality,
complexity and general human significance of experience otherwise
accessible to no one but the individual subject himself – and even then
only in fragmentary and intermittent form. In *La Jeune Parque* we feel
we can see into the human mind at a stage of this experience where it
is still striving towards fullness, and no small part of the reader's emo-
tion derives, perhaps, consciously or unconsciously, from recognition
of the power of poetic language to bridge a gulf in communication
between self and self, to express an experience which in the case of the
Parque herself at the time she undergoes it, is essentially lacking in the
intelligibility provided by words. In 'Au Platane', on the other hand,
the narrative inner voice has reached a further stage in its development.
Indeed, the voice of poetic consciousness itself – in the general sense
of self-aware creativity – makes its stylised entry in the form of the
poet-persona introduced in the third person near the end of the poem:

> Je t'ai choisi, puissant personnage d'un parc,
>   Ivre de ton tangage,
> Puisque le ciel t'exerce, et te presse, ô grand arc,
>   De lui rendre un langage!
>
> O qu'amoureusement des Dryades rival,
>   Le seul poète puisse
> Flatter ton corps poli comme il fait du Cheval
>   L'ambitieuse cuisse! . . .

$$\text{(P.I, 115)}$$

Consequently, a double frame of reference is set up in the poem
between the inner dialogue of a mind with itself in the face of the
object of its vision – the plane tree – and the outer dialogue of the
poet with the reader. In the line 'Je t'ai choisi, puissant personnage
d'un parc', for example, Valéry is surely finding a poetic means of
referring not only to the experience of the poet-persona within the
poem, but to the complex linguistic act I referred to at the beginning
of this discussion. It is one more instance of the fact that, given the
special properties of language, Valéry very often prefers the type of
verbal illusion which draws attention to, rather than conceals, its own

creative activity. Indeed, by using the image of the tree which is in turn itself a 'source' of imagery, Valéry comes near in a poem like 'Au Platane' to writing poetry which embodies the activity of the creative imagination itself. By handling the tree image in the course of the two poems in a way which suggests the highly flexible and perpetually shifting degrees of detachment and involvement at the heart of mental creativity, he is writing the kind of poetry which enables the reader to travel through the 'space of literary activity',[8] a space in which the mind is the freer in inventive powers of identification and empathy the more aware it is of the distance between itself and the object of its 'love':

> — Non, dit l'arbre. Il dit: *Non*! par l'étincellement
> De sa tête superbe,
> Que la tempête traite universellement
> Comme elle fait une herbe!

The 'proud head' of the tree-top is embodied throughout Valéry's poetry in a manner which suggests it still to be as 'untamed' and 'untameable' as the poetic spirit which draws upon it for self-replenishment — perhaps even more untameable than Pegasus, the horse of the Muses ('le Cheval').

Before concluding, it is possible to give a very brief idea of the many changes of framework Valéry brings in other poems of *Charmes* to what is virtually the same basic imagery of the tree. In 'Fragments du Narcisse', for instance, the image is diffused throughout the poem, the branches forming a half inner, half outer landscape in which is mirrored, like his own reflection in the pool below him, the relationship of Narcisse's mind with the physical world. One instance of the tree motif near the end of the poem is of particular interest here:

> Adieu . . . Sens-tu frémir mille flottants adieux?
> Bientôt va frissonner le désordre des ombres!
> L'arbre aveugle vers l'arbre étend ses membres sombres,
> Et cherche affreusement l'arbre qui disparaît . . .
> Mon âme ainsi se perd dans sa propre forêt,
> Où la puissance échappe à ses formes suprêmes . . .
>
> (P.I, 130)

From the personification of the trees — searching for each other in the
fading light, perhaps the coming of that symbolic darkness in which
the Parque herself had already been immersed — Valéry allows the
imagery to move towards a direct comparison in the mind of Narcisse
with the plight of his own consciousness seeking to preserve its
identity in the face of the immense disorders capable of overwhelming
it, the metaphor of the forest — a metaphor within a comparison —
working with Racinian totality. The region at the top of the tree where
individual branches picked out against the night sky merge with the
vast density of the forest — 'l'épaisseur panique' — has been directly
internalised to suggest a psychological truth.

It is interesting to note that of the four remaining poems of *Charmes*
where the same imagery occurs — 'La Pythie', 'Ebauche d'un Serpent',
'Le Rameur' and 'Palme' — the perceptual framework continues to
shift. After all, it is characteristic of Valéry's way of thinking and
creating that he should approach a limited number of themes from many
different critical perspectives, rather than pursue a diversity of themes
from a single point of view. 'Pauvre système — arbre de vie, platane
branlé par ses propres fureurs élémentaires inexplicables' (XXV, 571),
he once wrote of the human psyche, and it is easy to see how the first
of these poems, 'La Pythie', makes discreet use of the tree theme to
stage an internal drama of precisely this kind. 'L'arbre de ma vie' (P.I,
135) is how the Pythoness refers at one point to her writhing body,
and an image from 'Au Platane' — the tree as a bow ('arc') — is now
exended to apply to language itself, the language that the plane tree
could never give:

> Vois de tout mon corps l'arc obscène
> Tendre à se rompre pour darder
> Comme son trait le plus infâme,
> Implacablement au ciel l'âme
> Que mon sein ne peut plus garder!

(P.I, 131)

Valéry's brief, almost ironic use of the tree image here as a direct
metaphor for the body — in a sense the inverse of the personificatory
device by which a tree is compared with a human being — might be said
to reflect the traumatic overwhelming in consciousness of that same
potential distance between the self and its emotions which the Parque
was seen re-establishing in herself, which Narcisse contemplated
fixedly from the point of view of its potential disruption, and which

the speaker in 'Au Platane' exercises as the source of inescapable creative power.

In 'Ebauche d'un Serpent' and 'Palme', where so many of the themes and images I've been looking at occur yet again, Valéry seems to have continued to explore the metaphorical transfer of the tree imagery to perceptual processes, but this time processes of a more general kind. In the first poem, the tempting seduction offered by the plane-tree of 'Au Platane' to the individual imagination of a beholder has now been transferred metaphorically to the vigour of the human mind in general. In the second poem, 'Palme', the tree image has been used somewhat similarly, in a simple yet deeply symbolic manner, to set up a possible imitative interchange between the qualities of the mature mind — patiently deepening its own inner riches — and the slow, balanced, fertile growth of the tree, graceful intermediary between the earth and sky.

It is in 'Le Rameur', immediately preceding the culminating poem 'Palme', that an interesting and delightful twist to the previous perspectives on the tree image occurs:

Penché contre un grand fleuve, infiniment mes rames
M'arrachent à regret aux riants environs;
Ame aux pesantes mains, pleines des avirons,
Il faut que le ciel cède au glas des lentes lames.

Le cœur dur, l'œil distrait des beautes que je bats,
Laissant autour de moi mûrir des cercles d'onde,
Je veux à larges coups rompre l'illustre monde
De feuilles et de feu que je chante tout bas.

Arbres sur qui je passe, ample et naïve moire,
Eau de ramages peinte, et paix de l'accompli,
Déchire-les, ma barque, impose-leur un pli
Qui coure du grand calme abolir la mémoire.

                                                              (P.I, 153)

Now it is the human being himself who outwardly moves forward over the tree tops — over the reflection of trees in the calm water; he who wields with relative effectiveness the oars which the trees in 'Au Platane' beat in vain against the sky. However self-sufficient — 'Le Rameur' for instance is a beautiful evocation of the pleasures of the natural universe seen from the point of view of the oarsman enjoying the reward of his physical effort — the poems of *Charmes* undoubtedly gain, in my opinion, from being read in close conjunction with each other in this way, certain recurring word-patterns like those of the tree theme setting up echoes, sometimes, as in this case, even half punning jokes and parallels, even the most literal use of a word or image becoming highly metaphorical, while metaphors lead back in turn to the concrete relationships from which they grew up.

For me, the most exciting discovery made in the course of this study has been how Valéry's poetry constantly points to the reality of imaginative relational structures behind and at the root of the experience of language-making itself. When the centre of his poetry is described in this way, there is a tendency for one basic question to seem to remain unanswered: what is the relation of the texture of words and their own creative adventures to this central concern? Although much more could be said in answer to this important question than the particular orientation of this study has allowed, I have tried to show nonetheless that there is no real contradiction involved in Valéry's poetry from this point of view, rather a creative tension which constantly invigorates his work. Far from being rejected as inadequate in the task of expressing the reality of non-verbal experience, it is words themselves, their full suggestive, mimetic, conceptual range of qualities, which are used, through some of the structuring devices I have analysed in relation to the tree theme, to point to an imaginative physical reality of which Valéry shows the language-making activity itself to be a part at once relative and yet vitally necessary to the understanding and expression of human experience.

That Valéry's poetry entertains no contradiction between the one hand a 'suspicion' of words, common to so many contemporary novelists and poets, and on the other a delight in the humanising powers of words themselves, while at the same time fully incorporating the problems, consequences and creative values of that 'suspicion' itself, seems to me to be one of his most significant contributions to modern poetry, and one which definitely justifies his inclusion in a volume devoted to poets who point towards the future and who have lived out in their work many of the consequences of an anti-rationalist defiance of language itself. To communicate not the 'voice of language', as he thought Mallarmé had done, but the 'language of a voice', this was Valéry's poetic ambition (XXII, 435): to set in action the powers of 'Saint LANGAGE' proclaimed at the end of 'La Pythie' —

> ... cette auguste Voix
> Qui se connaît quand elle sonne
> N'être plus la voix de personne
> Tant que des ondes et des bois!

(P.I, 136)

but to do so in such a way as to preserve not so much the voice of no-one other than the trees and the water, as the voice of someone whose humanity and individuality the trees and the water serve to reveal.[9] It was indeed because of this mistrust of the impersonality of language that Valéry differentiated himself from those who saw the poetic principle as lying in imagery alone. For him, as I have tried to show, the true poetic principle lies not in imagery as such but in the way in which, through the critical use of all the resources of language at the poet's disposal, imagery is made to suggest the multiple avenues of human possibility that lie beyond, the polyvalency of self and reality which the rich flickering ambiguities of language can be made to reflect in the processes they set up in the reader's mind.

To return to the questions I posed at the beginning of this study: the poet affirmed in Valéry's own practice of poetry is one who, finding himself naïvely facing words on one side and the world on the other, refuses simply to turn to language as being immediately capable of expressing what he feels or sees. Instead, he detaches himself critically from both language *and* experience. Only then, like the oarsman in 'Le Rameur' striving *against* the current, 'rowing' with his whole mind and senses re-alerted in the resistant and partial medium of language itself, can he aspire to express, this time through the multiplicity of his own reactions to the mystery of the inexpressible, the threshold of self and reality, 'la source où cesse même un nom'. The goal of Valéry's poetry is not the poem itself — the 'voice of language' — but the creative capacities outside the poem which the poem has a privileged role in disclosing to the human mind. If the image of the tree occurs so frequently, it is not as a mere allegory of mental processes, nor as the remnant of an attempt at objective realism, but as a reminder of the power of the real tree to reveal a human capacity, the capacity to endow that real tree with the power to remind. The sensuous image of restlessly tossing branches, for ever outside the nets of both language and reductive self-analysis, expresses the nonetheless fertile interaction of mind and universe, the 'space' between mind and object, perception and language, which enables the real tree to act as the focus for moments of human refusal, moments of mystery or moments of fleeting, hard-won reciprocity and peacefulness which the poet, like the oarsman, selects and extends to spur him on.

Notes

1. Gaston Bachelard, *L'Eau et les Rêves*, Paris, Corti, 1942, p. 14. In an article entitled 'Les Sources de Valéry. Qual, Quelle' (*Modern Language Notes*, vol. 87 (1972), no. 4, pp. 563-99), Jacques Derrida suggests that 'La source serait alors ce qui pour Valéry n'a jamais pu devenir un thème' (p. 568). When Valéry writes of the tree's dream of becoming a source (e.g. *Cahiers*, IX, 428), perhaps he is playing on the double idea of water and 'total' expression.

2. Many of Valéry's direct comments on the tree theme are collected in Pierre Laurette's *Le Thème de l'Arbre chez Paul Valéry*, Paris, Klincksieck, 1967; see also the sections on imagination, on the tree and on plant growth in my book *Paul Valéry, Consciousness and Nature*, Cambridge, Cambridge University Press, 1972, pp. 75-84; 107-22; 133-8.

3. The abbreviations 'P.I' and 'P.II', followed by a page number, refer to the two volumes of the Pléiade edition of Valéry's collected works, ed. J. Hytier, Paris, Gallimard, 1957 and 1960. References to the *Cahiers*, Valéry's notebooks, are to the facsimile edition in 29 volumes published by the Centre National de Recherches Scientifiques, 1957-1961.

4. 'Ainsi le même arbre est un *but* de mouvement; / . . . / un *signe* de souvenirs; / . . . / un repère de pensées; / . . . / un fixateur ou un distracteur, un révélateur, un interrupteur; un réflecteur./ Il est en somme un objet privilégié' (P.II, 718). A passage in the first notebook concerns the 'psychology' of the image-making process called forth by a tree:

    > Arbre – bras dressé: on a 1. image. 2. la branche serait bras si bras était dressé. 3. idée de bras dressé – impulsion. 4. effort – énergie. 5. Quand? lutte – *victoire*. 6. développements etc. / 1. état statique. 2. etc. dynamique, activité – entre 1. et 2. activité très grande./ effort ici pour comprendre cette attitude d'arbre – langage métaphore tentative p. relation relationnelle. Opération pour réaliser = 2. quoi de plus profond? sentir et produire. sentir = 4. produire = 5, 6 etc.

    (I, 711)

5. Cf. the process of unification through self-awareness known as 'individuation' in Jungian psychology.

6. Cf. 'CERTES, d'un grand désir je fus l'œuvre anxieuse . . .' (*Le Philosophe et 'La Jeune Parque'*, P.I, 164). Valéry's poetics is centred on insight into the close connection between self-awareness and creative anxiety.

7. Gaston Bachelard, *L'Air et les Songes*, Paris, Corti, 1943, p. 235.

8. The term is used by Malcolm Bowie in *Henri Michaux – a study of his literary works*, Oxford, Clarendon Press, 1973, p. 16. See in the same work the discussion of opposite reactions to language in Valéry and Artaud (p. 177).

9.   I have studied in detail in *The Poetry of Valéry* (Cambridge, Cambridge
      University Press, forthcoming) Valéry's conception of a poetry modelled
      on the 'music' of the individual human voice.

2 APOLLINAIRE'S SOLAR IMAGERY

David Berry

On peut partir d'un fait quotidien: un mouchoir peut être pour le
poète le levier avec lequel il soulèvera tout un univers. (. . .) C'est
pourquoi le poète aujourd'hui ne méprise aucun mouvement de la
nature, et son esprit poursuit la découverte (. . .) dans les faits en
apparence les plus simples: une main qui fouille une poche, une
allumette qui s'allume par le frottement, des cris d'animaux, l'odeur
des jardins après la pluie, une flamme qui naît dans un foyer.

(OC,III, 907)[1]

The above lines indicate one of the essential means by which
Guillaume Apollinaire through his poetry aimed to transform the
ordinary into the extraordinary, by which he intended to practise his
central conception of a truthful yet surprising art: his purpose was
to seize, with ever vigilant eyes, upon the most apparently simple and
routine fact — a handkerchief fluttering in a wave of farewell, perhaps;
the striking of a match, the smell of rain-washed gardens — and to in-
vest it with a sense of revelation. There is an important emphasis,
therefore, in Apollinaire's work, on perceptual rather than conceptual
knowledge, with sensory perception leading towards poetic discovery.
At one point he called himself 'le flâneur des deux rives', who strolled
through Paris exploring both banks of the Seine with equal enthusiasm.
Such peregrinations allowed him to reconnoitre all zones of the
external world, to observe the visible signs of life in all their enchanting
profusion, to find poetic material in what is most plain and prosaic:

Tu lis les prospectus les catalogues les affiches qui
      chantent tout haut
Voilà la poésie ce matin . . .

(A,7)

In spite of Apollinaire's wanton eclecticism and his fascination with
all things curious and arcane, he was quite happy simply to wander and
watch, to give himself up to the full force and flow of life as it went on
around him, to transform his observations into enchantments. Indeed
his basic artistic ambition was to become a verbal enchanter who
brought the marvellous and the magical into the world by means of

poetry. His attitude is made quite clear in a letter of 1913: 'Ce n'est pas la bizarrerie qui me plaît, c'est la vie, et quand on sait voir autour de soi, on voit les choses les plus curieuses et les plus attachantes.' (OC,IV, 768.) As these words imply, truth can be stranger than fiction; it is simply a question of being on the look-out, of developing one's vision. Such delightful and mysterious sights can sometimes lie just around the corner:

> Au tournant d'une rue je vis des matelots
> Qui dansaient le cou nu au son d'un accordéon
>
> (A, 121)

For Apollinaire vision itself becomes a creative process; the faculty of sight must be sharpened before poetic insight can be obtained. Before the poet can experience the joy of knowledge and understanding, he must train himself to undergo the ecstasy of seeing. As he asks in one of the key poems of *Calligrammes*, 'La Victoire': 'Connais-tu cette joie de voir des choses neuves'. As defined in the conclusion to this poem, 'La Victoire' thus means creative conquest through vision:

> La Victoire avant tout sera
> De bien voir au loin
> De tout voir
> De près
> Et que tout ait un nom nouveau
>
> (C, 182)

As well as wishing to reveal what he called 'le merveilleux quotidien', the marvellous in what is apparently mundane, Apollinaire constantly strove to open up new perspectives for the imagination. Through his creative activity he sought to discover new artistic truths to match those technological miracles, like the aeroplane and the advanced utilisation of electricity, with which the scientists had revolutionised the physical picture of the world. Thus the poet-magician, through the power of his imagination, fired as it was by his vivid experiences of reality, would create his own new spiritual flights and poetic illuminations. For Apollinaire, therefore, the role of the senses becomes crucial in helping him to achieve this feeling of conquest and discovery. Through an exploration and exaltation of the senses he can embrace the world in its totality, thus helping to satisfy his inner desire, as a visionary poet, for omniscience and omnipotence:

J'écris seulement pour vous exalter
O sens ô sens chéris

(C, 23)

Throughout his work the external world is communicated with
sensorial immediacy. The senses bring a fragrance, a flavour and a
feel of reality to a world Apollinaire wants to render visible. They
also, through a process of association, help to enlarge and enrich his
inner life. They become important catalysts in an act of poetic
creation, contributing to the invention of a whole imaginative world,
providing the keys to unlock the doors of perception, and thus
increasing the poet's knowledge:

Je me disais Guillaume il est temps que tu viennes
Pour que je sache enfin celui-là que je suis
Moi qui connais les autres
Je les connais par les cinq sens et quelques autres
Il me suffit de voir leurs pieds pour pouvoir refaire
    ces gens à milliers
(. . .)
O Corneille Agrippa l'odeur d'un petit chien m'eût suffi
Pour décrire exactement tes concitoyens de Cologne
(. . .)
Il me suffit de goûter la saveur du laurier qu'on cultive
    pour ce que j'aime ou que je bafoue
Et de toucher les vêtements
Pour ne pas douter si l'on est frileux ou non

(A, 49)

As the above lines indicate, it is through the senses that the poet can
become a seer and a prophet, endowed with exceptional powers of
divination and insight: a mere laying-on of hands enables him to
decide whether one has a chilly disposition; the simple smell of a dog
allows him to conjure up the teeming sixteenth-century world of
Cornelius Agrippa, the cabbalist of Cologne.

Apollinaire realises that the most spiritualised perceptions of the
mind must find their expression in the forms encountered every day by
his bodily eyes. He thus thrusts himself towards the immediate and
physical experience of life. He goes out into the world in search of
events which can give him the impression of having tracked down the
secrets of existence, events which, as is suggested by the title of his

first major collection, *Alcools*, are subsequently distilled into the
burning, intoxicating alcohol of poetry. The title of *Alcools*, cruder,
less symbolist, less mannered and more violently modern than the
original title of *Eau-de-Vie*, has an immediate impact on the senses
and is charged with a spirit of energy, release and destruction — alco-
hol: burning, corrosive and volatile, yet envigorating and inspiring,
the element which emerges from the fusion of fire and water, both
of which are important sources of imagery for Apollinaire. Each poem
in the collection can be considered in terms of an alcohol which is
consumed, spontaneously transforming the essential nature of the
external world by plunging it into a state of intoxication and song.
Each poem, which, as Apollinaire has said, commemorates an event
in his life,[2] is savoured like brandy, stirring the memory and
sharpening the senses, then swallowed down like a life-giving liquor:

> Et tu bois cet alcool brûlant comme ta vie
> Ta vie que tu bois comme un eau-de-vie
>
> (A, 14)

For the poet the whole of life becomes an alcohol which he consumes
in an effort to savour the very quintessence of the cosmos:

> Mondes qui vous ressemblez and qui nous ressemblez
> Je vous ai bus et ne fus pas désaltéré
> Mais je connus dès lors quelle saveur a l'univers
> Je suis ivre d'avoir bu tout l'univers
>
> (A, 142)

The poem thus represents a creative means by which Apollinaire can
dominate a life of change and disintegration; can diminish the sense
that his personality is in a constant state of internal dissolution, can
reduce his awareness that, as time passes, his existence is submerged
in a flood of disassociated memories. In the alcohol of poetry, the
events of Apollinaire's sentimental, emotional and psychological life
are not just preserved but, in his own metaphorical terms, are
purified by water and transfigured by fire.

There is, then, all-pervasive in his work, this constant desire for
assimilation; this sense of devouring and consuming the world, almost
as if his creative method were motivated by an intuitive response to
the infantile oral stage, in which the child tries to take the external
world into his system by eating it. Thus, Apollinaire becomes, as has

been pointed out, 'le mangeur, l'avaleur de mondes'.[3] It is in such terms that Apollinaire himself has described the essential nature of the poet. The poet-hero of *Le Poète assassiné,* in order to feed his creative inspiration, gobbles up the universe with his eyes: 'Ses yeux dévoraient tout ce qu'ils regardaient et quand ses paupières se rapprochaient rapidement comme des mâchoires, elles engloutissaient l'univers qui se renouvelait sans cesse par l'opération de celui qui courait en imaginant les moindres détails des mondes énormes dont il se repaissait.' (OC,I,254.) Thus, the poetic process is seen as one of ingestion and absorption, magically transforming the raw material of the external world into energy for creative vision. And in this act of magic metamorphosis it is the eyes which become the vital agents of such vision. In his privileged and divinely inspired role, the poet has eyes which see into the life of things, eyes which, as we have seen above, focus on those 'moindres détails' which feed his imagination; he is blessed with what are called 'yeuz lyriques' (A,73). Apollinaire, therefore, as a poet of sight and inner vision, shows how the act of seeing is an active, dynamic and personal act, not just the passive recording of a given image. For him, to see is a unique experience, since it is through this act that he seeks to belong to the world about him and to make the world belong to him. In discovering the world he can discover not only himself: 'Pour que je sache enfin celui-là que je suis' (A,49), but also the new worlds born out of the poetic imagination. His mission as a poet, therefore, in the words of a collection of poetry by Eluard, is to *Donner à voir*.

Naturally Apollinaire's gaze, like that of any other poet, also turns inwards. The material objects of the outer world are absorbed by his sensibility and are used to interpret various introspective preoccupations. To a poet who was essentially a visualist, certain key images in his poetry offer natural sources and means of vision, images like the sun, light, fire and flames, stars, eyes, windows and mirrors. By the frequency of their appearance and through the sensitivity of treatment accorded to them, they occupy places of special distinction in the poet's work and represent nerve-centres of vision. To call these vital images simply symbols is perhaps to depreciate their value. Unlike symbols, these images are not merely denotative, standing for one thing only, but, by their richness and intensity, become multi-dimensional in significance.

For example, the image of light appears most strikingly in those poems where Apollinaire attempts to communicate his vision of an elusive transcendental reality, a vision of perfection in which light has become refined to an essence of pure thought:

> Descendant des hauteurs où pense la lumière
> Jardins rouant plus haut que tous les ciels mobiles
>
> (A, 92)

In this vision of a new reality, the gardens of paradise are creations
of the light, spinning like wheels of fire beyond man's normal vision,
unfolding, as is suggested by the verb 'rouer', like the plumage of a
miraculous cosmic peacock, in the manner of the luminous yet invisible
horizon in 'Chant de l'horizon en Champagne': 'Moi l'horizon je fais
la roue comme un grand Paon' (C, 131). These gardens of light,
symbolizing a spiritual ideal, appear, in 'L'Emigrant de Landor Road',
as lakes of light into which the refugees and wanderers long to be ab-
sorbed:

> Et des mains vers le ciel plein de lacs de lumière
> S'envolaient quelquefois comme des oiseaux blancs
>
> (A, 85)

As we see, it is a rising movement, a flight upwards, an act of ascension,
which takes the poet into the realm of this perfect light; the higher we
rise, the more breathtaking is the transforming effect of the light upon
us, even though, like the lady in 'Les Collines', we might be simply
going up in a lift:

> Elle monte dans l'ascenseur
> Elle monte monte toujours
> Et la lumière se déploie
> Et ces clartés la transfigurent
>
> (C, 36)

Light, therefore, in Apollinaire's imagination, is an image of the trans-
figuring power of poetry; it is also the prime mover, the symbol of a
divine force in the universe; the poet is its chosen agent and his poetry
is its earthly manifestation. But, as is typical with Apollinaire, he does
not always remain totally abject in his adoration and envisages a time,
in 'Cortège', where his own creative forces become so intense that they
take over from the power of light: 'Au point qu'il deviendra un jour
l'unique lumière' (A, 48).

Similarly, the image of the stars is multifaceted in meaning. For

Apollinaire the primary stellar quality is soft diffuse light and delicate
fluidity, a quality splendidly conveyed in the thrice-uttered refrain of
'La Chanson du Mal-Aimé':

> Voie lactée ô soeur lumineuse
> Des blancs ruisseaux de Chanaan
> Et des corps blancs des amoureuses
> Nageurs morts suivrons-nous d'ahan
> Ton cours vers d'autres nébuleuses

In these lines we see that starlight, for the poet, is essentially a wonder-
ful shimmering lactescence. The Milky Way captivates the poet's creative
vision and is transformed into a ravishing symbol of the ideal, in which
the promise of spiritual peace offered by the milky waters of Canaan
(the biblical land of milk and honey) and the bliss of sensual rapture to
be discovered in the flowing creamy contours of the female body are
fused together, suggesting that Apollinaire, like Rimbaud (who in 'Le
Bateau ivre' declares that '. . . je me suis baigné dans le Poème/De la
Mer, infusé d'astres, et lactescent'), longs to bathe, freed of all mortal
restraint, in the ocean of the cosmos, to fling himself, so to speak, at
the very maternal breast of the universe, from which flows this life-
giving stream of irresistible and influential starlight. Similarly, in
'Crépuscule', the creative powers of the poet-magician seem to be
nourished by the lactescence of stars and the full force of his magic is
demonstrated when, having grown miraculously before the eyes of his
audience, he is able to reach up to the stars and capture the very thing
which lies beyond the grasp of ordinary mortals and which for them
symbolizes a supra-terrestrial ideal:

> Ayant décroché une étoile
> Il la manie à bras tendu

(A, 37)

On the other hand, the distant stars, with their fluid and flickering
light, which seems to reflect the saddening flow of time and the im-
permanence of human feelings, also become, in Apollinaire's imagin-
ation, symbols of impurity, evoking the deceptions and the cold
inaccessibility of women. In 'La Chanson du Mal-Aimé' we find:

> Rois sécoués par la folie
> Et ces grelottantes étoiles

De fausses femmes dans vos lits

(A, 30)

stellar beauties whose fickleness and treachery have already been
suggested earlier in the poem:

Ses regards laissaient une traîne
D'étoiles dans les soirs tremblants

(A, 24)

These impure stars are flung on to the bonfire in 'Le Brasier', revealing
themselves as brutalized images of false women: 'Et les astres qui ont
saigné/Ne sont que des têtes de femmes' (A, 90), stars which have
also adorned the funeral pyre of suffering in 'La Chanson du Mal-Aimé',
female stars whose presence punningly signifies *désastre*: ' . . . ô bûcher
divin qu'ornent/Des astres . . .' (A, 25).

   Thus, as we see from these references to light and stars, certain
key images in Apollinaire's poetry, although they exist as physical
elements, affected by the emotional vibrations of their context and
with their degree of sensuality being directly related to their evocative
power, are also surrounded by a network of mental and cultural
associations. At times the physical element in such images tends to be
eclipsed as, through the transfiguring force of the poet's imagination,
they assume the status of myths in Apollinaire's own poetic mythology.
A study of the image of the sun in particular will help to illustrate how
Apollinaire transformed the *quotidien* into the *merveilleux*, how he
brought to traditional metaphors a new metamorphosis and how, in
the words of Aragon, he initiated in the realm of imagery 'l'ère d'une
sensualité nouvelle'.[4]

   Apollinaire's frequent use of the sun as an image has been shown to
reflect the Mediterranean aspect of his personality, to reveal a poetic
spirit which, in its earliest formation, was nourished by the fierce heat
and dazzling sunlight of the Riviera. He himself has said that the
people of the Midi are 'gens du soleil', living amidst 'la joie adorable
de la paix solaire' (C, 152). In his story 'Que vlo-ve?', as a poet of
light, radiance and illumination, he calls upon the patronage of the
sun-god, Apollo: 'Apollon! mon Patron' (OC,I, 166); whilst to Louise
Faure-Favier he confesses his own self-identification with the sun:
'Attendons ici, devant ce décor fluvial, le lever du soleil. Vous verrez

comment je renais à l'aurore. Car je suis le cours du soleil. Je m'éteins à son coucher, je m'éveille à son lever. Je suis solaire.'[5]

The sun, as a vital source of light, energy and life, is expressively celebrated in a number of contexts. The sunrise in particular, symbolising the renaissance of life and the genesis of creative forces, is given brilliant and vivid treatment. Writing on the eve of mobilisation in 1914, Apollinaire describes his return from Deauville to Paris, with the sun rising over the Seine as if heralding the dawn of discovery and the birth of a new era: 'C'est un merveilleux lever de soleil sur la Seine, merveilleux et inoubliable. Des barres noires nageant dans du blanc opalin et qui s'épure, puis mille bêtes célestes et sombres se violacent, les étoiles pâlissent, un feu profond et clair dore l'horizon.' (OC,II, 706.) The sense of wonder and enchantment in these lines, with their dramatic contrast of colour and movement, enhanced by the allusion to the hordes of mythical beasts which seem to take shape amidst the explosion of light, is characteristically accompanied with a sense of cruelty and violence: 'L'Orient blêmit encore pour fructifier enfin en prodigieux jarden des Hespérides. Quelle fraîcheur adorable! Ensuite, tout s'incendie avec grâce, comme si l'Amour même était l'incendiaire. Je sentis alors le vide enfin de mon cœur et me laissai gagner par le sommeil tandis qu'apparaissait le brûlant soleil qui nous tortura et finit par nous assoupir.' (*Ibid*.) Here the sun, with its solar flares and cauterising heat, 'un feu profond . . . tout s'incendie', is for Apollinaire an agent of both destruction and creation: its golden rays bring about the illusion of mythical wonderlands in the sky: 'pour fructifier en prodigieux jardin des Hespérides'; its fiery light consumes and oppresses: 'le brûlant soleil qui nous tortura', purifies and renews. Significantly, however, we notice that even though the sun is shown to be bright and burning, an item of strong sensory experience, its real importance lies in the fact that it becomes for Apollinaire a focus of vivid mental associations, a dynamic literary and cultural entity which stimulates his poetic imagination.

The sun generates the light and warmth which are necessary to the growth of the fruits of the earth. For example, in the richness of our sensual response to the physical world, we are, like grapes, children of the sun: 'Ces grappes de nos sens qu'enfanta le soleil' (A. 137). Although it is often cruel through the violence of its blazing rays, it nonetheless nourishes health and embodies splendour, opulence and fertility. The ritual of eating in 'Le Repas' is enriched by its presence since it turns the ordinary into the extraordinary:

Un rayon traverse un verre presque plein de vin mélangé d'eau
Oh! le beau rubis que font du vin rouge et du soleil

(GM, 192)

At the beginning of 'Zone' it is the sun which transforms Paris into
Poetry, where an ordinary street in the 17th *arrondissement* is
magically changed into a trumpet of gold, resounding with the music
of sunlight and providing a clarion call with which the sun announces
the beauty of the modern industrial world: 'J'ai vu ce matin une jolie
rue dont j'ai oublié le nom/Neuve et propre du soleil elle était le
clairon' (A, 8.). If the sun does not figure in the aerial display of this
same poem, then later, in 'Les Collines', it is nevertheless seen as an
immense celestial aeroplane, spraying down on the world its inexhaust-
ible supply of blazing fuel:

Tandis qu'au zénith flamboyait
L'éternel avion solaire

(C, 28)

The sun thus executes its immutable function as a source of psychical
as well as physical energy; it combines the twin powers of concentration
and radiation; it at once nucleates the energies of fire and light and
diffuses them across the world. In this respect it becomes for Apollinaire
a magnificent symbol of the sacred nature of cosmic forces. It is under-
standable, therefore, why man, as a poet or prophet, in his most frenzied
moments of megalomania as well as in his wildest dreams, should
attempt to demonstrate his supernatural power by bringing the sun to a
halt in its course across the heavens. Apollinaire alludes to such an
action in *La Femme Assise* when he brings the prophet, Joshua, on to
the scene and makes him comment sceptically on the miracle which he
has wrought and which has been recorded in the *Book of Joshua* (X:12-
13): 'Il faut être assez ignorant des lois de la nature pour arrêter le
soleil d'or afin que sa lumière soit un prétexte de victoire. (. . .) Le soleil
s'arrêta, froidit, et pendant la nuit solaire des ennemis, las de soleil,
s'enfuyaient' (OC,I, 424). Here Joshua, even though he has managed
to make the day last long enough for his enemies to be overcome,
seems rather to regret that he has had to go to such supernatural
lengths. Thus, elsewhere his name gives rise to a comic pun, with the
sun taking its revenge for his high-handed miracle by causing a certain
Josuette to die of sunstroke: 'Josuette, qui est morte d'une insolation
à Christiana, le soleil voulant ainsi se venger de Josué' (OC,I, 234).

Joshua's miracle, which caused the world to be flooded with constant sunlight, prevented the approach of darkness and so produced the phenomenon of the 'nuit solaire', is reflected in Apollinaire's own poetic universe. Night-time in the city seems to be so brilliant with light that there is a total absence of nocturnal gloom: 'Les villes chaque nuit ceignant une auréole/Feignaient d'être soleil tant qu'il n'était point né/Villes chair de ma vie j'aime vos nuits solaires (GM, 76). Similarly, there appear cities which ' . . . vomissaient la nuit le soleil des journées' (A, 53). By day, such cities, with their lights extinguished, seem deprived of all passion and vitality, as if no longer fulfilling their proper function in the world: 'Et les villes le jour ce sont des soleils froids' (GM, 77). This impulse towards what might be called 'solari-sation' is extended into images in which a bird's-eye view of the earth changes it into the sun, strengthened by the linguistic confusion of 'le sol' with 'le soleil': in L'Enchanteur pourrissant we find eagles which, looking down on the illuminated city,'Croyant voir, sur le sol, un soleil écrasé,/Eblouis, ont baissé leur seconde paupière' (EP, 30); whilst in 'Cortège' the strange bird flying upside down, 'A la limite où notre sol brille déjà', is told: 'Baisse ta deuxième paupière la terre t'éblouit/ Quand tu lèves la tête' (A, 48). Such images allow Apollinaire to dominate the world and the sun both at the same time. By the same token, the astral bodies of 'Onirocritique' are turned into 'feces et . . . oignons' (EP, 90), illustrating what has been called the 'gulliverisation' of cosmic elements in Apollinaire's work,[6] a process by which he asserts authority over them by metaphorically cutting them down to dwarfish size.

In his tendency to suffuse the night with solar radiance, Apollinaire again gives evidence of the extent to which the mythical invades his poetic imagination. In classical mythology the night is the incestuous mother of the sun, 'la nuit, ta mère incestueuse' (PL, 50).   Their mythical relationship is depicted in the frescoes of 'Le Larron', '(. . .) qui figurent/L'inceste solaire et nocturne dans les nues' (A, 70), and provides an erotic allusion for one of the love poems to Lou: 'Je voudrais que tu sois la nuit pour nous aimer dans les ténèbres' (PL, 171). In passing, it is interesting to note that, in pale contrast to the sun, the moon in Apollinaire's poetry plays a minor role, almost totally devoid of metaphorical significance. The moon generally provides a straight-forward lighting effect, as for example in 'Le Voyageur': 'Les cyprès projetaient sous la lune leurs ombres' (A, 53); or is treated with irrev-erence and sarcasm, fit only for burlesque or grotesque conceits: 'C'est la lune qui cuit comme un œuf sur le plat' (A, 120), and 'Lune

mellifluente aux lèvres des déments/(. . .)/Chaque rayon de lune est
un rayon de miel' (A, 123). The moon, for Apollinaire, does not
provide the same powerful stimulus for the kind of vivid and
enriching cultural associations which are conjured up by the image of
the sun.

In a letter to Madeleine Pagès, Apollinaire refers to his youthful
adoration of the sun and his habit of staring directly into its radiant
face, a practice through which he symbolically received spiritual
illumination and instilled himself with creative energy; but, as he warns,
such a practice is not without its dangers: 'C'est drôle que vous regard-
iez le soleil en face, je l'ai fait aussi souvent étant plus jeune et ma
vue a baissé depuis . . . faut pas.' (OC,IV, 489.) Apollinaire's remark
to Madeleine in a way relates to the whole of his poetic quest: the
desire to embrace an ideal which lies beyond the scope of human
capability and which can only end in failure, the longing to soar up,
like Icarus, towards the sun only to be blinded by its brilliance. The
aspiration towards that totality of vision whereby man, with impunity,
can stare at the sun necessarily brings with it, as Apollinaire indicates,
the danger of blindness and the threat of a terrible plunge into dark-
ness and death. This particular notion is clearly illustrated in the poem
'L'Ignorance' (PL, 49-50).

In the opening line Icarus declares that he holds the sun directly
responsible for firing his youthful ambition for adventure: 'Soleil, je
suis jeune et c'est à cause de toi' (PL, 49). At the same time his feelings
are charged with an almost sexual desire for the sun: 'Et j'ai pris mon
essor vers ta face splendide/(. . .) /Soleil, je viens caresser ta face
splendide/Et veux fixer ta flamme unique, aveuglement' (Ibid.). But
although the sun, the 'Dieu circulaire et bon', inspires the creative
spirit, it also immolates it before the point of ideal fulfilment is
reached. Its victims, nonetheless, like Icarus, even in death continue to
worship it: 'Au semblant des noyés il ira sur une île/Pourrir face tournée
vers le soleil splendide' (Ibid., 50).

Thus, in spite of its beneficence, the sun is a merciless master to those
who attempt to break out of their enslavement to it and enter into a
closer, more intimate communion with it. Then its blinding glare and
scorching incandescence become instruments of torture for a sadistic
solar tyrant. Its rays are frequently compared to whip-lashes, whipping
indolent nature into action:

    Mais soleil je veux te louer
  Car tu revins et fis claquer sur la nature

Des rayons tout à coup cinglés comme des fouets

(GM, 28)

Their stinging, stimulating effect on the world is comparable to the painful ecstasy of erotic flagellation:

Mon Lou je veux te reparler maintenant de l'Amour
Il monte dans mon cœur comme le soleil sur le jour
Et soleil il agite ses rayons comme des fouets
Pour activer nos âmes et les lier

(PL, 101)

and in the war-zone they become the perfect weapons with which to subjugate the German oppressor:

Entends braire l'âne boche
Faisons la guerre à coups de fouets
Faits avec les rayons du soleil

(C, 146)

In a counter movement of poetic feeling, during his moments of supreme creative confidence or in his attempts to convey the violence of the universal life force or, more especially, in his moods of profound psychological anguish, Apollinaire turns the tables on the torturing sun and subjects it to torture itself, a torture which frequently ends with its decapitation and death.

One of the first instances of the symbolical death of the sun in Apollinaire's poetry is found in an early adolescent piece, 'Aurore d'hiver'. After a rather drawn-out poetic labour, the winter dawn dies giving birth to a stillborn sun, bewitched by evil fairies: 'Et l'aurore joyeuse/(. . .)/Meurt/(. . .)/ Quasi honteuse/D'être mère d'un soleil mort-né' (GM, 129). The value of this poem lies simply in the fact that it provides an early example of what is later to become an important image in Apollinaire's work, the death of the sun. However, a poem from the same early period involves us in a more virile solar blood-bath. This poem, 'Les Doukhobors', through the revolutionary violence of its theme, with its reference to late nineteenth-century Russian terrorist activities, provides a full-blooded ferment in which the stillborn sun of 'Aurore d'hiver' is transformed for the first time into the decapitated sun of *Alcools*:

Les Doukhobors; le soleil qui radiait
Dut paraître à leurs yeux extasiés,
(. . .)
Le cou tranché d'une tête immense, intelligente,
Dont le bourreau n'osait montrer
La face et les yeux larges pétrifiés
   A la foule ivre,
Et quel sang, et quel sang, t'éclabousse, ô monde,
   Sous ce cou tranché!

                                                         (GM, 135-6)

In these lines we find all the elements connected with the image of
solar slaughter: the executioner, the decapitated head, and the profusely
streaming blood. For Apollinaire the act of decapitation itself symbol-
ises the innate brutality of human nature and also the violence of the
sexual urge, particularly when it has been thwarted by deceit and
treachery. For example, in 'Le Brasier' those false women who have
made the poet suffer are now made to pay for it with their heads:

Les têtes coupées qui m'acclament
Et les astres qui ont saigné
Ne sont que des têtes de femmes

                                                         (A, 90)

In 'Les Doukhobors' the decapitation of the sun is very clearly a
symbol for political assassination. However, the daily death of the sun
is also, to the Christian consciousness, an eternal reminder of the
death of Christ. At each sunset the blood of Christ is symbolically
spilled across the world, purifying the corrupt and redeeming the
sinful. In 'Le Dôme de Cologne' the stained-glass windows of the
cathedral at sunset are shown to assume sympathetically the aspect
of the stigmata, bleeding with light in imitation of Christ's passion:
'Pourtant par tes vitraux chaque couchant tu saignes/(. . .) /Le sang
du Christ-soleil . . .' (GM, 48). The association between Christ and the
sun is consolidated in a further series of images in which the return
of the sun at springtime, symbolising the resurrection of Christ at
Easter, seems to draw the poet out of the winter of his discontent,
warming up his heart, which is shown to be even more frozen and
persecuted than the forty Christian martyrs of Sebastia in Armenia
who were left to freeze to death on an ice-covered lake, and giving
him a sense of renewed religious faith:

> J'ai hiverné dans mon passé
> Revienne le soleil de Pâques
> Pour chauffer un cœur plus glacé
> Que les quarante de Sébaste
> Moins que ma vie martyrisés
>
> (A, 19)

In 'Les Fiançailles' we find a further stage in this cycle of solar decapitation. Here the poet, supremely confident of his ability to transmute the raw material of reality into poetic creations, begins by carrying out a savage assault on those very things through which his experience of the world is acquired, namely the senses. He transforms the five senses into the monstrous products of his own visionary fantasy and includes along with them a sixth sense, the sense of love and desire, or, more generally, the vital spark which inhabits all forms of life in the universe. Absolutely gigantic and tentacular in its magnitude, it is seen as a cosmic colossus, living paradoxically in a state of decapitation, with the sun forming its severed yet sentient head:

> L'un est pareil aux montagnes au ciel
> Aux villes à mon amour
> Il ressemble aux saisons
> Il vit décapité sa tête est le soleil
>
> (A, 119)

In a way it is Apollinaire himself who, feeling that he is, as he frequently suggests, a living and thinking centre of universal love, identifies with the 'soleil-tête' in the above image.

The stunning synthesis of all these metaphorical antecedents is brilliantly forged in the final line of 'Zone':

> Adieu Adieu
>
> Soleil cou coupé
>
> (A, 14)

In this laconic, yet highly charged and deeply reverberating image, the Christian and the cosmic are fused. The full impact of the image is concentrated into a dramatic ellipsis of five syllables. In 'Zone' the death of the sun takes place not at sunset, when it becomes a symbol of triumphant ritual sacrifice and renewal, but, tragically, at sunrise, the hour for guillotinings. The poem, which begins in a sunlit morning, expressive of hope and confidence, thus finally moves full circle, through various temporal and spatial zones and after a night of searching and self-questioning, to end in a dawn of utter despair. This summary execution of the sun, given the *coup de grâce* in the terse, staccato alliteration of 'cou coupé', symbolises from one point of view the death of Christ but, in a wider perspective, the terrible extinction of the source of life itself. All that has remained of the poet's early religious faith is finally killed off; all consoling belief in love is destroyed, underscored by the jeering pun of 'cocu' echoing in 'cou coupé'. In this painfully expressive image the poet symbolically cuts his own throat, indicating a state of inner anguish and self-loathing which is resolved metaphorically by his mutilating and annihilating himself. It is here that the sun, as a literary and cultural entity for the poet, achieves its apotheosis.

The poet's self-identification with the sun is apparent elsewhere in *Alcools*. In the third section of 'Les Fiançailles', dealing with the crisis of creative sterility through which the poet has recently passed, we find the lines:

Un Icare tente de s'élever jusqu'à chacun de mes yeux
Et porteur de soleils je brûle au centre de deux nébuleuses

(A, 116)

Here the poet has been transformed into a solar system, not simply a sun but a bearer of suns, suggesting his superhuman creative power. His struggle to give satisfactory literary expression to the ideal vision which blazes within him is conveyed by the reference to Icarus's striving flight. It is the poet's eyes which, as receptacles of vision, have been turned into suns, symbols of the potential brilliance of the poetry he carries within him, yet also symbols of an unattainable ideal. Like Icarus, the poet is blinded and burnt up by a vision so dazzling that he cannot find the words to express it. His powers of verbal expression fall short of his inspiration.

'Lul de Faltenin', a more arcane poem from the same period as 'Les Fiançailles', makes use of the same solar mythology. On one of the various levels at which this poem operates simultaneously, we find the allegory of poetry versus passion: the poet is torn between con-flicting forces, between the sky and the sea, between the stars and the sirens, between creative ambition and destructive sexual self-indulgence. Like the sun he consorts with the stars, yet each day he is submerged in a sea of troubles. The marine sunset of 'Lul de Faltenin' involves not just the symbolism of the sun's daily assassination, which is always a bloody spectacle: 'Le sang jaillit de mes otelles' (A, 76), but also the additional horror of death by drowning: 'Mer le soleil se gargarise' (A, 77), where the sun, symbol of the male, is engulfed by the sea, symbol of the female. The final stanza makes the assimilation of poet and sun complete: 'Le soleil d'hier m'a rejoint /Les otelles nous ensanglantent' (*ibid.*); their wounds, suggesting some kind of stigmata, are now exacerbated by the ravages of sexual desire, inflicted by the sirens with their 'terribles bouches muettes', dumb perhaps because the poet has been unable to provide them with those songs which he had so triumphantly proclaimed earlier in 'La Chanson du Mal-Aimé': 'Et des chansons pour les sirènes' (A, 21). The death of the poet-sun in 'Lul de Faltenin' is, therefore, the death of Apollo, who in Greek mythology was the god of both poetry and the sun: and as such it is an expression of the degradation and sterility of Apollinaire's creative talent during the period 1904-7.

Immediately before this period, however, in June 1904, when the poet composed the final victorious stanzas of 'La Chanson du Mal-Aimé', Apollo was still very much alive and providing his disciple with inspiration. In this poem, amidst the deadening heat of Paris in June, the sun at first evokes a feeling of physical malaise, which is then characteristically attenuated by means of more positive mythical associations. The poet escapes from the fierce physical power of the sun by seeing it as the lyre presented to Apollo by Mercury (A, 175) and thus transforming it into an instrument of creativity:

> Juin ton soleil ardente lyre
> Brûle mes doigts endoloris
> Triste et mélodieux délire
> J'erre à travers mon beau Paris
> Sans avoir le cœur d'y mourir

(A, 31)

The poet, even though saddened by unrequited love, feels the sun's rays like quivering, burning strings beneath his fingers and is stimulated into turning his suffering into song, a song which emerges as the celebrated 'Chanson du Mal-Aimé' itself.

However pre-eminent the symbolism of the sun might be in Apollin-

aire's creative vision, it is prevented from achieving absolute autocracy
by the controlling, countervailing force represented by the symbolism of
the shadow. In the poet's universe the shadow is not merely a symbol
for the powers of darkness which attempt to blot out the inspirational
light of the sun. It is not an element in a simple contrast of light and
shade. On the contrary, the shadow has its own complex nature, com-
pounded of several metaphorical factors, and it becomes a positive and
negative image operative in its own right. Nevertheless, in Apollinaire's
poetry, shadow and sun are shown to be intimately interrelated, involved
in a disconcerting metaphorical symbiosis.

To begin with, the shadow is an image of life, a symbol of vitality
and permanence, the dark projection of the living form. As such, as
Apollinaire shows in 'Sur les prophéties', it is too precious to be treated
with irreverence or to be subjected to necromantic scrutiny: 'J'ai
connu un sciomancien mais je n'ai pas voulu qu'il interrogeât
mon ombre' (C, 46). Icarus, in 'L'Ignorance', in his attempt to forsake
the human and embrace the divine, has flung away his shadow: 'Mon
ombre pour être fauste je l'ai jetée' (PL, 49), but in so doing has thrown
away life itself. When all else is lost, the shadow still remains faithful
and constant, representing, as it does for the friendless thief in 'Le
Larron', a companion in loneliness: 'Va-t'en errer crédule et roux
avec ton ombre' (A, 74). It becomes a projection of the poet's more
profound self yet also a reflection of death and destiny, doggedly
following him through life: 'Une épouse me suit c'est mon ombre
fatale' (A, 111). This same shadow-wife, playing Eurydice to the poet's
Orpheus, is found in 'La Chanson du Mal-Aimé', where it takes on
serpentine form, thus fusing Eurydice with the snake which caused her
death and becoming an object of both love and fear:

> Et toi qui me suis en rampant
> Dieu de mes dieux morts en automne
> Tu mesures combien d'empans
> J'ai droit que la terre me donne
> O mon ombre ô mon vieux serpent
>
> (A, 26)

This stanza is immediately followed by one in which the shadow, with
all its various associations, enters into communion with the sun, striking
up a duality which fits in with the overall pattern in *Alcools* of essential
paradox, ambivalence and contrast:

Au soleil parce que tu l'aimes
Je t'ai menée souviens-t'en bien
Ténébreuse épouse que j'aime
Tu es à moi en n'étant rien
O mon ombre en deuil de moi-même

(A, 26)

The shadow is, therefore, at once deeply disturbing, like the
'ombres infidèles' of the poet's defiled and guilt-ridden passion,
emerging from the 'demi-brume' of 'La Chanson du Mal-Aimé'
(A, 17-18); yet also deeply desired and sought after as if it were sun-
light itself: 'Passe il faut que tu poursuives/Cette belle ombre que tu
veux' (A, 47). In these lines this 'belle ombre' represents not the
projected image of the poet's personality, a shadow which, if inter-
rogated, might reveal the secret of his destiny; nor the fading vision,
in his memory, of a beloved woman; but perhaps more specifically
the shadow of poetry itself, a ravishing ideal which must be pursued
until the wavering outlines of inspiration have been transformed into
the 'ombre enfin solide' (A, 118) of real poetic creation. At the same
time the shadow is the sign of life: '(. . .) les pauvres fameux/Pour elle
eussent vendu leur ombre' (A, 19), and the emblem of death in life:
'O mon ombre en deuil de moi-même' (A, 26). As we have seen, the
poet might expose his soul to the sun: 'Mon âme au soleil se dévêt'
(A, 89), but he also clings to his shadow as if to life itself, refusing to
make this ultimate sacrifice to the sun-god:

J'ai tout donné au soleil
Tout sauf mon ombre

(A, 121)

For both the shadow and the sun are symbols of life, and the departure
of the shadow means the death of the sun, the one linked to the other:

Il y vient aussi nos ombres
Que la nuit dissipera
Le soleil qui les rend sombres
Avec elles disparaîtra

(A, 47)

The delicate balance of associations which is contained within the sun-
shadow duality is illustrated by one of the war poems from

Calligrammes, itself entitled 'Ombre'. Just as Apollinaire longed to
merge his own personality with the whole mass of humanity, or,
vice versa, to assimilate the mass of humanity into himself, so in
'Ombre' his own personal shadow merges with and assimilates the
shadows of his dead war companions. In this poem the shadow is once
again a multi-faceted symbol, signifying permanence and fidelity:
'Vous voilà de nouveau près de moi/ (. . .) /Un Indien à l'affût pendant
l'éternité/ (. . .) /Vous qui m'aimez assez pour ne jamais me quitter'
(C, 78); individual memories and collective memory: 'Souvenirs de mes
compagnons morts à la guerre/ (. . .) /Souvenirs qui n'en faites plus
qu'un/Comme cent fourrures ne font qu'un manteau' (*ibid*.); and, in
its elusive, reptilian form, death and the shades of the dead: 'Ombre
vous rampez près de moi/Mais vous ne m'entendez plus' (*ibid*.). Then,
in the final lines, shadow and sun are juxtaposed:

> Ombre multiple que le soleil vous garde
> (. . .)
> Ombre encre du soleil
> Ecriture de ma lumière
>
> (C, 78)

In other words, the solar radiance of the poet's own creative power
gives to the memory of the dead a firm and clearly outlined form,
a memory which is fixed forever by the printed words of the poem.
Thus Apollinaire, identifying with the sun, casts a shadow of words
on the page, a shadow which is 'Cette belle ombre (qu'il) veu(t)',
the 'ombre enfin solide', a shadow which is the poem itself, the inky
expression and printed projection of his luminous inspiration. But, as
the final line shows, since the poem has been inspired by death and
departed shadows, the poet is filled with grief, his divine songs are
interred with the bodies of his compatriots, and the sun-god is brought
down to earth: 'Un dieu qui s'humilie' (C, 78).

However, in 'La Jolie rousse', the final poem of *Calligrammes* and
the last significant poem of Apollinaire's life, it is the sun which
reigns supreme over the poet's world, the sun of summer which, at its
zenith, casts no shadow: 'O Soleil c'est le temps de la Raison ardente'
(C, 184). Thus the poet, feeling that he has reached a peak of maturity,
rejects the superstition of the shadow for the supralogical reason of the
sun. 'La Jolie rousse' again reveals the poet in his role as a seer and
enchanter, transforming the ordinary into the extraordinary, the
quotidien into the *merveilleux*, and using the senses as a springboard

to propel him towards an undiscovered world of myth and magic.
Returned to creative strength by means of a new love, 'la jolie rousse'
of the poem, with her halo of golden hair and embodying all the
sensual and restorative power of sunlight, he finally suffuses him-
self with solar force and bravely proclaims that he will continue his
struggle to keep his visionary powers alive and to communicate those
mysterious poetic enchantments which lie beyond the realm of
ordinary sensation and perception:

> Nous voulons vous donner de vastes et d'étranges domaines
> Où le mystère en fleurs s'offre à qui veut le cueillir
> Il y a là des feux nouveaux des couleurs jamais vues
> Mille phantasmes impondérables
> Auxquels il faut donner de la réalité

(C, 184)

Notes

1.   Quotations are from the Gallimard 'Poésie' editions of Apollinaire's works:
      Alcools (A); *Calligrammes* (C); *Poèmes à Lou*, together with *Il y a* (PL);
      Le Guetteur mélancolique, together with *Poèmes retrouvés* (GM); and
      L'Enchanteur pourrissant (EP). Other references are to the *Œuvres
      Complètes*, in four volumes, edited by Michel Décaudin, Paris, Balland et
      Lecat, 1965-6 (OC).
2.   In a well-known letter to Henri Martineau: 'chacun de mes poèmes est la
      commémoration d'un événement de ma vie ' (OC, IV, 768).
3.   Marcel Jean et Arpad Mezei, *Genèse de la Pensée Moderne*, Paris, Corrêa,
      1950, pp. 165-73.
4.   Louis Aragon, 'Calligrammes (Apollinaire)', in *L'Esprit nouveau*, no. 1,
      1920, p. 105.
5.   Louise Faure-Favier, *Souvenirs sur Apollinaire*, Paris, Grasset, 1945,
      p. 118.
6.   Jean Burgos, 'Apollinaire et le recours au mythe', in *Du monde européen
      à l'univers des mythes: Actes du Colloque de Stavelot* (1968), Paris,
      Minard, 1970, p. 122.

3 EYES AND SEEING IN THE POETRY OF PIERRE REVERDY

Michael Bishop

The poet's observation of the world about him is as eager and compulsive as it is persistent and long-suffering. It is, moreover, an observation that is not simply concerned to catch the surface gestures of a largely recalcitrant reality or to register the shifting and meaningless patterns of its disparate components. Like Baudelaire whom he so greatly admired, Reverdy seeks to establish the secret, but 'just' relationships between the things of the world. He must thus take care never to lose 'son rang de spectateur particulier et supérieur subtil, pénétrant, imaginatif, et capable de relier toutes choses par des rapports qu'il est seul capable de leur découvrir et de faire voir' (GC, 38).[1] The poet's seeing is, in consequence, of a most special order. Fascinated as the poet is with the wealth of phenomenal presence in which he is immersed, his seeing does not lead to a direct notation or catenation of the elements of this presence. Reverdy's poetry may be steeped in the things of reality, but it eschews any simple descriptive or discursive recording of them. It is true that, on the one hand, Reverdy allows his poems to become a place of meeting of world and poet, so that his art bears, of necessity, the traces of the joys and anguish, the aspirations and impediments of a primary mode of existence. Yet, on the other hand, it is equally true that, in accordance with Reverdy's strictly and obsessively articulated poetics, each and every poem constitutes a lasting testimony to the poet's transcendence of a purely natural and given condition and his attainment of a new, secondary level of being to which art alone can aspire.

The motif of looking and seeing lends itself in a particularly apt way to a discussion of such considerations inasmuch as it permits us to glimpse both sides of Reverdy's poetic equation. In the pages that follow I shall seek essentially to elaborate and demonstrate two points. Firstly, it will be shown that the eye is a prime carrier of the poet's relationships with the world of things and people and that the activity of looking and seeing constitutes a potent metaphor for the poet's desire to establish contact, to transform possibility into realisation and to achieve at least minimal fulfilment where nothingness and misery seem to prevail. Secondly, I shall attempt to show, rather more briefly, to what extent the poetry itself, taken as the living result of the poet's very act of seeing, may be said to achieve a tense and minimal, though sure and magical, transcendence of the lingering traces of existential data. If our first concern is therefore to reveal some of the primary emotions, sensations and volitional drives that cling to the activity of seeing, our final attention will be devoted to a demonstration of the fact that the poet's seeing may bring about a discreet aesthetic and ontological transcendence of the emptiness and distress they frequently offer.

The activity of seeing is of fundamental ontological significance to the poet, for it is one of the principal channels by means of which the essential openness of his being may be maintained and an apprehension of reality, both natural and poetic, brought about:

> Et je suis là
> Les yeux penchés sur la caricature
> Un poing sur la réalité bien pleine

> (PT, 279)

Both life and art are 'realised' by the subtle interplay of all of the poet's faculties and senses and by the relationships they lay down and continually remodel in and with the world. The hand, the heart, the mind and the ear, in particular, play equally important roles in Reverdy's work. Being is therefore constituted not only by virtue of the activity of seeing. It is, for example, as much a question of 'la vie avec son cœur', as of 'la vie avec ses yeux' (PT, 153). And this is so whether the poet is concerned with a purely primary mode of existence in which sight still remains for Reverdy 'le plus implacable des sens, celui qui saisit et domine le plus fermement, le plus nettement, ce qui concerne son domaine' (EV, 23); or whether he inflates the ontological significance and functional capacity of sight, so that it becomes an instrument of poetic vision whose powers of seizure and domination come to parallel those of the poetic imagination itself. In this case the original, merely perceptual control is cast off, as it were, in favour of an intuitive apprehension and conceptual mastery. For Reverdy, then, the fact of the poet's seeing is inseparably interwoven with the fact of his primary being in the world, just as it is intimately associated with the poet's special need to go beyond this level of being in an effort of imaginative, liberating and revelatory vision.

But patience and attentiveness are required in playing this deadly serious game of being and seeing. The poet's gaze does not achieve directly and without a struggle the fulfilment it craves, and Reverdy's poems often couple together the acts of looking and waiting, as in 'Jeux d'hommes sous la tente': 'Les regards/les attentes' (PT, 277), or in 'Dans les champs ou sur la colline': 'On attendait/On regardait' (PT, 222). If such a waiting reveals the poet's basic attitude of expectancy, his anticipation of a certain something, a later poem such as 'Attente', from *Ferraille*, shows that looking and expectancy may also point to the poet's state of nervous preparedness in the face of the endless 'risques et périls' (RP, 7) that life and creation may generate:

> Et mon désir glissait sur la route du temps
> Aride au bord du mystère des gouffres
> Mon cœur obscur jeté aux crevasses du doute
> Et l'œil inquiet qui regarde de temps en temps
> Par-dessus l'épaule du soir si rien ne vient
> Si rien ne sortira du sort que je redoute
>
> (MO, 351)

Ideally, the poet's looking will permit a transformation of possibility and desire into realisation and attainment, and 'Attente' begins with an affirmation of a tenuously continuing and positive expectation: 'Il se peut qu'on émeuve encore le dormeur/Enseveli sous des lambeaux de rêve à fond de cale/Il se peut qu'on atteigne encore la lueur/Qui grimpe à l'horizon de branche en branche' (MO, 350). But the closing lines already cited show just how fragile and impaired the desire may be, just how necessary a cautious, defensive scanning of the horizon may be, in order to avoid the unexpected occurrence and to salvage what is glimpsed on the horizon of a more glowing potentiality.

The poet's act of looking and seeing demands, therefore, a steady and at times uneasy vigilance. Such a vigilance, with its odd mixture of optimism and self-protectiveness, reveals the dual fact of the poet's openness and exposure to the phenomena, human and non-human, of the world. The eye's activity involves, in effect, a two-way movement. There is an out-going as well as an in-coming, a direct and forceful effort on the part of the poet to search and achieve contact, in addition to a less controllable arrival of phenomena into the 'searchlight' range of the scanning eye. The poet's gaze may thus, on occasions, be directed upon given spaces with a vague intentionality, but the precise nature of what arrives or comes about cannot be predicted: 'La tête qui paraît regarde dans le ciel/Attend ce qui peut arriver' (PT, 284).

No *foreseeing* is thus possible and the act of looking is shown to be steeped in contingency.

Expectancy may be rewarded, however, and things do indeed flood into the 'locus' of openness and anticipation that is the eye or the eyeing poet. 'L'eau et la clarté de la lune lui coulaient doucement dans l'œil', Reverdy tells us in the opening line of 'Flammes' (MO, 75); and in 'Filet d'astres', a poem that delicately fuses notions of voyaging, hope, arrival and union, we read of the enigmatic coming of 'Un navire indécis [qui] navigue vers mes yeux' (PT, 295). It is, moreover, via this essentially unforeseeable arrival of things into the eye's sphere of operation that an appropriation of the world may come about. Coming into revelation themselves, seen phenomena reveal the poet's inner being by their very constitution of it. In this sense, *eau, clarté* and *navire*, in the two poems above, not only come into being themselves, but in the complexity or simplicity of their own attributes and relationships, may be said momentarily to constitute the poet's own ever-becoming being. However, it would be inappropriate to believe that the modes of waiting and looking, allied to the notion of arrival, engender in the poet a dull, unresponsive passivity. Just as there may be an anticipated and desired coming of phenomena to the eye, so the act of looking possesses within itself the power and urge to respond actively to the deeply felt fascination of life's enigmatic signs and stimuli. With the placing of 'Un œil à la fenêtre/Tout le mystère humain se posera' (MO, 490), Reverdy declares; and, elsewhere, the strange magnetism of half-sensed things that brush past in their seemingly fleeting presence may be felt, as when the poet's attention is caught by 'le bout de l'aile blanche [qui] attire l'œil' (MO, 189). Life is definitely there, 'à regarder en face' (MO, 494); its things lure and attract the poet's gaze and demand that he confront the teeming spectacles and scenes in which they find themselves enmeshed.

But the poet, 'celui qui regarde en tremblant le roulement perpétuel et terrible du monde et son calme' (FV, 76), may find that his act of observation needs to be more specifically and searchingly directed. In principle concerned with all the things of life, his special mode of seeing, as an image of the poet's fundamental creative activity, strives intuitively towards selection. To 'see' in the midst of all that there is to be looked at, to apprehend in the midst of all that is thrust upon the poet's sensitive retina, requires a dedication to discovery and attainment that is quite beyond the ordinary. This dedication is reflected in Reverdy's poetry by the abundance of motifs which engage the eye in acts of scanning ('On suit de l'œil/Le pays neuf/La terre

propre' (PT, 360)); fixing ('les yeux fixant le cours limpide des nuages'
(PT, 338)) or measuring ('Les yeux mesurent l'altitude où vous êtes
placé' (PT, 188)). Seeing, in this way, is made to involve a rather more
deliberate and conscious out-going drive whose gauging activity may
embrace, all the better, discovery, knowing and contact alike. More-
over, in its somewhat dogged pursuit of objects of attention and the
potential significance which attaches to them, the eye will often shift
the direction of its gaze from the horizontal to the vertical plane.
In this way the poet may explore the recessed substrata of reality and
fathom those mysterious yawning chasms that stretch below: 'En
dessous/un trou/l'œil fonce sans limite/Et que trouvera-t-on au bout'
(PT, 200). Or else his gaze may soar upwards to seek the vital nourish-
ment, the soothing caress and the mysterious significance it so clearly
craves in poems such as 'Horizon' ('Et le ciel me soutient/Le ciel où
je lave mes yeux tous les matins' (PT, 71)) and 'L'homme aux étoiles'
('le regard frappe au ciel et la porte qui s'ouvre laisse entrevoir l'espace
où remuent les formes mortes sur les chemins tracés par un doigt
lumineux' (FV, 98)).

The recurrence in Reverdy's poems of these varied motifs of visual
search, measurement and interrogation underlines quite clearly the
poet's determination to bring into focus, by means of a seeing
alternatively described as telescopic (cf. RP, 198) and microscopic
(cf. LB, 166), the fine grain of reality's secrets. Fortunately the poet
has the telling advantage of possessing 'des yeux plus loin que les vôtres,
des yeux qui portent plus haut et plus loin que les vôtres' (PH, 104),
for his attempt to bridge the distance that stretches both between
individual things and between things and himself demands that he
carry out his observations 'd'un regard clair et sec' (SM, 14), even with
a measure of 'cruauté' (LB, 166). It is paradoxically only by way of a
dry limpidity and a hard detachment that seeing may make its contact.
Only then may the unobserved become visible. Only then may what is
normally concealed from — and even perhaps by — others, be brought
into the open:

Ce que j'avais vu
On ne se souvient pas
Personne ne remarque
Ce qui reste dedans après avoir vécu
Et j'emporte derrière moi
Sans que tu le saches
Les signes les visages et les mots

Et tout ce qu'on ne veut pas laisser voir
Qui se cache

(MO, 280)

What the poet's vision brings about is an at once aesthetic and onto-
logical appropriation of the world. The trail the poet blazes is one of
illumination and tempestuously sudden flashes of *insight*. His is a
seeing of what is overlooked or otherwise kept from his view; it is a
distillation of the substance of existence and a retention of its essence;
and it demands a dragging along, behind the self and finally out into
the open before other people, into the 'clearing' of the poem[2], not so
much of 'les choses telles qu'elles sont', but rather of things 'telles
que, sans lui [le poète], ils ne les verraient pas' (EV, 84). Confronted
with the variegated and yet oddly blank surfaces of reality, Reverdy
seeks to reach those high points of intense and visionary being
where he may declare that with 'un seul coup d'œil/J'ai surpris le
secret des sources' (MO, 405) or that 'cette prunelle regarde et touche
au loin/le corps blanc du mystère' (MO, 14). Only at such moments
will the ever-felt tensions between shallow appearance and profound
being be resolved. Only then will the poet perhaps be able to 'voir le
réel, ce qui est, rien que lui' (GC, 45).

While it is essential to appreciate the full and persistent power of the
advancing, embracing movement initiated by the poet's activity of
looking and seeing, an examination of many of Reverdy's collections
of poetry — and, in particular, later ones such as *Ferraille, Plein verre,
Le Chant des morts* or *Bois vert* — will soon impress upon us a
negative tonality and an increasingly pervasive aura of anguish and
failure. The poetic act of looking is by no means assured of a direct
and uninhibited passage from desire to fulfilment. The world's
phenomena and inhabitants possess a potential cruelty that is especially
damaging to the sensitive mechanism of an eye engaged in the finely
calibrated out-going movements to which it is committed. The poet's
eyes may thus be 'percés par les rayons brûlants' (MO, 178), provoked
to tears by a seemingly innocent encounter ('C'est le jour qui entre ou
quelque souvenir qui fait pleurer tes yeux' (PT, 316)) or inexplic-
ably reddened to the point of bleeding ('Mais le monde est ouvert à
tous les pas/Aux ailes/Et même au vent du soir/Pour passer la ruelle
où crie l'homme aux prunelles qui saignent' (PT, 341)). Those that
share the poet's world, too, often manifest a similarly grievous hostility.

In particular, the gaze of others, at times warm and caressing, may become, repeatedly though unpredictably, a gesture of shameful intent ('J'ai deviné ton regard qui transparaît sous tes paupières closes et le dessein qui fait rougir ton front' (PT, 34)) if not of outright aggression ('Ce regard/qui m'a laissé son dard dans le flanc' (MO, 528)). In such situations of phenomenal and human antagonism, Reverdy's poems may tell of an instinctive search for shelter and seclusion, as in 'Les poètes': 'Sa tête s'abritait craintivement sous l'abat-jour de la lampe. Il est vert et ses yeux sont rouges' (PT, 19). Eyes may often avert their gaze from danger and menace, withdrawing from a contact that is harmful. Indeed, despite the poet's continuing desire to discover and to know, a divergent wish may arise, whereby the poet 'ne veu[t] plus rien voir' (PT, 148; MO, 298). The eye's understandable evasive action is thus pushed to its extreme limit, although it is clear that this constitutes a decidedly desperate gesture and one that risks a fundamental denaturation of the eye's very *raison d'être*. Instead of bringing about a hoped-for fulfilment, 'les yeux se sont remplis d'un sombre désespoir' (PT, 233) — a filling has materialised, but it would seem to be purely negative. Instead of attaining to a realm of being and possession, the poet's seeing is reduced to non-apprehension and to a blank nothingness.

It is important to stress, too, that this fact of being left in a state of dark emptiness may come about by means of what may be thought of as an inverted hostility on the part of the world and its inhabitants. Whereas, before, the poet's gaze had been greeted with out-going but inimical gestures that had forced it to retreat, it now meets insufficient response or else bears witness to a disquieting withdrawal of the world's phenomena beyond the eye's zone of influence. Reverdy draws attention to a hiatus between the poet and other men, a hiatus which forces the poet into an isolation both distressing and privileged: 'Les yeux gris et leurs rêves/Des hommes plus petits/ (. . .) /Des haussements d'épaules/Et le pilote nu/seul/à la pointe du môle' (PT, 388). The poet's creative activity, like his special sight, maintains a degree of acute sensitivity quite beyond the caring capacity of the others 'qui passent sans regarder' (MO, 244), with their 'yeux indifférents' (PT, 79). Whereas the poet's seeing betokens a vigilance and concern and strives creatively towards contact in defiance of an at best painfully savoured solitude, the indifference of the others' gaze hovers between unwatchful negligence and an almost intentional shunning: 'Près de moi il y a des gens qui ne me regardent même pas/D'autres que j'ai vus et qui ne me voient pas' (PT, 132). Because of this the possibility of a simple and natural communion with others, via eyes, is often felt to slip away. In order that communion may not be totally thwarted by this seemingly impassable distance between self and others, in order that something may be salvaged from nothingness, the poet's gaze must become poetic vision, a vision capable of producing those astonishing 'cristaux déposés après l'effervescent contact de l'esprit avec la réalité' (GC, 18) — crystals that may lie there, in silence, until ultimately glimpsed by men.

This kind of slipping or ebbing of the possibility of human contact is mirrored in the eye's relationships with the world at large. The previously available light, on which the eye depends, may begin to fade 'et pour retrouver l'ordre à travers ce mystère/On n'a même pas la clarté intérieure de l'œil' (MO, 97). The world's potential wealth and profundity is, at such times, lost. Reality remains 'aplatie dans un angle' (*ibid*.), flatly housed in its quotidian dimensions, its fullness unglimpsed. Eyes weaken, perhaps 'réduits par la fatigue' (PT, 261), unable to maintain their hold on things that now live in terms of their bewildering departure: 'Tout ce qu'on voit/Tout ce qu'on croit/ C'est ce qui part' (PT, 196). Where, previously, access and apprehension had been afforded by the poet's persistent gaze, now feelings of severe deprivation and limitation reign. The poet can no longer see what he could see before and his restricted sight is often able to pick out only the most sombre and menacing fragments of reality, 'l'ombre dans la nuit' (MO, 230) or 'la nuit noire et le mur qui soutient la maison' (PT, 330).

This withdrawal of sought phenomena and the unhappy narrowing of the poet's field of vision are further complicated by the frequent interposing of barriers between the eye and what it seeks to contact. The poet may thus experience the discomfort and confusion of 'un nuage sur l'œil' (MO, 532) or else 'un voile de neige qui tombe pour nous empêcher de voir' (PT, 87). At its worst, as for example in the poem 'Mais pourquoi', such blockage spells not the innocence of the evening's restorative sleep, but rather the nightmare of the closing day, and indeed of death itself, with the dark and irremediable imprisonment of its blindness:

Le soir déroule enfin son immense visière
qui tombe sur mes yeux et partage mon cœur
Les pierres du malheur s'entassent sous le lierre
Et le rocher distille les perles de la peur

(MO, 513)

With the dropping shut of the night's visor comes a reign of terror, one that nullifies the promise of a morning 'luisant d'allégresse' and replaces it with the chilling prospect of finality and nothingness. Thus the poet's seeing, powerfully searching and receptive as it may be, is reminded of its vulnerability by the very diurnal flow of time. In the midst of being, a nothingness is always imminent; the poet may at any time be obliged to confess to himself that 'On n'a rien vu/De tout ce qui passait on n'a rien retenu' (PT, 177), or else that 'Tu ne peux rien voir/Ni rien saisir malgré tes bras/La nuit a glissé sur ton front/Elle a soufflé sur tes paupières/Eteint ton regard' (MO, 198). The poet's blindness — which may, moreover, combine occasionally with other malfunctions to produce a more general debility, a state of near-complete mental and physical collapse ('Aveugle/sourd/Et sans savoir/Les jambes plient' (PT, 380)) — this blindness, no matter how apparently temporary, carries the threat of permanent deprivation and blank absence. External and internal limitations upon the eye's functioning may be countered with vigour, as profound horror is experienced at the thought of a complete void, a vertiginous nothingness. Yet, for Reverdy, the experience is far from uncommon and its menace fundamental in that non-seeing, temporary or permanent, constitutes an extinction of the self, a suppression of being. The Reverdyan imagination tends to present its subjective assessments as objectively possible. If nothing is seen, perhaps there is, objectively, nothing: 'Mais derrière on ne voit plus rien/Il n'y reste peut-être rien' (PT, 360). At all events the subjective orientation of the imagination is such that an objectively relative datum becomes a subjectively absolute datum. If there is nothing to be seen, the poet is reduced to being as nothingness — at least inasmuch as the eye is a partial metaphor for being. The Reverdyan imagination finds itself locked within its own forces. It cannot leap beyond its own relativity. The structures of the imagination are not *felt* to be relative, and, indeed, they are not, psychologically, relative. The danger of the closing of eyes is therefore felt to be real, and its frequency in Reverdy's poetry thus all the more disturbing. For, whenever 'Les yeux se ferment/On pourrait mourir' (PT, 208). The mundane and banal event of eyelids closing, as of evening falling, is transformed into a consciousness of the permanent contingency of death and non-being. Just as it manages to impress upon us the fact that any attainable fullness of being and seeing will necessarily be fragile, pressured as it is on all sides by the violent and recurrent incursions of a nothingness fostered by the poet's sightless, impotent groping.

*   *   *

Like all great poetry, that of Reverdy is non-acquiescent in character This is true, moreover, in two ways. Firstly, despite the increasingly oppressive atmosphere of Reverdy's poems, a tenaciously clinging, yet lucid optimism continues to inspire them. No matter how grim or anguishing the conditions of the poet's primary mode of being, the poetry always manages to maintain traces of bare survival. Secondly, the poet's non-acquiescence is, paradoxically, most strongly felt by virtue of the existence of the very poems in which the spectre of nothingness is most visible — strongly felt, but often pushed out of sight, wedged in the metaphoric and syntactic interstices of the poet's act of visionary transformation of the banal and the natural. The poet does not so much speak of such a survival, such a minimal yet magical transcendence, as demonstrate or enact, via his poetic production, the rejection and domination of a nothingness that had threatened to crush him. The closing pages of this essay will be devoted to a short examination of these two inter-related points and will reveal just how delicately paradoxical the resolution of the tensions of being and nothingness may be for the poet's act of seeing.

Confronted with inhibitions of varying intensity, the poet's gaze remains, in effect, available. Vision may be impeded, but, inevitably, 'l'œil . . . cherche une meilleure trace' (MO, 65); for as long as eyes can maintain their will to feed upon an albeit scant and intermittent success, they may retain their status as instruments 'qui n'ont jamais fini de regarder' (FV, 48). In this way, in the seemingly frequent absence of finely focused seeing, a persistent looking may still be rewarded with 'un reflet de fleur dans la prunelle de la vieillesse' (MO, 386). And death itself is defied, if not denied, by the poet's sightless though insistent gaze: 'La cendre des yeux morts pourtant toujours ouverts' (MO, 361) — a gaze that continues through suffering and frustration until a seeing may become truly possible, until a more positive modification of the poet's relationships with the world may be, however fleetingly, brought about. It is this persistent determination that enables the eye to hold on through the anguish of blindness and 'negative' being so that a certain adaptation or habituation may set in: 'Le globe est fermé/On ne voit plus rien/Puis les yeux s'habituent' (PT, 268). What the poet shows he understands is that although the inhibitions affecting vision may threaten and even momentarily impose the non-being of non-seeing, they may yield to a certain — perhaps equally momentary — transcendence.[3] These are features that may just be coped with via a recovery of possibility. For just as possibility may ebb and nothingness may loom, so may the movement be reversed. A compensatory up-swing of possibility may thus be achieved in what can now be recognised as a vacillation between seeing and blindness, something and nothing. This is the case, for example, in an early poem from *Cale sèche*, 'Comme chaque soir', where the protective closing of eyes is deliberately executed with the youthfully buoyant assurance of a cyclical resumption of the possibility of seeing: 'Attention prends garde à la lumière/Ferme les yeux tes cils sont chargés de poussière/Quand se lèvera la lune/Tu pourras les rouvrir' (MO, 480). Dust, like other agents of harm, may be tolerated, perhaps only barely, in anticipation of an ultimate retrieval of conditions of lighting appropriate to the poet's clearer vision; and it is because such anticipation continues to be feasible that the poet deems it worthwhile to remain available, 'la prunelle accrochée à la lueur naissante' (MO, 391), vigilant in the midst of blindness and death, still ready to grasp after the slightest budding potentiality. After all, as Reverdy reveals in 'Convoitise', 'Il suffit d'un mouvement imperceptible de tes lèvres/D'un changement dans la clarté de ton regard/D'un muscle sous la peau qui danse/Ou encore d'un geste de tendresse qui arrive en retard/Tout est changé' (MO, 341). Change and vacillation, whether down-swing or up-swing, may result from the most minimal modification in self-world relations. The slightest gesture and everything may be transformed. Out of the hollow of nothingness a miraculous kind of fullness may emerge. This is indeed the central tenet of Reverdy's aesthetics; it is a notion deeply embedded in the thematics of his work; and it is, as we shall finally see, the marvellous practice of his art. The poet, to remain a poet, cannot succumb in meek surrender to non-seeing. He must remain forever sensitive to the 'lueur à peine perceptible' (SM, 33) that resides within him and without and that may be converted into fire and vision. Reduced as he increasingly is to admit 'Je n'ai plus assez de lumière/Assez de peau assez de sang/La mort gratte mon front/Et la meme matière/S'alourdit vers le soir autour de mon courage', he must still find the stamina to remain conscious of the 'but', of the 'yet', that can modify his condition, the fact that there is 'toujours le réveil plus clair dans la flamme de ses mirages' (MO, 333).

It is appropriate to speak of a delicate, tense and varyingly expressed equilibrium governing the basic movements of the Reverdyan imagination. Certainly there are, as we have observed, many occasions when non-seeing dissolves to permit a glimpse of fragments or even the attainment of substantial visionary goals. And there are, equally, many instances where, despite the closure of the eye's channel of being, other channels may remain at least partially open: 'On entend tous les bruits mais les yeux sont éteints' (PT, 360). Eyes may be extinct, but sounds are registered in their totality and the poet's being is thus paradoxically constituted not only in terms of extinction, but also, almost simultaneously, in terms of wholeness. Such evidence of the poet's occasionally joyous, though more often woefully painful transcendence of nothingness and the establishment of an ontological equilibrium, is of course articulated within the thematics of the poetry, within its metaphoric-discursive flow. The transcendence, the vacillation and the compensatory balance are, however minimally, stated. But it is clear that transcendence is achieved not merely by the fact of statement; indeed, it reflects the 'anti-natural' accomplishment of the poet's creative vision within the bounds of a natural condition that tends to erode the very basis of such accomplishment.[4] In effect, the greatest paradox and the greatest feat of transcendence and equilibration lie in the existence, and especially the manner of existence, of Reverdy's poems. Such transcendence is constantly obscured by the very traces of original being and emotion out of which poetic transcendence has been spun. What must be understood is that, wherever there is, within the thematics of the poems, a surface pullulation of 'negative' being, fading vision or blindness, at the same time equilibrium and 'positive' being are quietly and deftly derived from the fact of the re-created, figurative form of that negativity.

In accordance with Reverdy's own ideas, I have argued that the poet's seeing and being are inextricably woven together, so that the poet becomes, and is, *what* he sees. Should his vision lapse into blindness, his being is beset with the dark night of nothingness, 'la nuit de velours/masque du vide' (MO, 373). Should he glimpse contact and splendour, his being is correspondingly exalted. The *what* of this Reverdyan equation implies, however, not only the simple agglomeration of its component parts, for it includes within itself a *how*. It is this *how* — this *how the poet sees what he sees* — that accounts for the poet's magical transformation of emptiness and torment into a form of at least minimal fullness and beauty, into that 'light and happiness' in which Reverdy considered Matisse's art, and in consequence his true being, to be steeped. Thus, when Reverdy speaks, in 'Chair vive', of 'Ma vie dans la coulisse/D'où je vois onduler les moissons de la mort' (MO, 522) or when, in 'Mais pourquoi', he declares, as we have heard earlier, that 'Le soir déroule enfin son

immense visière/qui tombe sur mes yeux et partage mon cœur/Les
pierres du malheur s'entassent sous le lierre/Et le rocher distille les
perles de la peur' (MO, 513) — on such occasions when death is seen
and a frighteningly sudden blindness descends upon the poet, the
negative composition of his being is transcended by the poet's own
imaginative seizure, domination and reconstitution of it. Seeing does
not merely offer the nothingness of death and blindness, for it
functions miraculously over and above such inhibitions thanks to the
new poetic figures it manages to shape from the old, terrifying stuff
of concrete experience and psychological obsession. Death, just like
the masking of eyes, is thus recast in metaphoric mould, and it is out
of this newly moulded form that the poet achieves the creation of a
new form or mode of being — one that retains the things and events
of nature, but in the transmuted, anti-natural form of art.

This dual mode of natural and anti-natural seeing and being is
evoked by many of Reverdy's poems. In the poem 'Santé de fer', for
example, we recognise that on the one hand the poet's being is
diminished to little more than a locus of disintegration and skeletal
decay, whence he may do no more than transmit a desperate signalling
of his wrecked condition: 'Ma place est au niveau des cercles désunis/
Appels désespérés/Signaux de ma détresse/Voile désemparée/Carcasse
de la nuit' (MO, 428). On the other hand, however, as the same poem
actually tells us, the poet may manage an occasional transcendence of
this condition by means of his poetic riding of 'La vague qui parfois
soulève ma nature/Et rejette une épave à l'approche du soir'. Such a
piece of poetic flotsam, one of those miraculously salvaged 'épaves du
ciel'[5], at once maintains and strains away from the immediate, daily,
terre à terre contact with nature. 'C'est le carré chantant d'une source
limpide', as Reverdy puts it, a finally sub-transcendent locus of
limpid gazing and melodious form — sub-transcendent because the
poem is caught between the distress of its elements of natural being
and the 'singing limpidity' of figurative being, the latter straining away
from and just transcending the former. But, as we must insist, the
poet does not achieve transcendence merely by telling of its occurrence.
It is the manner of telling that finally convinces us that transcendence
is occurring. It is the reality of the demonstration that finally per-
suades. Transcendence must be spoken, not just spoken of, for it
resides within the imaginative vision underpinning the poetry's abund-
ant modes of figuration. In Reverdy's poems there is not, therefore,
the often flat articulation and discursive logic of his notebook entries.
'Santé de fer', like so many of Reverdy's poems, emerges out of the

blue, thrusting upon us its unrooted elements. Its discursive-thematic development is metaphoric and elliptical, proceeding via the accumulated flurries of at once distinct and loosely dovetailed or opposed fragments. In this way the poem is able to create an inner coherence and offer a series of richly obscure revelations by means of a 'visionary' interplay of imagery and syntax whose degree of poetic *écart* is constantly shifting. The poet's place may be 'au niveau des cercles désunis', his condition that of the capsized vessel splintered into a corpse-like débris and flashing its final and futile signals of distress. But such a state is astonishingly overcome by virtue of its being so articulated, so imagined, so woven into the fine fabric of a complex and 'just' figuration.[6]

Many, many examples could be given of this tense equilibrium between what is often a negatively charged thematics and a virile, magnificently restless imaginativeness. All would serve to demonstrate the tensions of seeing and non-seeing, being and nothingness, that haunt Reverdy's poetry. All would point to the poignant paradox inherent in the dual fact that Reverdy is, perhaps more than any other modern poet, a poet of failure, a poet obsessed with non-attainment and non-seeing; and that he yet manages to achieve so much, to seize and to see so much, to create, out of a primary experience hovering between drabness and anguish, a kind of 'critique d'or de la misère' (MO, 390), a form of luminous and visionary being enabling survival in the midst of a dark nothingness. And even if, after all, as Reverdy is bold enough to suspect, art were to prove to be merely the other face of such nothingness — 'si tout ce que j'ai vu m'avait trompé/S'il n'y avait rien derrière cette toile qu'un trou vide' (MO, 18) — the poet's continued commitment to poetic vision would not be wasted. There would remain the satisfaction of leaving 'sur la terre un léger souvenir/Un geste de regret/Une amère grimace/Ce que j'aurai mieux fait' (*ibid.*). Besides, the poet has no choice, if he is to continue to be a poet. His nervous looking is an inevitable part of his struggle through, against and yet for, life. 'On ne peut plus dormir tranquille quand on a une fois ouvert les yeux' (PT, 126), Reverdy affirms. To be born to seeing is to realise the unceasing uneasiness of life. Yet, strangely, it is out of the very substance of such a peering, out of the gaining of poetic insight into the distressing experience of life, that for Reverdy, a truer and purer being may be fashioned.

Notes

1. The following abbreviations are used: SD *Self-defence*, Paris, Imprimerie Littéraire, 1919; LB *Le Livre de mon bord*, Paris, Mercure de France, 1948 (1970 edition); MO *Main d'œuvre*, Paris, Mercure de France, 1949 (1964 edition); SP *Au Soleil du plafond*, Paris, Tériade, 1955; EV *En Vrac*, Monaco, Editions du Rocher, 1956; SM *Sable mouvant*, Paris, Louis Broder, 1966; PT *Plupart du Temps*, Paris, Flammarion, 1967; GC *Le Gant de crin*, Paris, Flammarion, 1968; FV *Flaques de verre*, Paris, Flammarion, 1972; RP *Risques et périls*, Paris, Flammarion, 1972; NEP *Note éternelle du présent*, Paris, Flammarion, 1973.

2. The notion of the poem as *clairière*, a special place of being and illumination, seems to be firmly lodged in Reverdy's imagination. See the preface to SD and, for example, these poems: MO, 397; MO, 471; PT, 235

3. This is not to deny the subjective absoluteness of such motifs as inhibition and non-seeing, which present themselves as 'stopped' moments, as it were, in the poem's temporal flow of being and imagining. It should be observed, too, that the non-relativity of the poem's thematic structures is not cancelled by their figurative transcendence but, rather, is simultaneously compensated on a different level of being that is *purely* that of the poet.

4. For an understanding of Reverdy's idea of art as anti-nature see, for example, his essay on Georges Braque, 'Une Aventure méthodique' (NEP, 39-104).

5. The title of Reverdy's 1924 selection of his poems previously published between 1915 and 1922.

6. To obtain a better impression of the importance Reverdy attaches to *justesse* in art, see the following: GC, 9, 30, 174; SP, 23-4; EV, 157; NEP, 110, 124.

4 FROM THE LABYRINTH OF LANGUAGE TO THE LANGUAGE OF THE SENSES: THE POETRY OF ANDRE BRETON

Michael Sheringham

Je reviens à mes loups à mes façons de sentir

(S, 32)[1]

While many poets require us to go beyond the evident themes and modes of statement in their poems to the latent sensibility from which they emerge, Breton involves the reader immediately in his personal response to the world around him. Before we can appreciate the significance of this profusion of the sensibility on the surface of Breton's poetry, it is helpful to examine the importance which he attaches to sense-experience. For Breton it is in man's sensory contact with the world that an intuition of his personal identity is most available to him: self and world are reciprocally defining concepts, the individual is inhabited by the accretions of his sensory contact with things:

Je ne suis pas seul en moi-même
Pas plus seul que le gui sur l'arbre de moi-même
Je respire les nids et je touche aux petits des étoiles

(CDT, 65)

The things to which we are drawn — objects, landscapes, textures — and our reception of the sensory signals they emit, form an ever-evolving constellation (SEP, 260) which is the figure of our sensibility. Breton refers to the 'sensations électives' (Na, 22) which together constitute an individual's 'lumière propre' (Na, 128), and frequently in his work we come across lists of things to which his response seems particularly self-illuminating. But to discover the self is, simultaneously, to discover the world. Breton gives the initiative to his senses, allowing them a free rein: 'Je pique les coursiers de mes sens/Les uns sont montés par de belles Amazones/Les autres se cabrent au bord des précipices vermeils' (CDT, 66).

It is not to the usual run of sensations that Breton introduces us — nor to the circumscribed, rational world which these alternatively license and betray. Indeed if he himself contributes to the discrediting of ordinary sense experience, it is not in the name of any rational

evidence but to assert the cognitive role of less familiar sensations
in respect of aspects of reality which the rational mind ignores but to
which the individual sensibility gives testimony. There are certain
sensations which reveal a hidden face of the world which corresponds
to the hidden side of the mind — the unconscious. Revelation of the
unconscious is directly linked to revelation of the world, and the
senses are the agents of this process. The senses, however, can reveal
the world only in so far as they have been activated by it, and in this
lies the crucial role of the individual sensibility. Yet Breton does not
propose a reversion to primitive modes of consciousness — pure
anoesis or Lawrentian 'blood-knowledge'; the role of the poet is to
'dégager l'intelligible du sensible' (V, 141). What is essential is that
the senses should *lead*; if we permit them to, argues Breton, a wider
horizon will be available even to the conscious mind.

Breton frequently addresses himself in his work to the problem of
how we can incorporate into our everyday conception of the world
fleeting moments of revelation which have fashioned our sensibility.
The individual's unconscious bears the imprint of its encounters with
the hidden aspect of the world, achieved through the process of
reciprocal illumination which I have outlined, and it is by gaining access
to the unconscious that he can avail himself, in a more permanent way,
of the gifts which his sensibility has amassed for him. In Breton's view
it is the office of poetry to provide the means for this access.

The surrealists discovered that it was possible to accede to the
unconscious if the mind was allowed to express itself spontaneously
in a manner which minimised the control of reason. In a second stage,
the poem or text produced in this way acts as a catalyst through which
the moments of perception which have made a deep impression on our
unconscious can be re-precipitated in the mind. The poem itself comes
to embody the trace of sensation on the mind; in so far as they
manifest the poet's unconscious, his poems present a map of his sensi-
bility, a sheet at a time. Yet there is comparatively little direct
evocation of sensation in Breton's poetry; indeed on first acquaintance
his poems seem merely to enact the strange and ambiguous behaviour
of language when the customary semantic grid is lifted, allowing words
to improvise provisional, individual compacts with one another —
finding their own level, floating now perpendicularly, now obliquely,
by turns luminous with meaning or opaque as the letters from which
they are formed, merely words. But even if language is granted an
autonomy seemingly incompatible with customary schemes of literary
communication, this does not signal any evacuation of human presence

in Breton's poetry: the new space into which words are projected by the practice of his poetry is not infinite, or circumscribed only by the finite permutations of the vocabulary he uses; and far from being remote from the human, the true space in which the words negotiate their meaning is that of his sensibility. But the sensory register to which it corresponds is a particular one, and the sensations which concern Breton are not the common sort. I hope to show presently that there is a parallelism of linguistic texture and type of sensation encompassed by Breton's poetry; but it is important to stress from the outset that, even if we accept that highly metaphorical discourse is not necessarily inappropriate to the true nature of our emotional and perceptual experience of the world, nevertheless it would be to misconstrue Breton's poetics if we assumed that he deliberately used language in a particular way so as to convey particular sensations. For Breton the poetic process does not consist in a sequence of perception followed by expression through images. Rather, the inarticulate sensation, not rationalised into appropriate terms of comparison, finds an outlet in the gush of language. Far from presenting us with the reminiscence of sensation, Breton generates language to which he then responds sensorially himself, thereby recuperating original and fleeting sensations and more besides. Inasmuch as Breton's images allude to any context of actual sensations, it is not in a local and descriptive way. The phrase 'la fourrure de la nuit' (S, 74) does not record a particular moment of experience when night was suddenly like fur — a local epiphany subsequently enshrined in the poem — even though the coherence and force of the image are totally grounded in sensory reciprocities. As a deliberate strategy the surrealist seeks to 'dépayser la sensation' (M, 279), 'delocalising' it, thereby enabling sense-experience to by-pass rational channels and obtain immediate purchase on the unconscious, and to apprehend the extended reality which corresponds to it. This view does not derive from a dissatisfaction with language as a medium of profound experience and knowledge of the world. For Breton, words, in the state of language proper to poetry, constitute 'le véhicule même de l'affectivité' (CC, 95); An essential corollary to this is that words can in other states be hollow — Breton refers to 'les carapaces vides des mots' (M, 277) — and it is only language emanating from the unconscious which can transmit the true apprehension of things. Our emotional experience is continuously forming chains of sensations, and to these there correspond language-chains ('groupements verbaux' (CC, 95)) which the poet records. It is, ideally, a discourse dense and quick with its emergence from the unconscious that Breton presents on the page. For all its irrationality and apparent arbitrariness the state of language which characterises Breton's poetry has a special relation to that area of the mind in which survives an unfragmented, unmutilated vision of the world.

But how can the reader share this experience, and profit from this inner adventure of the poet? If the words register the imprint of sensation on the unconscious, how can a response to language which *our* unconscious has not mediated be equivalent to a response to those aspects and that condition of things which such language designates? Michel Riffaterre has suggested that the coherence of an apparently arbitrary image derives from the peculiar semantic resources (one might say resourcefulness) of language.[2] The initial semantic hostility of two terms, apparently simply yoked together in an image, is waived by our capacity and tendency to select from the semantic spectrum of each term those qualities which correspond with one another. 'Night' and 'fur', in the image I quoted above, attract and repel each other until we find the equilibrium proposed by the image—grounded in this case, say, on density of texture, darkness and so on. What must be stressed, then, is that surrealist metaphor, far from taking us away from sensation, that is, our broadest experience of the world of things, forces us to refer to the sensory presence and properties of things, even if we may sometimes eventually reject the image as incomprehensible, or worse, banal.

As the patterns of Breton's sensibility emerge, we become aware of the aspect of things with which their presence in his poems habitually confronts us: their potentialities as objects of sensation. By a kind of reversed synecdoche, objects in Breton's poems generally represent, to the exclusion of others, one or a few of their aspects—those which correspond to sensation rather than to our intellectual knowledge of them. Form, texture, mass, mobility, and so on, are the defining categories which shape the object in the poem, switching its sphere of operation from the labyrinth of language to the language of the senses.

Breton's poems become comprehensible when we have weighed and touched and visualised in our minds, as far as we can, the things which inhabit them. No inventory of Breton's habitual material will afford us much insight into the mechanisms of his poetry unless it takes into account the particular sensory aspect which defines the meaning of a given object in his poems. The many animals in his poems are not cognate in respect of their status as animals and require classification not into the familiar genera of animal life but according to their shape, their gait, the texture of their pelt and outer surfaces, and so on, for it is these attributes which define their role in Breton's sensibility and their meaning in the space of the poem. It is these individual qualities or aspects which combine, transferring and translating themselves on to other objects and qualities. The process is an emotional and sensory one; it originates in and, through language, provokes a special kind of emotion. The field created by these sensory and linguistic interactions can be compared to the virtual space of a kinetic sculpture by Gabo: at once absent and present, it gives us a sense of something simultaneously stirring us and eluding us: the emotion proper to poetry, and as Borges once suggested, to all art.

In Breton's poetic practice, the potential arbitrariness of the way he uses language is obviated in two principal ways, Firstly, through recurrences of kinds of sensations associated with certain objects and categories of object. The referential valence of words and images — types of plant, references to climate and so on—which had seemed circumstantial, is seen, through recurrence, to be almost stable. Secondly, apparently gratuitous connections are themselves consonant with the manner in which the senses apprehend the world. The way our minds, if we let them, confer meaning on images—despite semantic anomalies— and respond to amalgams of mental and physical, abstract and concrete, corresponds to the way in which, truant to reason, we in fact receive and respond to the world. And Breton sees in this space created by the language of poetry, this space always at one remove, always beyond, the intimation of a new life-space, a source of new values and a mode of living which would embody them.

The sensory world of Breton's poetry is more than an index to the sensibility out of which his poetic creations emerge and to which it might provide a key. Rather, it constitutes the vocabulary through which Breton, enlisting the connections between the sensation and the unconscious, between the unconscious and language, and between language and sensation, presents his apprehension of an extended reality accessible to man. While it does record his individual response, it is important to remember that the evidence of the senses argues the possibility of a universal response through which man might accede to the lost plenitude of his condition. It is not only the identity of the individual self which the poem's condensations manifest, but the collective self. Although particular stimuli—individual things and relations— are personal, I think it can be shown that the particular range and quality of sensations is not, despite the fact that their expression may make it seem otherwise. The sensations correspond to

and translate a total apprehension of reality and, it would seem, evince
a literally *impending* domain of possibility and futurity. Although
language has a special pertinence to these sensations, not merely
describing them but presenting them according to its own means, it
can only act as a signal for them. But equally, the sensation itself is,
in an important sense, only a metaphor, the sign—which can be made
available to the conscious mind—of a total ontological engagement
to which it gives credence. There is a certain range of sensory experience
which Breton, in common with a number of other modern writers—
poets, philosophers, and theologians—sometimes refers to as *presence*.

There is a constant dialectic of absence and presence in Breton.
Presence indicates fulness of being, achieved through our relation
with things. But while in an early poem he had appealed for 'La vie de
la présence rien que de la présence' (CT, 72), he came to regard the
intermittence of presence as an essential attribute. Indeed to possess
wholly that to which we aspire would be to infringe the authenticity
of desire. So that, in his love for the woman whom he addresses in
these lines, he regards ' . . . la fusion sans espoir de ta présence et de
ton absence' as a positive quality in which he finds ' . . . le secret/De
t'aimer/Toujours pour la première fois' (CT, 181). What is essential is
that a balance (Breton writes of 'le balancier de l'absence . . .'(CT, 118))
should be found between absence and presence, or rather that their
complicity and intrication be recognised: ' . . . l'absence et la présence
qui sont de connivence' (CT, 138). This interrelation derives from the
individual's role: the moment of presence is less an instant when the
world, the thing, is present, as a sort of *Urphänomen*—though this is
sometimes the impression we are given—than a moment of the *self's*
presence in the world. The two are of course connected, as Wallace
Stevens conveys when he writes that '[poetry] is an illumination of
a surface, the movement of a self in the rock'.[3] Since consciousness,
in the broadest sense, is to the world as light and dark are to the earth—
divided, though by infinite degrees, in their appropriation—this self-
presence is related to the modulations and intermittences of the world
itself, as apprehended by the mind. Breton therefore frequently denies
the primary reality and sensory properties of things while drawing
attention to the fleeting nature of presence in reality, embodied in
aspects or dimensions of reality—in a gleam, an incandescence, an
atmosphere.

In doing so Breton is often simply transcribing the poet's own
emotional response to the world. In a letter to Breton's friend Antonin
Artaud, Jacques Rivière wrote: 'Proust a décrit "les intermittences du

cœur"; il faudrait maintenant décrire les intermittences de l'être.'[4]
For Breton, it might be said, these are in essence identical: it is in an
emotional response to reality that the moment of presence—the moment
of being—is made possible. Emotional response is, in Breton's view, the
mark of profound experience, and such a response was generally,
he believed, the outcome of sensory, rather than intellectual, activity
(though Breton, it should be stressed, believed that one responded to
ideas in a sensory manner). Consider the 'émotion très spéciale' which
registers his response to those things in which he finds himself:

> J'avoue sans la moindre confusion mon insensibilité profonde en
> présence des spectacles naturels et des œuvres d'art qui d'emblée,
> ne me procurent pas un trouble physique caractérisé par la
> sensation d'une aigrette de vent aux tempes susceptible d'entraîner
> an véritable frisson.

(AF, 11)

Some caution is required here: the physical component in the sensation
serves only as a signal of the fact that the writer has been *moved* at a
profounder level than the physiological – just as in Plato's *Ion*, the
shiverings of the poet are only the outward manifestation of inspiration.
In the egret's plume playing on his temples, there is an echo of
Mallarmé's

> lucide et seigneuriale aigrette   de vertige
> au front invisible

The parallel with Mallarmé, a poet who kept the sensory world at some
distance in his verse, offers a corrective to any exaggeration of the
strictly physical aspect of sensory-emotive response, and of the
precedence of powerful sensations in Breton.

The delicate oscillations of sensory activity which attract Breton
are at the origin of the emotional texture of his poetry. Emotion is
present at a primary level in the poet's frequent direct references to
the priority of emotive experience: 'Plutôt ce cœur à cran d'arrêt'
(CT, 72), he writes, or, in a striking apposition, 'cœur lettre de cachet'
(CT, 66). Even more common is the presentation of a reality in the
throes of the emotion which apprehends it. For instance we read
'Ce jour-là je tremblerai de perdre une trace/Dans un des quartiers
brouillés de Lyon' (S, 66). Here the poet's emotion has been imparted
to reality itself: the adjective *brouillés* suggests, of course, the labyrinth-

ine streets of the ancient city; but it also represents a projection of the
indeterminacies of the poet's quest, the quest for a dimension of
experience consonant with the confused intuitions of the deeper self.

The fleeting and febrile quality of the emotion is transmitted to the
reader in two distinct manners: firstly by a poetic tone owing much to
the nature of automatic writing, and secondly by the way the world
itself is presented in the poem. A few words must be said about the
former and then more extended treatment is called for by the latter.

The state of language actualised in automatic writing, rational and
analytical faculties being suspended, tends to favour the direct
exteriorisation of emotion through the diction and form (or formless-
ness) of the poem. Indeed, Breton's poetry often has the confidential,
intimate, tone of the 'murmure' (M, 39) and Breton sometimes, although
by no means always, sacrifices some of the characteristic felicities of
modern poetry—ellipsis and rhythmic control, shall we say—by allow-
ing the intricate patternings of the inner voice to guide the poem.
At a second degree, a further aspect of automatic composition is
involved. It should be remembered that the emotions referred to
register an *inner* experience, an adventure of the inner self. A curve
has been made from the world through the senses to the unconscious;
for the individual to become aware and to benefit, it is essential that
the rational intellect be excluded lest it reduce such experience to the
level of ordinary sense-data; for the circle to be completed, language
must participate, ferrying the sensory information unalloyed. This
is the basis of Breton's poetics: the poet is the amanuensis of the
unknown self.

Quite apart from the tone, then, Breton's poems bear the imprint
of the experience in which they originate in a less observable
fashion. We need to be attentive, beyond the direct notation of
emotional reaction, to the way the material world presented in the
poems reveals itself to be the world apprehended in unconscious
experience. But in so doing we must observe how things in the poem
articulate more than the emotion which has appreciated them, how
they are made to serve as the sign-language for a certain experience
of the world generally, to which in themselves they may be irrelevant.
Before going on to look at this in detail, it is as well to trace one or
two intermediate stages in which objects serve this role in a more
explicit way.

We might begin with a stage at which the poet's subjective response
to reality is conveyed merely by a linguistic contrivance: qualities
equivalent to emotive response are predicated of a reality in itself

stable. Thus we read of a 'château qui tremble' (S, 52), or of 'pièces frissonnantes' (CT, 159). There is next a further stage at which the poem registers a movement in reality and imbues it with human mystery— for instance the rustle of branches and the intermittent glimpses of sky this permits: 'le bois qui tremble s'entrouvre sur le ciel' (CDT, 47). Here the words are set the task of corroborating for the reader the poet's experience of reality: they acquit themselves of it in a manner independent of the experience itself—by exploiting the ability of language to operate in a range analogous to the sensory one. But the poem's foundation on the ability of the reader to recognise this *as* experience is of central importance. For this is how a thematic reality, in the network of the poetry, becomes a 'poetic' or super-reality. It is the semantic margins of words which create the area of play in which an extension of the customary *presence* of things can take place. Thus, in the last quotation, the verb *s'entrouvrir* engenders possibilities, or indeed obligations, of reading which transport us from a literal (habitual) zone—trees waving in the breeze— to a metaphysical (un-familiar) zone—an experience in which an intermittent sense of liberation and unveiling of reality is achieved. Yet the passage to metaphor is not a projection outside experience, but rather to the rim of experience—its exalted fringes of being.

To see how this is fully achieved in Breton's poetry we need to go beyond the two stages I have outlined to a thematic network not particularly identifiable by any direct appeal to sensory-emotive response. Let us examine, for instance, the thematic structure con-stituted by recurring references to favoured times of day and atmospheric conditions, and see how it translates, beyond a heightened awareness of the phenomenal world, an inner experience whose true nature and significance are independent of its literal reference.

Breton frequently refers to certain features of climate and times of day when the world seems spontaneously to partake of the emotion it occasions: 'Le temps est si clair que je tremble qu'il ne finisse' (CT, 159). The first light of morning appeals particularly to him. 'Chantier qui tremble chantier qui bat de lumière première' (S, 69); here morning is associated with the mystery of constant renewal and resurrection. In the same poem Breton writes 'c'est à croire/Que le ressort du soleil n'a jamais servi': the first rays of the sun form a diaphanous hedge: 'Pleine de velléités d'essors tendue de frissons/Une haie traverse la chambre d'amour' (S, 67); everything is re-created:

La maraîcher va et vient sous sa housse

>Il embrasse d'un coup d'œil tous les plateaux montés
>   cette nuit du centre de la terre
>
>   (S, 45)

The image of morning revealing things which have been freshly made
in the night is extended elsewhere, when the *chantier* becomes quarries,
and everything—leaves, snow, human flesh—is laid out in the first ray,
the 'premier rayon' of sunshine (CT, 164).

There can be no doubt of Breton's solidarity with Night. But, as
some of the above quotations imply, night is not so much a time of
revelation as of germination, when energies are marshalled for the day.
Night is a time for promise, 'les promesses des nuits étaient enfin
tenues' (CT, 86), and of invisible activity, 'la nuit/Qui fait bien ce
qu'elle fait' (CT, 87); an extreme time of disorientation which precedes
revelation, 'le mal prend des forces tout près' (CT, 69), but also a
time of dream and apparition: Breton refers to 'la nuit qui décalque
mes images' (CT, 69); and the night can be transfigured, just as flares
of imagery light up the page: 'C'est la plus belle des nuits, *la nuit
des éclairs*: le jour, auprès d'elle est la nuit' (M, 46). Night and Day,
like absence and presence, are relative: 'Moi qui n'accorde au jour et
à la nuit que la stricte jeunesse nécessaire/Ce sont deux jardins dans
lesquels je promène mes mains/. . .' (CT, 79.) Night is transformed by
light; day, by the paradoxical density of shadow: 'Sous l'ombre
il y a une lumière et sous cette lumière il y a deux ombres' (CT, 88).
The essence of daylight is not its clarity. Breton was attracted to the
play of sunrays, and in the list of things which he cites in one poem
as conditioning his poetic space, he includes, with evocative
ambiguity, 'le sens du rayon de soleil' (S, 123). It is often the para-
doxical solidity of light rather than its transparency to which he
draws attention. There is no feeling in Breton for the Mediterranean
éclat in which both a Camus and a Valéry could descry the Pindaric
realm of possibility; indeed his opposition to Graeco-Latin civilisation
increasingly nourished an intuitive enthusiasm for the more nubilous
art and culture of the northerly Celts. Breton is dismissive of what
he calls 'fallacieuse clarté' (S, 133); he once gave this report of a
projected visit to his favourite Tour Saint-Jacques in Paris: 'Ce dimanche
27 avril, force fut, très vite, d'en rabattre. Il faisait d'ailleurs très beau
et trop clair: l'insolite se fût en tout cas dérobé. L'air n'était même
pas pesant autour de la statue de Pascal.' (A. 153.)

It is to the transitional hours of the morning and evening twilight
that Breton most frequently refers us. In the evening it is the *last*

ray of light which is magical: ' . . . le rêve des chants d'oiseaux du
soir/Dans l'obliquité du dernier rayon le sens d'une révélation mysté-
rieuse' (S, 49); here again there is a play on the word *sens* – signifying
'meaning' and 'direction'. It is perhaps from the evening that one may
hope 'for the revelation when:

> Les lits faits de tous les lys
> Glissent sous les lampes de rosée
> Un soir viendra
> Les pépites de lumière s'immobilisent sous la mousse bleue
>
> (CT, 115)

It is characteristic of Breton that he uses two tenses in the same
sequence, for when, a little before, he writes 'l'avenir n'est jamais'—
this does not signify despair, but that the evening which will come is
already present, implicit, in the evening he experiences and 'describes'.
The twilight is, then, the transitional hour when 'le jour et la nuit
échangent leur promesses' (S, 33).

And it is of course a time when the air often has that *density* Breton
missed round Pascal's statue (which, appropriately, marks the spot
where his experiments confirmed Torricelli's theories about the weight
of atmosphere). At twilight the atmosphere is either enlaced with mist
or laden, perhaps illuminated as the quotations above suggests, with
dew. The morning dew has, of course, connotations of freshness and
nascence, so that it is the first dewdrop, like the first sunray which
makes it iridescent, which encapsulates ' . . . le mystère de l'existence/
Le premier grain de rosée devançant de loin tous les autres follement
irisé contenant tout' (S, 118). Of the scores of references to dew in
Breton, perhaps the most beautiful occurs in 'L'Union libre' where,
in his litany of celebration of the woman he loves, he writes of 'Ma
femme . . ./Aux seins de spectre de la rose sous la rosee' (CT, 94).
Here language mimes the lover's trembling apprehension of the woman's
breasts in half-light, when they might themselves resemble roses
sparkling but muffled in the morning dew. In one dimension, the rose
seen is spectral because the dew, and perhaps accompanying mist,
would give it an ethereal, remote quality; in the complementary
dimension of language, the word *rose* 'haunts' the word *rosée*. Mist,
related to dawn, embodies the persistence of dream in daytime. In a
lyrically complex extended metaphor, Breton associates mist with the
daily alchemy through which night becomes day—the 'Art des jours
et des nuits' (elsewhere he refers to 'La vapeur des alambics' (S, 161)).

He presents day and night as poised on the scales of a balance so sensitive that the flight of the first bird suffices to tip it towards day and release the mediating mist:

> Balance rouge et sensible au poids d'un vol d'oiseau
> Quand les écuyères au col de neige les mains vides
> Poussent leurs chars de vapeur sur les prés (. . .)
> Les roues du rêve charment les splendides ornières
> Qui se levent très hauts sur les coquilles de leurs robes
> Et l'étonnement bondit de-ci de-là sur la mer
> Partez ma chère aurore n'oubliez rien de ma vie

(CT, 109)

Taking the opportunity to show how Breton's imagination, and sensory mechanisms, operate, one might draw attention to the way, in these lines, the departure of the bird suggests travel, thereby introducing the idea of a chariot or waggon, on which mist arrives and in which dawn will depart, bearing with it some of the central elements of the poet's life, because it is party to his dreaming and his waking. The *roues* relate to the *char*, but also (as evidence in other poems suggests) represent sunrays, through the idea of spokes. The dresses of the horse-women, presumably wispy and diaphanous, suggest the curves of shells (and the connection may have been generated via the scallop's radiating lines, like sunrays); but there is probably also a telescoped reminiscence of Botticelli's 'Birth of Venus' here. The shells introduce the sea, which is also connected with departure, while *étonnement*—conveying the miracle and surprise of waking—seems to me to owe its context to a linguistic echo of *tonnerre* or *tonner*, and to refer to the frequent agitation of the morning sea.

The ethereal movement and insubstantiality of mist is further conveyed elsewhere, when it is invoked to convey the lightness and grace of a woman's arms: ' . . . des bras si légers que la vapeur des près dans ses gracieux entrelacs au-dessus des étangs est leur imparfait miroir' (CT, 122).

In the network so far established we might be tempted to subsume all references to climate and time of day into the general category of *air*. Very little that is extraneous to such classification—for instance purely visual aspects characterising different times of day— occurs in Breton's poems. Even references to the play of light-rays generally relate to the apparent solidification and shaping of the atmosphere, as do dew and mist. Yet it may be that air is only incidentally the

common factor. For it is not so much air that is important as the
processes for which it is the medium. Going further, we might say
that the experienced phenomenon is in itself less important than the
associative field of the concept—partly linguistic, partly cultural—in
determining the function of air as a poetic signifier in Breton's poetry.
Which is to say that we must avoid the tautology involved in a purely
literal reading which would lead us unequivocally from poem to
sensory experience. On the other hand, to opt for a totally symbolic
reading would lead to obligations which we could not fulfil on the
basis of the poetry. Air, once identified as a common ground for
multiple references to dew and sunlight, is by no means the con-
sistent symbol of anything in Breton's poems. Indeed, this may perhaps
account for its prominence as the hidden centre of a thematic network.
For it is not reference to *things in themselves* which characterises
modern poetry so much as *the interrelationship of things*—often, though
not exclusively, suggested by sensory analogy. Air is favoured precisely
because it is susceptible of a great variety of relationships, defining
itself only with reference to a multiplicity of contexts. It is, indeed,
in this slightly abstract aspect, rather than in particular sensory features,
that air is remarkable. Air is flux, transitivity, a catalytic medium in
which various degrees of substantification can occur.

The states of air which appeal to Breton are those which manifest
an insubstantial presence—as light, vapour or water. In certain con-
ditions—the bogus clarity of bright sunlight which hides and separates
rather than reveals—air is vacuity and nothingness. But when it blows
bits of paper around in a windy city (S, 55); rustles mistletoe—'Dehors
l'air essaye les gants de gui' (CT, 158); or when, as 'les vêtements de
l'air pur' (M, 99), it makes a billowing costume for the walker, the air
becomes shape and presence—animated space. It has the miraculous
capacity to precipitate itself: 'l'air est sur le point de fleurir' (SEP, 219),
and Breton once expressed the aspiration to a sense of participation
in the universe in these terms: 'Si seulement j'étais une racine de l'arbre
du ciel/Enfin le bien dans la canne à sucre de l'air' (CT, 81). For Breton
is fascinated by the mystery of precipitation, in both the chemical
and the meteorological sense. In one moment of discovery, the sun's
rays are associated with the falling rain, both solidified: 'Je vois les
arêtes du soleil/A travers l'aubépine de la pluie' (CT, 138). Elsewhere
rain becomes a 'colonne de cristal' (M, 85) or 'une haute verge de
tourmaline sur la mer' (S, 122). Solidification, modulation into sub-
stance, represents the apotheosis of the insubstantial; and it serves as a
metaphor for the shift from absence into presence and the mystery of

the advent of being. References to air and to the atmosphere therefore
have a multiple function in Breton's poetry. Far from any one-to-one
symbolic function or any stable sensory experience, air refers the reader
to a particular cluster of processes, relationships and metamorphoses
which are homologous, rather than directly analogous, to mental,
spiritual and emotional shifts. The broad wave-band of sensory reality
embraced by references to air—and grounded on experience—becomes a
semantic space in which can be articulated experiences which are non-
sensory but which relate to the deep springs of the psyche. Indeed the
grace of substance is often explicitly related to the emotion and desire
of the individual through motifs such as crystallisation, arborescence,
ramification. Sartre once wrote perceptively of Breton: 'Ce qui le
passionne, ce n'est pas le désir à chaud mais le désir cristallisé, ce
qu'on pourrait appeler, en empruntant une expression à Jaspers, le
chiffre du dèsir dans le monde.'[6] In the following, for instance, the
poet's desire is the catalyst which brings about a crystallisation
(here chemistry and meteorology join!): 'J'attends la pluie comme une
lampe élevée trois fois dans la nuit, comme une colonne de cristal,
qui monte et qui descend, entre les arborescences soudaines de mes
désirs' (M, 85).

The processes of desire register the imbrication of natural and
individual necessity, and through its operations—often manifest in
limpid emotion—self and world are mutually illuminated and discovered.
As Breton helps his wife step off a boat, a moment of physical con-
tact animates desire which 'creates' the transformed world within
the self:

> Ta main (. . .) réfracte son rayon dans la mienne. Son moindre con-
> tact s'arborise en moi et va décrire en un instant au-dessus de nous
> ces voûtes légères où (. . .) le ciel renversé mêle ses feuilles bleues.
>
> (A, 22)

Elsewhere dust suspended in the 'premier rayon du soleil', as the
poet wakes beside the loved one, is the insubstantial but tangible
legacy of the previous day: 'c'est toute la vie d'hier qui se ramifie en
un corail impossible de la couleur de tes mains' (CT, 185). In one place
we read 'toutes les branches de l'air' (AF, 12). Breton's poems are full
of references to things which present the quality of ramification:
trees of course, leaves, many plants, particularly ferns, coral; and of
things which *form* themselves: coral again, crystals, stalactites.
Because they are emblems of desire, as much as the talismans of an

individual sensibility, there is another way in which these things elude
the simple arbitrariness of preference. If desire manifests the unity of
mind and world, then these highly organised but delicate things seem
to have a special pertinence to, and our relation to them a special
purchase on, the generative processes of the mind:

> . . . les rameaux du sel les rameaux blancs
> Toutes les bulles d'ombre
> Et les anémones de mer
> Descendent et respirent à l'intérieur de ma pensée

(CT, 114)

The individual's discovery of these things has not taken place at the
level of his everyday life and self, but along the parallel inner traj-
ectory constituted by his emotional and sensory experiences, which
leave their trace on the sand of our unconscious and of the page:

> Ils viennent des pleurs que je ne verse pas
> Des pas que je ne fais pas qui sont deux fois des pas
> Et dont le sable se souvient à la marée montante

(CT, 114)[7]

It is possible to discern something of Breton's feeling for the morning
twilight in Baudelaire's line from 'Le Crépuscule du matin': 'L'air est
plein du frisson des choses qui s'enfuient.' Breton's poems record the
endeavour to dispel a customarily accredited reality by encouraging
words to give voice and vestment to an absent presence at the heart
of things. Accordingly, it is not the substantial massiveness of the
world in broad sunlight, but the flickering light of dawn and of
certain atmospheric conditions that corresponds to the 'frisson' which
registers sensory response. If poetry, in Stevens's phrase, is the illumin-
ation of a surface, then it is a feature of twilight to dissolve appearances
into a changing spectacle of momentary impressions. If we now turn to
this combination of the transient and the 'superficial' we shall be able
to extend our survey of Breton's poetic world into some of its more
paradoxical regions.

In a wide range of images Breton suggests that it is on the shimmering
surface of things that their true substance and profundity lie. His
poetry is characterised by a shifting of 'essence' from a putative depth
to surfaces, a modulation which, issuing from or paralleling *Gestalttheo-*

rie and phenomenology, or the aesthetics of a Focillon with his
'profondeur cachée sur la surface', underlies so much of contemporary
art and thought. 'O substance', exclaims Breton, 'il faut toujours en
revenir aux ailes du papillon' (CT, 187). The sudden glitter and flutter
of a butterfly's wing correspond better to Breton's sense of what is
'real', to presence, and to the context of our relation to the extended
reality he postulates, than the monumentality of the permanent everyday
scene. Permanence lies within, in our emotional and imaginative annals:
'Il n'est que de fermer les yeux/Pour retrouver la table du permanent'
(S, 48).

Yves Bonnefoy has it that 'le fugace, l'irrémédiablement emporté
est le degré poétique de l'univers'[8]; for Breton, too, what is fleeting
and momentary in experience is ontologically privileged. One image in
which this is expressed is that of the glow or glimmer—the *lueur*, which
is both within the individual: 'Cette lueur que le surréalisme cherche
à déceler au fond de nous' (M, 136) and outside. In one of the
Constellations—prose-poems which accompany paintings by Miró—
Breton takes up the painter's title 'Personnages dans la nuit guidés par
les traces phosphorescentes des escargots' and comments:

> Rares sont ceux qui ont éprouvé le besoin d'une aide
> semblable en plein jour, — ce plein jour où le commun
> des mortels a l'aimable prétention de voir clair (. . .).
> A l'éveil, le tout serait de refuser à la fallacieuse
> clarté le sacrifice de cette lueur de labradorite qui
> (. . .) est tout ce que nous avons en propre pour nous
> diriger sans coup férir dans le dédale de la rue.
>
> (S, 133)

In another place Breton writes of 'le brillant, quand on les coupe, de
métaux inusuels comme le sodium (. . .), la phosphorescence, dans
certaines régions, des carrières (. . .), l'éclat du lustre admirable qui
monte des puits' (Na, 128). Equally Breton is sensitive to the play of
light and shadow, for instance as sunrays filter through trees in a
wood giving the earth '(des) reflets plus profonds que ceux de l'eau'
(CT, 188). Elsewhere, he refers to 'la lueur qui pêche les cœurs dans
ses filets' (R, 101), which, through the idea of the net, subtly conveys
the patterns of light and shade cast by vegetation or anything latticed
(the thematic structure of the *ajour*, the *dentelle* and so on is an
important one in Breton) and also the dimension of our sensory and
emotive 'captivation' by the spectacle.

The *lueur* is thus a real property of certain places and things given emotive amplification in Breton's sensibility[9]; but it also commands other metaphors: the *lueur* is also present in the flickering gleams of the fire: 'Le fond de l'âtre/Etincelant et noir/Le fond de l'âtre où j'ai appris à voir' (CT, 166). One of Breton's most famous poems, inspired by Heraclitus, celebrates many aspects of the flame; in one passage the flame seems to represent that aspect of things which engages the individual's imagination: 'Et la flamme court toujours/C'est une fraise de dentelle au cou d'un jeune seigneur' (etc.). And just as the *lueur* was a guide in the labyrinth of the street, so Breton, splendidly enjoins the flame to guide him, here to an apotheosis: 'Flamme d'eau guide-moi jusqu'à la mer de feu' (CT, 113).

The intermittent *lueur* in things corresponds to a particular modality of our apprehension, and particularly vision, of them. A recurring theme in Breton's numerous writings on painting is the redefinition of our powers of vision. Breton bemoans the poverty of our customary ways of seeing, while at the same time celebrating the potential capacities of the eye. The eye is valorised specifically by its capacity to discern the unity of the world (cf. SEP, 200), and, above all, to catch what is delicate or only fleeting. Nadja has 'des yeux de fougère', not simply because her eyes are green but because they are open and sensitive to 'les battements d'ailes de l'espoir immense' (Na, 130), and because her way of seeing deserves the compliment of association with one of the prizes of vision, the subtle structure of ferns. For Breton there is a reciprocity of what is at the fringes of seeing, and the hidden self. The ambiguity of vision engenders a gyroscopic poise of the self in its quest and trajectory: Breton presents himself as 'fixant un point brillant que je sais être dans mon œil mais qui m'épargne de me heurter à ses ballots de nuit' (Na, 183). But this brilliant point can also be a point in time, a moment when outer and inner correspond, when we attain 'cet angle toujours fuyant sous lequel les 'choses' s'estompent jusqu'à disparaître, au prix de quoi commence à se dévoiler l'*esprit* des choses' (SEP, 341). This theme of the angle of vision at which things transmute so that we can see and relate them fully, can be well documented in Breton's poems — expressions such as *de biais, oblique, tangence, diagonal* are common. The revelation which this vision implies accounts for the frequent association of these terms with the curtain:

> Tu rentres à telle heure de la nuit dans une maison oblique
> à ma fenêtre/ (. . .)
> L'angle fugitif d'un rideau

(. . .)/ une route des environs de Grasse
Avec ses cueilleuses en diagonale/ (. . .)
Devant elles l'équerre de l'éblouissant
Le rideau invisiblement soulevé

(CT, 180-1)

This spontaneous and imperceptible unveiling of reality, indicated in
the last line, is what the eye can momentarily achieve; thus 'chaque
paysage nous trouve dans la même attente qui est celle du lever d'un
rideau' (PJ, 56). Returning to the angle and the curtain, we find 'Entre
le rideau de vie/Et le rideau de cœur' (CT, 171), or '. . . adorable
rideau de tangence' (S, 53). Essentially this tangential vision is akin
to the one which Bonnefoy ascribes to memory: 'la vision absolue
qu'elle nous donnait des choses, nous semble-t-elle la mère des plus
furtives lueurs que l'instant arrache, pour notre joie, à la substance
de ce qui est.' [10] Such vision, the *lueur*, is above all momentary, and
with this can be associated the fact that the theme, and sometimes
structure, of some of Breton's most successful poems is constituted
by recreating through images the shared instant of a momentary
encounter. In one poem a meeting-place with a woman is presented
not as a location in space but as the point defined by the trajectories
which separate evocations of it describe, or inscribe, on our senses.
Here is part of the passage:

Tout au fond de l'entonnoir
Dans les fougères foulées du regard
J'ai rendez-vous avec la dame du lac /(. . .)
C'est là
A la place de la suspension du dessous dans la maison
    des nuages

(S, 17-18)

This is not the definitive encounter which will re-shape the
individual's life around the adventure of love, it is the context in which
it is awaited: through the invocation of chance by an open, lyrical
mode of living in which, as Breton wrote elsewhere, 'toute femme est
la Dame du Lac' (S, 161). It is the improvised space and tangent of
Char's 'angle fusant d'une rencontre'. Such encounters, like that
celebrated in 'A une passante' (which marks one of the many moments
in Baudelaire which stand as paradigms of the modern poetic sensibility),
are of course the prize of the *flâneur* and, as is so manifest in Breton's

major prose works, one of the most familiar avatars of the surrealist is as wanderer of the city labyrinth. But in this context it is not the carnality of the libertine which characterises him; even the existence of the central woman in the poet's life, at a time of love, is refracted through the city: 'Ton existence le bouquet géant qui s'échappe de mes bras/(. . .) s'effeuille dans les vitrines de la rue' (CT, 163).

Even what is possessed is fleeting, ever escaping, needing to be lost and found again: 'les amants au défaut du temps retrouvant et perdant la bague de leur source' (S, 33). Between these poles of losing and finding, absence and presence, lies the experience of the encounter—the sudden flare of sexual energy, and yet more than the mere surge of lust, a source of revelation:

Oracle attendu de la navette d'un soulier
Plus brillant qu'un poisson jeté dans l'herbe
Ou d'un mollet qui fait un bouquet des lampes de mineur
Ou du genou qui lance un volant dans mon cœur
Ou d'une bouche qui penche qui penche à verser son parfum
Ou d'une main (. . .)

(S, 53)

In this poem, appropriately entitled 'Frôleuse', it becomes clear in the last line, which in retrospect conditions and focusses the poem as a whole, that it is around a fleeting encounter with a woman that the poem's images are congregating their defining beams: 'Et dis-toi qu'aussi bien je ne te verrai plus.' The sensual 'moments' celebrated in the poem may not refer to the same woman, but whether they are taken to do so or not, the power of the encounter to transcend the individual's customary experience lies outside its possible historical or anecdotal development or antecedents; it resides in the eternal instant. Of these moments Breton writes:

O ménisques
Au-delà de tous les présents permis et défendus
A dos d'éléphants ces piliers qui s'amincissent jusqu'au
    fil de soie dans les grottes
Ménisques adorable rideau de tangence quand la vie n'est
    plus qu'une aigrette qui boit
Et dis-toi qu'aussi bien je ne te verrai plus

In such fragmentary encounters, the poem tells us, may be heard the
voice of an oracle. These are not merely moments of sensory joy but
crucial particles of experience whose fleetingness and randomness
subvert the proprieties of space and time, and out of which might one
day be shaped a new sort of human destiny. These experiences are
meniscuses (the meniscus is a lens which is convex on one side, concave
on the other), through which the tremors of sensation diverge to fill
and embrace the whole of an individual's existence. Their gift is beyond
all gifts because it is not possession but transmutation; a process
illustrated in the next line where the twisting conical pillar on the back
of the decorated circus elephant modulates, via its visual similarity,
into the stalagmite ('dans les grottes'), which tapers into a silken
thread—the extreme point or drop of emotive and sensory experience,
and equally, as the manifold variations on this theme attest throughout
Breton's works, the thread which leads through the labyrinth: of the
street or of the mind. At such moments life takes on a limpidity which is
a revelation—'Quand la vie n'est plus qu'une aigrette qui boit'; space
and time blur; the individual lives a parenthesis, and floats in a pocket
of air.

The poem's function is to *summon up* these experiences by
embodying in itself something of their structure. Many of Breton's
poems have a parenthetical structure, creating autonomous worlds of
their own, which nonetheless match the exceptional nature of the
experiences to which they correspond. One poem 'Monde dans un baiser'
(CT, 157) generates through its images the autonomous world of the
kiss. It is this tendency for the poem to recreate exceptional mental
experience in all its unfamiliarity that can lead to an initial impression
of incoherence, a feeling that Breton's poetry is fanciful, gratuitously
'surrealist' in the banal sense, and antithetical to experienced reality.
It should be clear by now that for Breton poetry is not a flight from
reality but a confirmation and reinforcement of its deepest aspects
whose more permanent enstatement at its surface would transform
life. For it is not in the first instance in poetry that the transmutation
of the finite into the infinite comes about. The achievement of presence
precedes the poem: it is at the heart of reality, in the matrix of
experience that it occurs and that the key or thread of existence is
found. But only through language does the moment find a home; so
the poem is the homecoming and harbour of experience, not the
voyage:

Les araignées font entrer le bateau dans la rade

Il n'y a qu'à toucher il n'y a rien à voir (. . .)
Mais c'est l'aube de la dernière côte le temps se gâte (. . .)
Le ventre des mots est doré ce soir et rien n'est plus
    en vain

(CT, 83-4)

But in the eternal simultaneity of language and experience Breton can exclaim:

Je ne touche plus que le cœur des choses je tiens le fil

(CT, 138)

The movement of Breton's thought as of his poetry is to find the 'infinite' in a dimension of reality and experience. The theme of the star brings this out well. 'Tiens une étoile pourtant il fait encore grand jour' (CT, 139) he writes playfully. For there is nothing intimidating in stars; just as it does for the navigator 'à la recherche moins des pays/ Que de leur propre cause' (CT, 176), so for Breton the star orientates his quest, as something towards which he moves: introducing eschatological urgency into Hernani's melodramatic posturing, he writes

Je suis celui qui va
On m'épargnera la croix sur ma tombe
Et l'on me tournera vers l'étoile polaire

(S, 72)

And at the climax of *Les Etats généraux*:

La flèche part
Une étoile rien qu'une étoile perdue dans la fourrure
    de la nuit

(S, 74)

no longer foreseeing his death but registering the sudden influx of being which an event, a moment of sensation, has brought. The star can be found, and the experience and sensations with which Breton's poetry is concerned, are those which, as he writes, 'me servent à planter une étoile au cœur meme du *fini*' (Na, 183), and begin an answer to the question, at once urgent and hesitant, that he asks of Nadja: 'Est-il vrai que l'*au-delà*, tout l'au-delà soit dans cette vie?' (Na, 172). But

even the star, that 'pure cristallisation de la nuit' (Ar, 95), is not
abstracted; its metaphysical meaning is grounded in its sensory
properties. 'La vraie vie est absente' Rimbaud had written; so it was for
Breton: but the wanderings of the *flâneur*, the abandon of the lover,
and the poet's sudden tapping of the spring of language ever flowing
within him, may catch the ripples in the pool of absence; then, as the
everyday world recedes, the individual experiences 'le frisson de la
vraie vie' (CC, 101)—a moment of presence. The sensations which
manifest this presence, and their crystallisation into images as they
etch themselves into words, are those which evince a relative
dematerialisation of the immediate object and a materialisation of some-
thing beyond it—lying in its relation to other objects and to the
individual. The disorientation of sensation derives from a recognition
that it is experiences of sensory disorientation which convey and reveal
the attainment of privileged states of being.

Breton therefore focusses on the perimeter of sensory response.
The relation to things which he seeks maintains the object as and in
the process of our apprehending it, ever becoming itself in the corner
of our eyes, or at our fingertips: 'tout ce qui doit faire aigrette au bout
de mes doigts' (AF, 109). In *L'Amour fou* Breton writes of
'l'intrication en un seul objet du naturel et du surnaturel', and he
associates this with 'l'émotion de tenir et en même temps de sentir
s'échapper le ménure-lyre' (AF, 97). Such an experience is a paradigm
of relation to the world of things and this is frequently expressed in
terms of the hand's simultaneously grasping and releasing: 'la main
dans l'acte de prendre en meme temps que de lâcher' (S, 74). It is an
experience which translates a particular view of man's capacity and
channels for apprehending the extended reality, the Real, or the surreal,
of which he may have an intuition. It is not in a total abandoning of
physical reality that the individual may arrive at it. While Breton had
once called on man: 'lâchez la proie pour l'ombre' (PP, 110), he later
wrote of 'cet état particulier de l'esprit (auquel) le surréalisme a tou-
jours aspiré, dédaignant en dernière analyse la proie et l'ombre pour
ce qui n'est déjà plus l'ombre et n'est pas encore la proie: l'ombre et
la proie fondues dans un éclair unique' (AF, 32). This conjunction
and indeed the metaphysical view it embodies, can only be experienced —
it is a sensation, and Breton celebrates it in an image which shows
clearly the subordination of intellect to sense-experience, in the grasping of
what we cannot hold but which can illuminate us, when he writes of 'Cette
royaut sensible qui s'étend sur tous les domaines de mon esprit et qui tient
ainsi dans une gerbe de rayons à portée de la main . . .'(AF, 14).

*   *   *

It is, then, in what I will term the *limit-sensation*, that this relation, and the importance of the senses for Breton, is most significantly manifested. Sensations of this kind, and we have come across many in examining the emotional texture of Breton's poetry, are registered in the poems in a variety of ways, though generally not through direct evocations as in the example of the lyre-bird. More often, Breton directs our attention to the edges of sensory response by using language, or perhaps we ought to say presenting us with language behaving, in a certain manner. For example, he frequently assimilates abstract notions to concrete entities. He writes of 'la moire énigmatique de la ressemblance', or 'la menthe de la mémoire' (S, 119). Both these images are of course to some extent amenable to rational analysis— in the latter case, it might be agreed that Breton is appealing to the widely accepted relation (endorsed by Schopenhauer and Proust), between smell—the most characteristic property of mint—and remembrance. In other cases the connection is less definable: 'Dans les fougères foulées du regard' (A, 18). Of course a great many poets have used this device, but Breton's use is particularly vivid: luring the mind to give sensory definition to what is logically alien to such definition, as when he writes, about the news he awaits in a letter— 'les nouvelles qu'elle m'apportera leurs formes de rosée' (CT, 143). In this instance there is a double process; dew is certainly concrete, and yet we do not usually think of it as having form: just as a sensory habitation is made for what is otherwise a concept, then this too elides, leaving us nevertheless, I feel, with the aftertaste of a sensation.

Thus, a second operation taking place in Breton's poetry is that of starting from the concrete, and allowing language to deny its customary sensory properties, letting the material taper to the almost immaterial, to the limit of what we can feel and sense. This, again, is often achieved by the play of concrete and abstract, but the emphasis is reversed: 'Des bras qui ne s'articulent à rien d'autre qu'au danger exceptionnel d'un corps fait pour l'amour' (CT, 122); 'Une région plus délicate que l'impossibilité de se poser pour certains oiseaux' (CDT, 47). While constantly forcing us to a sensory reading, Breton's poems do not use sensation to give us a strong impression of the sensory presence of real objects. Rather, he exploits the sensory properties of things (and the capacity of word-combinations to present themselves as the tokens of sensation) in a way which often denies or, alternatively, exaggerates their primary sensory qualities, so as to assert sensory analogies at a remoter level: ' . . . la femme nue/Dont les cheveux glissent comme au matin la lumière sur un réverbère qu'on a oublié d'éteindre' (CT, 117). Here the movement of the simile is towards the dematerialisation of hair, whose static flow and gleam resemble the ebb of artificial light melting into that of the early morning, just as the curving hair of a naked woman emerges from and merges into the curves of her body. Breton's use of sensation in this way is further amplified in another more complex passage involving hair, flesh and light: ' . . .les guetteuses nues (. . .)/cambrant leurs cous sur lequel le bondissement des nattes libère des glaciers à peine roses/Qui se fendent sous le poids d'un rai de lumiere tombant des persiennes arrachées' (CT, 134). The context here is that tenuous and often paradoxically chaste eroticism which is characteristic of Breton. The *glaciers* relate to the warming flesh of the *guetteuses* in the cold morning. Locked into the typically intricate metaphorical texture of this sequence is an image which conveys admirably the apparent solidity of the oblique rays of the sun in the morning. We would normally expect *fondent* (melt), as being appropriate to the effect of sunshine on ice. Here Breton exploits a phonic resemblance and translates the impalpable process of sunrays melting ice into an active force—the 'weight' of the sun as it falls, dislodged by the opening of the shutters, is sufficient to make an incision in the ice,—or the woman: *fendent* evidently has sexual connotations here. For the glaciers were 'only' a metaphor; that is, we can only understand their presence or function in the poem if we see them 'as' rendering the texture of the naked flesh of a woman; in this particular case, when the movement of the vertebrae, imparted to it by the bending of the neck, is contrasted with the more vigorous tossing hair which also accompanies this gesture and which, itself, might seem to be the cause of the movement of the flesh. Indeed another aspect of the limit-sensation is Breton's frequent tendency to confound our normal rationalisation of causes and effects and present things in the magical, animistic way in which the child or so-called primitive might see them. Thus the toss and bounce of hair releases 'pink glaciers'; shutters opened abruptly dislodge sunrays. Or in another poem hands ravish a nighingale's nest *in order that* it should rain for ever (CT, 122). Returning to the original quotation, we might say that the lines were leading us back to a primary situation whose complex sensory and emotional texture the metaphors rendered—in this case the sight of a woman stretching her neck towards a window in the morning.

But this is insufficient. Breton does more than evoke the situation for us, or simply insert it in a fictional setting: firstly because the connections he makes are important in themselves; and secondly because the movement of his act as poet has been to allow sensation to crystallise, through language, into something more. So that it is not enough for the reader to go back through the mouth of the funnel to the original sensation, he must receive the fundamentally new sensation. The 'dépaysement de la sensation' is not merely negative but anticipates a new *pays*, a new world for man.

A further aspect of the limit-sensation is implicit in my remarks about metaphorical texture. The metaphorical process results not so much in presenting things in deliberately unfamiliar contexts but in denying all rational context (just as much modern painting dispenses with any consistent pictorial plane), and in bringing together elements from disparate semantic fields. This occurs even when the metaphoric development does have a stable tenor[11] (or initial term), as in 'L'Union libre' or in these lines: 'Je vois leurs seins qui mettent une pointe de soleil dans la nuit profonde (. . .)/. . . leurs seins qui sont des étoiles sur des vagues' (CT, 129). Here sun, night and sky are introduced into a process of metaphorical exchange; and there is a greater inter-relation than we might normally expect (and which tends towards the conceit), between these various vehicles of the metaphor: that of the first line could itself be a metaphor for the star in the second (though, paradoxically, the first line depends to some extent on suggesting a starless night sky); while the waves are prefigured aurally in 'profONDE'. When, however, as is frequent, the metaphor lacks a notionally stable tenor (like *seins* in the previous example), or when the whole fragile world of the poem is a vehicle for a tenor which is the theme or situation of the poem as a whole—so that direct statements, snatches of scenario, and so on, all contribute to a metaphor whose process is a constant generation of linguistic energy—then the *dépaysement* is even more extreme. 'Les pieuvres ailées guideront une dernière fois la barque dont les voiles sont faites de ce seul jour heure par heure' (CT, 106). Here there is no literal meaning which the images transmit, and it is perhaps the differential between what we can apprehend and what is meaningless which is the limit-sensation. We can detect no consistent context: totally different spheres of experience are assembled in the compass of a single line or sequence in the poem. The play of one against the other, in the absence of any stable metaphorical dynamism or single corresponding life-experience, produces a flurry of sensations since reference is so consistently made to concrete entities. 'What is

more abstract than a fortuitous collocation of sensations?' asks Randall
Jarrell;[12] yet it is not really towards abstractions that such colloc-
ations, in Breton's poetry, direct us, but to other sensations against
which reason may discriminate, but which are actual, though remote
and fleeting, and which have no language of their own. The metaphoric
process presents us with a limit-reality, yet it can operate only in so far
as we register the connections it makes in a sensory way—even if their
origin is in language. The licence Breton allows language to suggest
connections between things—whether through metaphor, homonymic
equivalence or phonic resemblance—is always grounded to some extent
in other sensory relations.

The limit-sensation also relates to the theme of transition in Breton's
poetry. Many poems have as their basic structure the evocation of a
moment of transition: from winter to spring, day to night and the
reverse; the associated themes of waking and falling asleep also being
common. But it is not only at this thematic level that the importance
of transition is indicated: the extraordinary dynamism of many of his
poems, particularly in the early collections, imparts to them, through
language, a feeling of constant organic transformation. The impossible
scenarios of a kind of mental picaresque are generally punctuated by
the vocabulary of transition: active verbs coloured by a sophisticated
use of tense, frequent occurrence of temporal words and phrases—
'alors', 'ensuite', 'tout devient', etc. But although the subject, the
je of the poem is frequently bustled through time and space, we are
often reminded that he is, in the first instance, hurtling through the
wonderland of language; and this awareness gives the poem a paradox-
ical immobility: the transition is never consummated and the itinerary
of the poem, the trajectory of its subject, like the lived experience it
transmits, does not reach a goal. Rather, in its 'vertige fixé', it gives him
access to the mystery of transition and imminence, and gives him the
sensation of what is about to be, and of what a total transformation
of existence might bring. It is not the fall of Adam and Eve that Breton
describes but that of Alice; if he acknowledges man's diminished state,
it is not to original sin that he attributes it but to man's error and loss
of the keys to himself. The limit-sensation is itself a transition; a foray
into 'la frange changeante et chantante par laquelle un âge révolu
anticipe sur l'âge à venir' (SEP, 346). It is a sensation too which, like
those around which Proust constructed his masterpiece, reaches out of
time into eternity.

Breton often plays on the ambiguity of the word *temps*, meaning both 'time' and 'weather'. Thus there are moments when 'Le temps se brouille à la fois et s'éclaire (. . .)/A la vie à la mort ce qui commence me précède et m'achève' (S, 45): that which is just beginning goes ahead of us into the future which will see man's resurrection. Man's progress will be impeded 'tant (qu'ils) ne feront pas *la part sensible* de l'éphémère et de l'éternel'; while the mediating role of the artist is to act as a conductor of the lightning apparitions of the future: 'l'œuvre d'art n'est valable qu'autant que passent en elle les reflets tremblants du futur' (PPS, 74).[13] But it is essentially in his own emotions and sensations and his own tentative approach towards the limits of experience, that the apprehension of the eternal, of the delicate balance of absence and presence, and of a new possibility for man, is available to the individual. These lines of great aural beauty, at once lucid and mysterious, resume succinctly the themes I have been seeking to elucidate:

> Et très loin dans les bois l'avenir entre deux branches
> Se prend à tressaillir comme l'absence inapaisable d'une
>   feuille

(R, 133)

The extreme delicacy which characterises the sensations in Breton's poetry is not arbitrary; if it indicates a preference, then this preference originates in intuitions of universal validity. There is no decadence or elitism in Breton's poetry, nor any full withdrawal from the world; but instead the desire to monitor and mime every smallest quiver of reality, and to greet what he can from beyond the normal horizons of experience. It is on the marches of reality and of experience that Breton concentrates his attention, and it is so as to capture the intimations of a deeper reality that he diverts his and our attention from 'le terre-à-terre de la sensation' (M, 162)—everyday sense-experiences—to 'la dentelle de mes sensations' (M, 84), those in league with the once and future state of man, present at the heart of things and self. The future is less a division of time than a dimension of man.

It is more than a quirk of Breton's sensibility that the scale of his poetic universe should so consistently be reduced. Apart from the diminutive quality of the habitual 'properties' of Breton's poems, the commerce which the *je* —a sort of Gulliver—enjoys with things, through the extraordinary mobility which the discourse lends the human subject (mirroring the rapidity of sense mechanisms) results in a

constant miniaturisation. A constant shrinking and metamorphosis of
the self, as it seeks a relation with things, characterises the poems;
Breton lives in the heart of a thistle (CT, 159), refers to 'Nous les
plantes sujettes aux métamorphoses' (CT, 130), writes 'Je goûterais le
long des marais salants la paix inconnue des métamorphoses' (R, 96),
or 'Tu te promèneras avec la vitesse/Qui commande aux bêtes des
bois' (CT, 107). It is with the fusion of self and world that the poems
are concerned. Emerging from the unconscious, objects present them-
selves in those aspects through which the poet has been able to relate
to them. The incidence of small and delicate things in Breton's poetry
seems to be connected with their special relation to the mind and senses.
It is as if there were something particularly apt about the mode of
existence of small, particularly small, living, things, in conveying the
processes of the unconscious: as if their micro-movements rendered
more plausible the capacity of the human brain to generate images of
the exterior world, and to reflect and recreate reality. Certain things,
and certain types of movement or potentialities for movement, seem to
press themselves with particular insistence on the mind, introducing
themselves into, and reflecting, its hidden processes which can only be
conveyed through metaphor. And so, in Breton's poems, rather than
the succulence or symbolism of Valéry's pomegranates; the universe of
fable, however individualised, in which Supervielle's horses gallop; or
the conventional botany and entomology of Gide; we are presented
with a miniature world populated by the darting softness of small
mammals, the glitter of minerals, the intermittent brilliance of king-
fishers' wings, the hieratic attitudes of flower and fern, the micro-
dramaturgy of eye and hand. On the edges of sensation, perception
is reconciled with imagination, while a further shrinking permits the
miniature world of language to stand for heightened encounters with
the world of things. The poem with its correspondingly emotive
texture, can become a receptacle in which endures what Eluard called
'La Vie Immédiate', and what Breton calls, 'La vie telle que je l'aime et
qu'elle s'offre (. . .): la vie à perdre haleine' (Na, 173). Through discourse
the universe is appropriated. Or rather, an earlier, unconscious appro-
riation is consolidated for as long as the intermittent aesthetic force of
the poem continues to operate.

The universe of Breton's poetry is, then, a gravitational field, pulling
more and more things into its orbit. His miniaturised inscapes and
scenarios are precipitates of desire; for Breton, language, mind and
sensation modulate into each other in a chain of precipitations. The
limit-sensation is a moment of coincidence of self and world. Some

sensations register 'des échanges mystérieux entre le matériel et le mental' (AF, 49). Yet the self is more than a composite mirror of the aspects of the world in which it has found itself; and the critic's task should not be to build up an anthropomorphic portrait, like one of those by Arcimboldo.[14] The relation of self and world is a dialectic, an ascesis; in the process of reciprocation the mirror, as in Yeats's line, turns lamp. What better to illustrate this than an image provided by the *réverbère*—half lamp, half mirror, and the butterfly—emblem of the limit-sensation? 'Les papillons de l'extérieur ne cherchent qu'à rejoindre les papillons de l'intérieur: ne remplace pas en toi, si elle vient à être cassée, une seule glace du réverbère'.[15] There are moments of experience which break the barriers between the outside world and the inner, between subject and object, creating that inner space or *Weltinnenraum* of which Rilke wrote.[16] The sight of a bird flying home momentarily reveals the continuity of self and world:

> Je vois l'ibis aux belles manières
> Qui revient de l'étang lacé dans mon cœur

(CT, 109)

The fluttering of a butterfly, like a human pulse; a glimmer of light; the fine point of sensation which the semantic resources of language can encapsulate: such things cross a divide and seem to participate more readily than others in this new space, and manifest better the possibility of a 'contact, entre tous éblouissant, de l'homme avec le monde des choses' (AF, 49).

My argument has been that the meta-world of Breton's poetic universe is the product and instrument of ethical and heuristic strategy. The tyranny of abstract reason has choked the natural channels through which we incorporate the evidence of the senses into our model of the world, so that our everyday perceptiveness gives only a partial, distorted view of things which we enstate as Reality. It is only through the reunification of the sensibility that the unity of the world, and of man with it, can be found again. The means for this are to be found in an openness to the world, in the passion of love, and in attention to the flow of subjective experience available to us in the speech always imminent in the mind. In these areas of experience the individual sensibility is integrated with sensory experience which challenges the familiar set of things, and may intuit a different way of the world. The senses are the garden in which man may await 'la fleur enfin éclose de la vraie vie' (M, 301); in any case 'on n'en finira jamais avec la sensation' (AF, 95).

Notes

1. I have used the following abbreviations: CT *Clair de Terre*, Gallimard Poésie, 1966; S *Signe ascendant*, id., 1968. (These contain a high proportion of Breton's published poems, but I have also referred to: CDT *Clair de terre* Collection de *Littérature*, 1923; and R *Le Revolver à cheveux blancs*, Cahiers Libres, 1932). Other works published by Gallimard: Na *Nadja*, Folio, 1972; AF *L'Amour fou*, 1968; V *Les Vases communicants*, Idées, 1970; SEP *Le Surréalisme et la Peinture*, 1965; PJ *Point du jour*, Idées, 1970; PP *Les Pas perdus*, Idées, 1970; En *Entretiens*, 1969. Published by Jean-Jacques Pauvert: M *Les Manifestes du surréalisme*, édition complète, 1972; CC *La Clé des champs*, 1967. Other publishers: Ar *Arcane 17*, 10/18; PPS *Position politique du surréalisme*, Denoel/Gonthier, 1972. All published in Paris.

2. M. Riffaterre, 'La Métaphore filée dans le poésie surréaliste', *Langue française*, 3 (Sept. 1969).

3. Wallace Stevens, *The Necessary Angel*, Vintage Books, 1951, p. viii. Cf. Breton 'C'est moi l'irréel souffle de ce jardin' (CT, 124).

4. In Artaud, *L'Ombilic des limbes*, Gallimard 'Poésie', 1971, pp. 44-5.

5. Cf. Rimbaud: 'Le monde vibrera comme une immense lyre/Dans le fremissement d'un immense baiser', *Poésies*, Garnier, 1966, p. 43.

6. In *Situations II*, Gallimard, 1968, p. 324.

7. Cf. '. . . puiser aveuglément dans le trésor subjectif pour la seule tentation de jeter de-ci de-là sur le sable une poignée d'algues écumeuses et d'émeraudes' (PJ, 165); also '. . . le secret impérissable s'inscrit une fois de plus sur le sable' (A, 148), where language itself proposes an image which conveys its generative processes (impérisSABLE).

8. Yves Bonnefoy, *L'Improbable*, Mercure de France, 1959, p. 120.

9. With a painter's eye Breton detects the magical quality of light in certain places: the moors of Britanny for instance (En, 222) or along the Hudson (En, 227); or '. . . Cette lueur vert-orangé qui me cerne du même fin pinceau . . . le décor romantique conventionnel et ce quartier presque enfoui de la Boucherie de Paris' (CC, 7).

10. Bonnefoy, *op. cit.*, p. 122.

11. 'Tenor', 'Vehicle' and 'Ground' are the terms coined by I. A. Richards in *The Philosophy of Rhetoric*, New York/London, OUP, 1936, to describe the elements of a metaphor.

12. In *Poetry and the Age*, Faber, 1955, p. 214.

13. Cf. Shelley: 'Poets are the hierophants of an unapprehended inspiration; the mirrors of the gigantic shadows which futurity casts upon the present . . .' (Quoted by Robert Gibson in *Modern French Poets on Poetry*, Cambridge, 1961, p. 33).

14. Although Breton sometimes encourages this: e.g. '. . . mon apparence de miroir mes mains de faille/Mes yeux de chenilles mes cheveux de longues baleines noires' (CT, 146).

15. *L'Immaculée Conception*, in Paul Eluard *Œuvres complètes* I, Gallimard

'Pléiade' 1968, p. 355. This work was written by Breton and Eluard in collaboration; the 'Pléiade' edition identifies the quoted passage as Breton's.

16.   'Durch alle Wesen reicht der *eine* Raum/Weltinnenraum. Die Vögel fliegen still/Durch uns hindurch. O, der ich wachsen will/Ich seh hinaus, und *in* mir wächst der Baum . . .' R. M. Rilke, *Sämtliche Werke*, Wiesbaden, 1955-66, Vol. II, p. 93.

17.   Cf. 'A toi mon amour il y a une escarpolette assez légère pour les mots/ Les mots que j'ai trouvés sur le rivage' (CDT, 53.).

5 JULES SUPERVIELLE: A POETRY OF DIFFIDENCE

Graham Dunstan Martin

André Breton once remarked that any critic who refused to accept that a horse could gallop inside a tomato was a fool. Certainly, said Supervielle, but what interested *him* was how the horse got into the tomato in the first place.[1] This statement is suggestive: what matters to this poet is not so much his 'favourite things' as the favourite *processes* which such things undergo. To list frequently recurring images like sun, stars, night sky, ocean, heart, tree and horse, takes us some part of the way,[2] but misses the fundamental character of his world. These images communicate their full meaning only if we observe that (in one poem) affection and tenderness *turn into* the hard wood of a tree, that (in another) someone's death causes an apple-tree to *grow*, that the outer darkness of night is 'poreuse et pénétrante', *mingling* frighteningly with the inner darkness of the poet's mind and body, [3] that even the most concrete elements of the world commonly suffer from a disquieting *instability*, and so on. In 'La Table',

> Tout à coup le soleil s'éloigne jusqu'à n'être
> plus qu'une étoile perdue
> Et cille.
>
> (G, 98)

The solar system's controlling centre is suddenly banished to the frontiers of awareness, reduced to the uncertain flicker of a star. Certainty and light have been transmuted into fear and the threat of oblivion. Such changes in the behaviour of an image suggest that Supervielle inhabits a world of shifting sand, whose features are radically unstable. The images are perhaps less important than the metamorphoses which they undergo, in the interplay between the poet's emotions, his senses and the outside world. And we may well expect what he tells us of his own very unusual sensibility to cast light upon the causes for these shifts and uncertainties.

It has often been suggested that the unborn child has no clear understanding of the differences between self and non-self. He has not yet learnt to distinguish his body from its surroundings. And to the adult Supervielle this distinction seems to have been by no means so

103

clear-cut as it is to most of us. When he walks abroad in the country, he tells us:

> . . . la campagne me devient presque tout de suite intérieure grâce à je ne sais quel glissement du dehors vers le dedans, a quoi ne participe pas seulement l'esprit, mais aussi les yeux, le nez, la bouche Et j'ai l'impression d'avancer dans le paysage comme dans mon propre monde mental, soit que l'air très léger semble n'avoir pas touché terre, être l'odeur même du ciel, ou qu'il s'épaississe, au voisinage des fermes, jusqu'à devenir presque aussi nourissant que du lait frais tiré.
>
> (BS, 20)

As we can see him insisting himself, this is not merely a psychological process: it has at least the appearance of being intensely physical: it is as if we were in the presence of a persistent hallucination, a habitual distortion of the senses.

Now, again according to the poet himself, his state of mind when writing poetry usually bore a distinct resemblance to the experience related in the last paragraph. 'L'inspiration se manifeste en général chez moi par le sentiment que je suis partout à la fois, aussi bien dans l'espace que dans les diverses régions du cœur et de la pensée' (N, 63). Or rather, this feeling looks like the converse of the other. On his country walks, Supervielle felt himself pleasurably invaded by the outer world, while under the influence of inspiration he, on the contrary, pleasurably invaded it.

Besides this strange osmosis between the inner and outer worlds, a second factor needs to be mentioned here: the poet's poor memory. In *Boire à la source* he writes:

> Ah! mémoire, que veux-tu que je fasse de ce peu que tu m'accordes quand tu ne fais pas la sourde, l'aveugle, ou même la rancunière, quand tu ne me disperses pas à tous les vents? Ici tu me livres un nez et des oreilles, tu m'interdis la bouche et le front. Et ces yeux, de quelle couleur étaient-ils? Et cette voix, chantait-elle vraiment ainsi? Là tu avoues une tête et me refuses les mains et tout le reste. Ou bien tu m'obliges à saluer dans la rue des inconnus interloqués. Comment faire dans ces ténèbres? En avant et à tâtons!
>
> (BS, 47-8)

Now the importance of memory to the human mind can hardly be overemphasised. It is clear that the ability to recognise phenomena, and hence the stability of perception itself, depend on it. So does our ability to interpret the world, for we must always guess at its future behaviour in terms of what we know of it already. Not to be able to rely on one's memory may lead to a sense of the outer world being unstable. And if memory of one's own past experience is chancy and fitful, one's very sense of identity may be uncertain. Thus, Supervielle confesses in this passage to feeling as if he is himself 'scattered to the four winds'. His is a mind changing in a changing world. Thus too, in 'La Chambre voisine', the poet is locked in the darkness of his inner self, while from his room there emerges a dog which has lost its memory and which seeks its master without ever finding him; and he himself is left behind in a catatonic state resembling death (FI, 84).

But I do not take Supervielle's poor memory to be a cause; it is rather an indication, to be understood along with the other shifting and obsessive phenomena of his strange sensibility. I have already mentioned *invasion*, one of the central experiences of his poetry. External objects may approach him: the mountain seeks to enter the poet's house; the trees press close around it (AI, 96). Finally, the outer world may actually enter the poet. Thus, in one poem he speaks of swallows 'volant de climat en émoi' (N, 27). The pun 'en moi/en émoi' gives some of the image's meaning: the swallows become part of the poet's own emotions; the outside world places its stamp upon his receptive mind. But the birds' very presence inside him deludes his senses: he sees them 'même errantes sous la lune'. The fluidity of his boundaries has led him to disquiet with regard to the outside world. And in the final line, where the birds are 'Oiseaux de jour perdus dans mes ombres sans fond', their original joyful meaning has been lost: they are threatened by an abyss of darkness within the poet.

The poet's mind, in fact, is hungry for images and experience, which it greedily engulfs:

> Je ne vais pas toujours seul au fond de moi-même
> Et j'entraîne avec moi plus d'un être vivant.
> Ceux qui seront entrés dans mes froides cavernes
> Sont-ils sûrs d'en sortir même pour un moment?
> J'entasse dans ma nuit, comme un vaisseau qui sombre,
> Pêle-mêle, les passagers et les marins,
> Et j'éteins la lumière aux yeux, dans les cabines,
> Je me fais des amis des grandes profondeurs.

(AI, 83)

From the point of view of the poem's readers this suggests the some-
times alarming experience of entering someone else's psychic world:
there is a danger to ourselves, we may feel, in making ourselves too
receptive to an emotional world that is foreign to us. But from the
poet's point of view, as the phrase comparing himself to a sinking
ship shows, things are hardly less alarming: he is himself afraid of the
darkness he describes; and the fear seems to be connected with the
disappearance into himself of features of the external world. It is
as if the poetry-creating mind were a devouring mechanism dragging
down the outer world and itself into darkness and destruction.

The complementary process to invasion, is *dispersion*. The poet's
surroundings may desert him, as if they were a dream from which he
is waking:

> Le monde me quitte, ce tapis, ce livre
> > Vous vous en allez;
> Le balcon devient un nuage libre
> > Entre les volets.

('Réveil', G, 108)

If the relief of freedom is momentarily implied by the third and fourth
lines, later in this poem anguish is reflected in what remains of the
poet's surroundings:

> Le plafond se plaint de son coeur de mouette
> > Qui se serre en lui,
> Le parquet mirant une horreur secrète
> > A poussé un cri . . .

And the poem ends on an image of disaster:

> Comme si tombait un homme à la mer
> > D'un mât invisible
> > Et couronné d'air.

(G, 109)

A nameless man finds himself caught between two vast emptinesses,
sky and sea, and falls from his position of perilous balance between
them. At this point the poem ends, but one is reminded of the dis-
appearance of the poet into the ocean after a similar fall in a much
later poem: 'Je deviens de l'eau qui bouge/Puis de l'eau qui a bougé'

(FM, 81). The image implies a death, or at least a total disappearance
of identity.

At the opening of 'Saisir', both an initial movement of grasping
and a succeeding movement of dispersal are followed by a threat of
amputation:

> Saisir, saisir le soir, la pomme et la statue,
> Saisir l'ombre et le mur et le bout de la rue.
> Saisir le pied, le cou de la femme couchée
> Et puis ouvrir les mains. Combien d'oiseaux lâchés
>
> Combien d'oiseau perdus qui deviennent la rue,
> L'ombre, le mur, le soir, la pomme et la statue.
>
> Mains, vous vous usurez
> A ce grave jeu-là.
> Il faudra vous couper
> Un jour, vous couper ras.
>
> (FI, 35-6)[4]

The poet grasps and understands. But he thereby removes objects from
the world. We have seen some of the fears of destruction and even of
self-destruction which may result from this process. In 'Saisir', the
poet then opens his hands and restores the objects to the world. He
thereby loses them; his grasp upon the world is diminished. And in
the last four lines quoted above, grasping and restoring are succeeded
by a threat of losing the very faculty by which contact is made, namely
the faculty of 'grasping', which, in French as well as English, means
also 'understanding'. There are overtones of guilt and punishment in
the image, which doubtless have to do with the poet's fears of tamper-
ing with the world, fears that I touched on above. For to grasp objects
and remove them from the world, is to attack the world's integrity.
Hence, not only letting go, but grasping too, may produce a sense of
loss of contact.

Not surprisingly, when Supervielle for once uses an image which
suggests firmness, strength and solidity, it is still loss of contact that
it symbolises:

> Et voici la muraille, elle use le désir
>
> (FI, 14)

Vous avanciez vers lui, femme des grandes plaines. . .
Vous fîtes de cet homme une maison de pierre,
Une lisse façade aveugle nuit et jour.

(FI, 37-8)

The hardness and coldness of stone is an apt element in the impenetrability of this curtain: experience has become lifeless and foreign, and silence has succeeded communication. And when experience is dispersed, almost totally lost, so that only a tiny and diminished fragment of it remains, we have the lines: 'Amérique devenue/Cette faible main de pierre/Séparée d'une statue' (FI, 145). The hand, the organ of contact, is amputated and of stone.

Dispersal may also entail a risk to the integrity of the self. This too produces a loss of contact with the world, since for an object to be grasped implies a subject to grasp it. The poet's inner self is as subject to uncertainty as the outer world. He depicts his organs, for instance, as uncomfortably independent, speaking of them as 'Ces bêtes à l'abandon dans leur sanglante écurie' (FM, 67). Man has no resource against his condition: besieged by vastness from without, he is equally besieged from within by forces beyond his control. His heart 's'agite prisonnier/Pour sortir de sa cage' (FI, 20). And in 'Le' (FI, 129) the cat bounding along the avenue turns out to be the poet's own heart; he is then in agony whether to wish for its return (for it is the source of life) or to settle for the calmness of emotional death (for it is a tormentor). And with these fears we may associate those numerous poems where the image of horses conveys some nameless terror, death, or the abolition of time, as in 'L'Allée' (AI, 14) or 'Les Chevaux du Temps' (AI, 11). It is reasonable to guess that the rhythm of hoofs evoked, for Supervielle, the irregular beat of his own heart, the 'intermittences' which caused him such anxiety during the larger part of his adult life.[5] The very centre of his physical world, the source of life itself, he felt to be constantly in peril.

And not merely the centre of his *physical* world. The heart, in Supervielle, is used with the full multiplicity of meanings which European languages give it. It is, from the physical point of view, the source of life; it is also the seat of the emotions.

The threat to the heart is thus one form which the poet's recurrent fear of the *loss of the centre* may take. But often this is explicitly psychological, as in those numerous poems where an Alter Ego appears, and the poet himself is left behind, a helpless and diminished fragment of himself, separated from his own soul:

Tout seul sans moi, tout privé de visage,
Me suffirait un petit peu de moi,
Mon moi est loin, perdu dans quelque voyage,
Comment savoir même s'il rentrera . . .

Comment ne pas trembler dans ce qui reste,
Mince enveloppe où j'essaie d'avoir chaud . . .

                                                    (FI, 112)

The poet trembles with cold, for his psychic vitality has been dimin-
ished; but also with fear, for his identity is under threat.
    Supervielle's world is thus a place of great insecurity: his personal
boundaries are uncertain, the world may invade his mind, or may be
scattered out of his reach, and his own psychic centre is threatened by
dispersal and by loss. The very act of grasping objects, of seeking
contact with the exterior, implies a threat both to the outside world
and the inner self. But not to have contact at all is equally disastrous,
for it is described in terms of a diminution or freezing of the self.
No position could be more anguished.

Now of course this is not the whole picture. Supervielle is by no means
always a poet of anguish, and his strange sensibility is also a source of
power or the illusion of power. We saw at the beginning of this essay
that he describes inspiration as giving him a sense of being everywhere
at once; and this is often presented as an almost entirely positive
feeling, containing barely a shadow of metaphysical disquiet.

Dans l'esprit plein de distances qui toujours se
    développent
Comme au fond d'un télescope
L'homme acceuille les aveux de sa pensée spacieuse,
Carte du ciel où s'aggravent Altaïr et Bételgeuse.

                                                    (G, 91)

This poem is not just a record of the poet's personal experience: it
goes on to describe a sound of battle 'Venant de l'âge de pierre',
villages being built and falling into ruins, and 'la lumière des visages
morts'. The same picture of man as a tiny point lost amid vast spaces,
which is so often used by the poet to express his own disquiet, here
communicates a modern view of Man as poised between enormous

expanses of space and time. And the sense of power at the start of the poem expresses an undoubted truth: that, despite Man's physical insignificance, his mind can indeed grasp and contain such immensities.[6]

Similarly, the ability of certain elements of the poet to vacate their owner, can be turned to good creative use:

> Il vous naît un poisson qui se met à tourner
> Tout de suite au plus noir d'une lame profonde,
> Il vous naît une étoile au-dessus de la tête, . . .
> Il vous naît un oiseau dans la force de l'âge,
> En plein vol, et cachant votre histoire en son cœur . . .
>
> (AI, 9)

and so on, through a whole range of creatures, including even human beings. The creations of the imagination are as solid and real as any object—as far as the imagination is concerned. For both the real and the unreal have to be imagined. And their equal reality in the imagination is particularly striking in this poet, not least because of the agonising uncertainties which attach to the notion of 'reality'. I have suggested elsewhere[7] that Supervielle's poetry has an unusual tendency to extended personification. Many of these personifications are visualised as possessing a whole mass of emotional attitudes of their own. Thus, in 'Sans murs' (a rather prosy poem, it is true, but a particularly clear example of the process, for that very reason) the poet remembers himself as a sixteen-year-old schoolboy sitting in his Paris classroom feeling bored with his Latin lesson. He raises his eyes from his book, and experiences a sort of sexual hallucination:

> Lorsque je lève les yeux, à l'Orient de la chaire/(. . .)/
> Une jeune fille est assise, elle fait miroiter son cœur/(. . .)/
> Un nuage de garçons glisse toujours vers ses lèvres
> Sans qu'il paraisse avancer.
> On lui voit une jarretière, elle vit loin des plaisirs
> Et la jambe demi-nue, inquiète, se balance.
> La gorge est si seule au monde que nous tremblons
>   qu'elle ait froid/(. . .)/
> Elle aimerait à aimer tous les garçons de la classe/(. . .)/
> Mais sachant qu'elle mourra si le maître la découvre
> Elle nous supplie d'être obscurs afin de vivre un moment
> Et d'être une jolie fille au milieu d'adolescents.   (G, 55-6)

The vague longings of the adolescent schoolboys are given definition in
the vision of a girl: she personifies their sexual desire. She also reflects
other features of their emotional mood: her leg is 'inquiète' and 'se
balance', her bosom is 'seule au monde', and 'elle nous supplie d'être
obscurs'; all these details reflect the boys' unease, shamefacedness and
secretiveness.

But this is not all: the vision does not only have the schoolboys'
feelings but also feelings of her own: 'Elle aimerait à aimer tous les
garçons. . .'; and it is she who would like to live for a moment among
them. This kind of thing occurs frequently in Supervielle: the feelings
of the observer are not merely passively attributed to the object in
question; instead, he attributes reciprocal feelings to it, so that it
appears to be responding to its creator's yearnings.[8]

The effect of this is a picture of the world where longing strongly
distorts appearances, rather as gravity bends light in Einstein's
universe. The best instance of this process is Supervielle's recurrent
ghosts.[9] In 'La Revenante' a series of uncanny happenings, ravens
tearing shreds of cloud from the sky, deer crying with human voices
and causing firs to fill with white roses and fall to the ground, are
succeeded by this tormented appeal to the ghost:

> Jurez, jurez-le-moi, morte encore affairée
>   Par tant de souvenirs,
> Que ce n'était pas vous qui guettiez à l'orée
>   De votre ancienne vie,
>
> Et que la déchirure allant d'un bout à l'autre
>   De la nuit malaisée
> N'était votre œuvre, ô vous qui guettiez jusqu'à l'aube
> L'âme dans la rosée.

> (G, 128-9)

The reiterated imperative expresses considerable anguish: superficially
it asks for reassurance that the mysterious ghost was not responsible;
but the very force of the demand shows a strong impulse to believe that
she was.[10] And even were she to answer as he 'wishes', that it was
not she, that answer would paradoxically assert her presence. The poet
is in fact appealing to the ghost to confirm something that he longs
to be true; and the negatives in his appeal have a strange and ambiv-
alent function to perform, which is not far from the heart of the

problem of uncertainty.

To explain their function, we must first recall Supervielle's remarks in a letter to Etiemble about the negatives which appear in so many of his poems. Whether a thing is negated or not, he says, whether we know it to be a fiction or not, its mention still evokes it. 'Remplacer une affirmation par une négation n'implique en rien un désaveu en poésie, ce qui compte c'est la chose même peu importe qu'on l'affirme ou qu'on la nie: la nommer c'est la mettre devant les yeux ou dans l'oreille et voilà ce qui importe.' (S/E, 78.) A close examination of Supervielle's poetry, however, reveals that it is not as simple as that. There is still a difference between statement asserted and statement denied; though the negative performs a more subtle function than in prose. It stands rather as a reluctant and wistful barrier between longing and reality.

Thus, in the poem just quoted, the negatives help to express the poet's grief that reality is not as he longs it to be, that the dead woman has not survived; but also his fear that she might have. For the images of the poem are expressive of pain. Whose pain? The poet's, doubtless. But what if the ghost were real, and they expressed *her* pain and grief? This alternative too would be intolerable.

Another example of the use of negatives and of expressions equivalent to them, can be found in a poem about his mother, 'Les Yeux de la morte':

Cette morte que je sais
Et qui s'est tant méconnue
Garde encore au fond du ciel
Un regard qui l'exténue. . .

All she has left is a 'look', which, moreover, exhausts her. Perhaps the look is the poet's; but there is also an implied parallel with the light of a star, which is of course progressively weakened by the enormous distances it has to travel to reach us. Her only other possessions are 'Une rose de drap, sourde/Sur une tige de fer,' (funeral regalia, in fact) 'Et des perles dont toujours/Une regagne les mers' (a very uncertain possession). She is inconceivably distant: 'De l'autre côté d'Altaïr/Elle lisse ses cheveux. . .' So she does have hair. But does she have eyes, or not? Is she conscious?

. . . Et ne sait pas si ses yeux
Vont fermer ou s'ouvrir
                                              (G, 119-20)

Now certainly it is implied that the poet would *like* to believe in her existence. He longs to assert his mother's survival, and talks as if it were almost established; and he transfers to her his own desire to see her survive. Yet the flimsiness of her imagined survival is so great that the poet's sense of loss is also communicated. In the last two lines, for instance, simple though the language is, it is rich in suggestion. 'She does not know . . .': literally, it is clear that if she is dead she has no knowledge. She apparently has no control over her eyes. This in turn has somewhat pathetic overtones: she is powerless, uncertain and bewildered. Finally, the opposition between 'open' and 'shut' suggests an indefinable no-man's-land between consciousness and unconsciousness, between life and death, as if nothing so positive as even a negative statement were possible. Negatives, in short, are so common in Supervielle because of the radical uncertainty which torments him. He dare not assert, but neither do his negatives quite dare to deny.

It is clear that we cannot claim literal existence for Supervielle's ghosts. But his sensibility is (if I may so express it) haunted by them. Just as real objects approach the point where they alter, fade or vanish, so such figments of the imagination as ghosts approach the point where they are almost believed in. The poet moves in a world of shadows, of half-existent beings. Reality is distorted by longing and by fear.

It follows that no attachment to a concrete guarantor is possible in Supervielle. Contact with the outside world is sometimes blocked, often uncertain, and usually subject to distortion, strange metamorphoses and difficulties of recognition; the outside world may invade the poet with irresistible force, it may overwhelm him, and bereave him of a sense of his own reality; he may be 'scattered to the four winds'; and then he may be unable to distinguish reality from dream, so that the reality of the invading world itself is called in question; and many of the most persistent objects in the world are creations of his own mind. Nor are such creations of the mind necessarily confident ones: their fluidity and ephemerality reflect the diffidence of their creator.

But this diffidence does not exist merely at the level of perception and sensation. It will be clear that it is very deeply rooted: its centre is the problem of identity itself. As I said above, for an object to be grasped implies a subject to grasp it; and, when there is no longer an observing subject, things are (rather as in Bishop Berkeley's universe) no longer reliably themselves:

> Quand nul ne la regarde,
> La mer n'est plus la mer . . .

(FM, 150)

> Un sapin, la nuit,
> Quand nul ne le voit,
> Devient une barque
> Sans rames ni bras.

(FI, 172)

For the core of the problem of the self's relationship to the world is this: that relationship itself alters the two participants in it, and thereby makes them both unstable. We no longer have a clear and separate consciousness mapping a clear and separate world, but a shifting state of affairs in which self alters world and world alters self. In a mind so uncertain of itself, so much at the mercy of outside forces, interaction is instability.

And if uncertainty about identity is the source of Supervielle's diffidence, it will not be surprising if we find that this diffidence is expressed, not only in his negatives (for instance) but in the whole texture of his verse. He will sometimes explicitly state his own doubts when faced with the task of writing:

> Comment fait-on pour se mettre en un vers (. . .)
> Lorsque l'on est plus dispersé au monde
> Qu'une comète à la queue vagabonde,
> Comment fait-on pour être de ce temps
> Quand l'éternel vous mord à tout instant,
> Et pour loger dans son petit espace
> Quand tout le ciel vous le change de place.

(OM, 153-4)

On the face of it, the poet's confidence is great and his claims large: his vision is too wide-ranging to fit into the narrow confines of a poem. But the mention of dispersal, and of the refusal of the space he occupies to keep still, as also something hesitant and tentative in the very tone of the first line, make one feel rather his uncertainty. And this is conclusively confirmed in this poem's last three lines:

> Un vers requiert plus de travail qu'un mur!
> (Ah l'on voit bien qu'il n'a rien d'un mâçon

Et qu'il bâtit la chose à sa façon).

(OM, 154)

Some of Supervielle's diffidence, in fact, attaches to his *language*:
words are as difficult to grasp and manipulate as the world itself.
But this fact, in the case of a poet, may have an unfortunate effect:
it may produce hesitancy and imperfection in his very means of
expression. We find him disavowing his own way of putting things,
even self-consciously appealing to the reader's tolerance. The honest
reader will admit that, in effect, Supervielle's poetry may occasionally
not so much express hesitancy as hesitate to express. This is of course
not true of his best work, but does some of the poetry not suffer from
prosiness and lack of compression, from a diffidence that is usually
charming but sometimes clumsy, a humour that is usually effective but
sometimes over-defensive; and is some of it not poised on the verge of
sentimentality? It is my belief that these reservations are at times
valid; and that the very problems which make Supervielle's sensibility
so original, cause further problems for his expression of it.

Doubtless these occasional failings are connected with the curious
fact that, until Supervielle was between thirty-five and forty, his
poetry was conventional, slight and sentimental. Popular myth would
have us believe that poets die young, but in this case we have a 'late
developer'. He himself comments on his early works, 'Je ne dirai pas
que tout cela est bien *jeune* mais plutôt bien *vieux*.'[11] And in
explanation of his late development as a poet, he had two things
to say. Firstly, he had read little modern poetry, and indeed little
in general; and his surroundings were uncongenial to the practice of
modernism. Secondly, and this is the point I want to emphasise here,
he feared self-exploration. He writes, 'Si je me suis révélé assez tard,
c'est que longtemps j'ai éludé mon moi profond. Je n'osais pas
l'affronter directement . . .' (N, 58).[12]

Yet even after 'finding himself' in the mature poetry of *Débarcad-
ères* and *Gravitations*, Supervielle plainly continued to fear his inner
world, and his exploration of it always remained cautious. He tells
us again:

J'ai toujours plus ou moins redouté de m'attaquer aux
monstres que je sens en moi. Je préfère les apprivoiser avec les mots
de tous les jours, lesquels sont rassurants entre tous. (Ne sont-ils
pas ceux-là mêmes qui nous ont tranquillisés lors de grandes peurs
enfantines?) Je compte sur leur sagesse et leur amitié maintes fois

éprouvées pour neutraliser le venin de l'insolite, souvent précurseur
de panique. Et peut-être dois-je le meilleur de ma sagesse à ce que
j'ai eu souvent à dompter un peu de folie.

(N, 65.)

He had, in fact, to tread warily: he felt sometimes that madness was
not far away. As for what these inner monsters were, it is clear that
they were precisely the anxieties and terrors I have been describing
in the early part of this essay.

This then is one explanation for his youthful failure as a poet.
But it is also the explanation for a fairly consistent refusal, throughout
his poetry, to explore fear and anxiety otherwise than cautiously.
When one treads on shifting sand, after all, care must be taken. Or, to
change our metaphor to one that is more Superviellian, the poet prefers
to enter the dark places of the mind carrying a candle. He has two
enemies: too much light would be as dangerous as too much darkness.
He goes armed into the darkness of his inner self; and he must take
care not to shed too much light there, lest this destroy him:

> Guerrier de l'obscur,
> Vous vous étoilez,
> Prenez garde à vous,
> Vos yeux vont brûler!
> Vous ne pouvez rien
> Sans obscurité.

(FM, 72-3)

Besides, the soul is a timorous creature, all too easy to scare away.
'C'est beau', he writes,

> . . . d'avoir atteint l'âme
> A petits coups de rame
> Pour ne l'effaroucher
> D'une brusque approchée.

(39, 56)

A frontal attack upon these psychic mysteries might have, in short,
two unfortunate results: the poet might be overwhelmed, or he might
be blinded to the very truths he is seeking. Supervielle prefers therefore
to content himself with small certainties:

Suffit d'une bougie
Pour éclairer le monde ...

(G, 101)

And his most common metaphor for the state of inspiration, and for
the poetic image, lighting poets in obscurity, is that of starlight. Night
is

... la couche où poser la tête qui déjà
   Commence à graviter,
A s'étoiler en nous, à trouver son chemin.

(AI, 139)

Supervielle's exploration of his sensibility, then, is an attempt to
shed light in dark places—but in a cautious way. 'L'image est la lanterne
magique qui éclaire les poètes dans l'obscurité. Elle est aussi la surface
éclairée lorsqu'il s'approche de ce centre mystérieux où bat le coeur
même de la poésie.' (N, 61.) He is, he claims, 'naturellement obscur',
but 'Je tâche d'y mettre des lumières sans faire perdre sa vitalité à
l'inconscient.' (N, 60.) It is therefore not surprising that he should
turn out to be one of the least obscure of modern poets. And this
double fear of his own monsters and of appearing too obscure a writer,
may have had at times an inhibiting effect upon his poetry. Thus, one
may detect a prosy defensiveness that rings far from true in the poem
'Le' (the title is both definite article and object pronoun, and suggests
some nameless fear). Here he addresses 'quatorze voix en même temps',
inner voices of the mind which haunt and terrorise him. He first
commands and then asserts:

Allez ailleurs, brûlez ailleurs...
Laissez ce corps d'homme tranquille
Jamais vous ne pourrez l'atteindre
Dans les lointains qui sont en lui.

But can such nameless fears be kept at arm's length by mere apostrophe
and assertion? The prosiness of this attempted exorcism gives one no
confidence in the poet's victory. One is more inclined to accept the last
two lines of the poem:

Silence! On ne peut pas offrir l'oreille à ces voix-là.
On ne peut même pas y penser tout bas

> Car l'on pense beaucoup trop haut et cela fait
>   un vacarme terrible.

(FI, 129-30)

Similàrly, the hesitant delicacy of the poet's approach to the denizens
of his world risks collapsing into sentimentality in those cases where his
touch becomes *too* delicate, where his reluctance to gaze too hard and
too long at a violent or unpalatable fact wrings from him a pity that is
merely whimsical. Such a poem is 'Le petit bois', where a wood (and
possibly a number of people sheltering in it) appears to have been
blown up in an artillery bombardment. The first and last verses typify
the poem, and show that the poet's reaction is surely not adequate to
his subject:

> J'étais un petit bois de France
> Avec douze rouges furets,
> Mais je n'ai jamais eu de chance
> Ah! que m'est-il donc arrivé?

> (. . .)

> Mon Dieu comme c'est difficile
> D'être un petit bois disparu
> Quand on avait tant de racines
> Comment faire pour n'être plus?

(39, 24-5)

His best work thus falls into two categories, first, those poems (Usually
brief and using a simple and direct vocabulary) where a series of delicate
and enigmatic images are presented, and hesitation is absent from the
actual mode of expression. 'Les Yeux de la morte' and 'Guerrier de
l'obscur' may serve as instances. The touch is always light, sometimes
almost cautious, but the imagery is dense, and a sense of underlying
insecurity is communicated by the imagery itself, and by the character-
istic changes and metamorphoses which it undergoes.

But secondly, tentativeness itself may, when it finds full expression
in the poem's language, become a virtue. The poem 'Figures' is an
example:

> Je bats comme des cartes
> Malgré moi, des visages,

   Et tous, ils me sont chers.
   Parfois l'un tombe à terre
5 Et j'ai beau le chercher
   La carte a disparu.
   Je n'en sais rien de plus.
   C'était un beau visage,
   Pourtant, je l'aimais bien.
10 Je bats les autres cartes.
   L'inquiet de ma chambre,
   Je veux dire mon coeur,
   Continue à brûler
   Mais non pour cette carte,
15 Qu'une autre a remplacée.
   C'est un nouveau visage,
   Le jeu reste complet
   Mais toujours mutilé.
   C'est tout ce que je sais,
20 Nul n'en sait davantage.

                                          (CP, 138; AI, 18-19)

Now here the poet's uncertainties certainly do not get between him and
the reader: the poem expresses them, not merely through its content,
but also through its manner. A tissue of hesitant disavowal weaves in
and out of the poem's texture in such expressions as 'malgré moi'
(1.2), 'j'ai beau le chercher' (1.5), 'Je n'en sais rien de plus' (1.7), 'C'est
tout ce que je sais' (1.19). And the self-correction 'L'inquiet de ma
chambre/Je veux dire mon coeur' places hesitation within the very
language of the poem. (Incidentally, this phrase is not the mere mood-
painting it might appear: for in the context of 'brûler' the words
'L'inquiet de ma chambre' suggest, though dimly, the flickering light
of a fire or a candle. The suggestion is dim, but so perhaps is the
flame.) And in fact the sentence structure of the poem is as if con-
versational, as if improvised by the ordinary spoken word, and seems
therefore to suggest a similar mood of hesitation and approximation.
Brief phrase succeeds brief phrase as in conversation, and the subord-
inate clause is on the whole eschewed. Line 15 is of course an exception.
But that this effect is intentional is proved, I think, by the fact that in
the text given above (which is the amended text in the 1947 *Choix
de poèmes*) Supervielle has suppressed a subordinate clause which
appeared in the 1934 *Les Amis inconnus*. Originally line 9 read 'Pour-
tant, que j'aimais bien'. The later text reads more conversationally,

more spontaneously, and fits the mood of hesitancy better.

We may of course rightly say that such poems as 'Figures' lack the overpowering force that some poets achieve, and that since they are almost more like parables than structures of images, they do not have the intangible and haunting quality of 'Les Yeux de la morte' or 'Guerrier de l'obscur'. But it cannot be denied that they achieve a very special tonality, delicately and precisely accomplished. 'Je suis', wrote Supervielle, 'd'une famille de petits horlogers qui ont travaillé, leur vie durant, la loup vissée à l'œil' (N, 62).

The dangers to Supervielle's poetry are only too evident: they are sentimentality and an avoidance of the dark or painful. He most success-fully resists these temptations in the four collections *Gravitations* (1925), *Le Forçat innocent* (1930), *Les Amis inconnus* (1934) and the second half of *La Fable du monde* (1938). His best work shows either firm but delicate images devoid of expressed hesitation, or (by turning a necessity into a virtue) tentativeness itself expressed as a fully realised element of the poem. But perhaps a diffidence that strikes so deep, beyond his vision into his very sense of identity, could hardly have been expected not to affect, disturb, and sometimes undermine the language of his poetry. An occasional uncertainty in expression is the price we have to pay for the poet's universe, a universe whose originality resides precisely in the bewildering instability that afflicts the earth and its creatures, the sky and its stars, and the poet's own diffident self.

Notes

1.   Quoted in Christian Sénéchal, *Jules Supervielle, Poète de l'univers intérieur*, Paris, Jen Flory, les Presses du Hibou, 1939, p. 67. André Breton's remark can be found in 'Exposition X. . ., Y. . . ', where he writes: 'Les valeurs oniriques l'ont définitivement emporté sur les autres et je demande à ce qu'on tienne pour un crétin celui qui se refuserait encore, par exemple, à *voir* un cheval galoper sur une tomate.' (*Point du jour*, Paris, Gallimard, Collection 'Idées', 1970, p. 57.) Supervielle's presumably unconscious alteration of the horse galloping *on* a tomato to one galloping *in* it, is interesting, for I should take it to be further evidence of his concern with processes of change. A horse *on* a tomato is but a strange juxtaposition; a horse *entering* a tomato adds the sense of a continuing process. (I am indebted to Michael Sheringham for pointing Supervielle's misquotation out to me.)

2.   Such a list is given in Tatiana W. Greene, *Jules Supervielle*, Geneva/Paris, Droz, 1958, p. 91. She proceeds to study certain of these.

3.   AI, 139. References are as follows: AI *Les Amis inconnus*, Gallimard, 1934; BS *Boire à la source*, Gallimard, 1951; CP *Choix de poèmes*,

Gallimard, 1947; FI *Le Forçat innocent*, Gallimard, 1930; FM *La Fable du monde*, Gallimard, 1938; G *Gravitations*, Gallimard, 1925; N *Naissances* suivies de *En songeant à un art poétique*, Gallimard, 1951; S/E Jules Supervielle/Etiemble, *Correspondance 1936-1959*, Paris, Société d'Edition d'Enseignement Supérieur, 1969; Sh *Shéhérazade*, Gallimard, 1949; *39 1939-1945 Poèmes*, Gallimard, 1946.

4. It should be noted that these last four lines were removed by the poet from the version of 'Saisir' which appears in his *Choix de poèmes* (1947). An unfortunate, if by no means isolated, lapse of judgement.

5. Cf. Greene, *op. cit.* pp. 16-17.

6. One could list many other poems where the mood is optimistic, or at least mainly so. But there are almost always hints of anguish. In the poem cited, for instance, 'L'âme d'obscures patries/Rôde désespérément dans le ciel indivisible.' And 'On voit monter la lumière des visages morts sur terre' has not only comforting overtones of the unity of human history, but clearly also disquieting ones that contradict the comfort.

7. See my article 'Metaphors in Supervielle's Poetry', *Modern Language Review*, Vol. 59 (1964), pp. 579-82.

8. Somewhat altered and paraphrased from the above article. This particular type of image is there termed 'transferred attribution'. Perhaps 'reversed' or 'reflexive attribution' would have been better.

9. Another is his image of God, who is a persistent figure of longing in Supervielle. The subject is interesting, but I have no room here to discuss it.

10. Cf. William Empson, *Seven Types of Ambiguity*, Harmondsworth, Penguin Books, 1961, p. 205: 'Thus in Keats' *Ode to Melancholy* "No, no; go not to Lethe; neither twist" tells you that somebody, or some force in the poet's mind, must have wanted to go to Lethe very much, if it took four negatives in the first line to stop them.'

11. S/E, 28, pp. 27-9 reprints a few brief fragments of his first collection *Brumes du passé* (1900, no editor's name), which will sufficiently bear out the poet's own comment.

12. Cf. S/E, 29, where he mentions again his psychological fears and his unfamiliarity with any literary milieu.

6 THE WORLD AND THE WORD IN SAINT-JOHN PERSE

Roger Little

In his Nobel Prize speech in 1960, entitled simply 'Poésie', Saint-John Perse declared: 'Par son adhésion totale à ce qui est, le poète tient pour nous liaison avec la permanence et l'unité de l'Etre' (Pl, 446).[1] The role of the poet is thus seen as that of mediator between two poles worthy of human attention, physical reality on the one hand and the essence of Being on the other. He is, in his poetry, a creator of relationships through the medium of language, and in the case of Saint-John Perse these relationships are claimed to be between 'le monde entier des choses' (a phrase used in 'Poésie' after re-echoing throughout *Vents*) and 'le mouvement même de l'Etre'. By the latter phrase, he implies an interaction between *being* and *becoming* which underlines the dynamism of our developing selves.

The absolute nature of the presentation of this dialectic brings both its stimulus and its problems, however. For Perse's poetry is bifocal in the extreme, pivoting around the mediating stance of the poet. He sees—as we in turn must try to see— the wood for the trees, but at the same time sees the wood *of* the trees. 'Au poète indivis d'attester parmi nous la double vocation de l'homme' (Pl, 447).

What Perse understands by the dynamic essence of being is, on his own admission, close to the sense of everything being a state of flux, as expressed by Heraclitus and other pre-Socratic philosophers.[2] Nearer to our own time, the idea has been reinterpreted by Bergson, Heidegger and Teilhard de Chardin, each involved in different ways with the problems of moral philosophy and notions of man's progress— and, in the case of the two Frenchmen, his perfectibility—in society. Saint-John Perse is undoubtedly closest to Heidegger without ever having read him.[3] For it would be quite wrong to treat the poet as a systematic philosopher. Rather is he attempting in his own way to probe the unknown, putting to himself such questions as are by their nature insoluble and in consequence the most interesting. But the poet's way is not the philosopher's; since his task is to mediate, he cannot indulge in abstractions or detach himself from two very concrete realities: the phenomena he perceives and the language he uses. In an interview with Pierre Mazars, Perse said:

> Le poète a parfaitement le droit, et même le devoir, d'aller explorer
> les domaines les plus obscurs; mais plus il va loin dans cette direction,
> plus il doit user de moyens d'expression concrets. Aussi loin qu'il
> pénètre dans l'au-delà irrationnel ou mystique, il est tenu de
> s'exprimer par des moyens réels, même tirés de sa vie expérimentale.
> Gardez votre emprise au sol et bâtissez avec tout cela une œuvre
> hors du temps, hors du lieu, édifiée dans cette récréation.
>
> (PL, 576)

For present purposes it seems appropriate therefore to concentrate on
the creative aspect of Perse's writing, the forging through language of
a personal relationship between the world and the word.

To what extent is his metaphorical claim to embrace 'le monde entier
des choses' fruitful as a stimulus or goal? It certainly tallies with the
cosmic scope of his preoccupations with the elemental forces of nature
and the fundamental drive of man in relation to them. But Perse's
attention is necessarily selective; his interest is not indiscriminately
aroused by everything the sensible world has to offer. Within certain
areas of predilection, he responds actively to those things and events
which seem to him worthy of praise. Of these there seem to be two
main categories which often coincide: things that spark off a sense of
the marvellous and things that seem to fulfil their natures most
completely. In a letter to André Gide, Perse wrote of the title of his
first collection of poems, *Eloges*: 'Il est si beau que je n'en voudrais
jamais d'autre, si je publiais un volume—ni plusieurs' (Pl, 769). What-
ever cannot elicit Perse's praise is, in the main, disregarded in his poetry.
The realms of knowledge that particularly excite his curiosity seem to
be: zoology (including ornithology and entomology), ethnology,
botany, geology, the sea and ships (including navigation and so the
stars) and law. In all these fields he shows not only a keen interest
but accurate knowledge based on first-hand experience. It is important
for his sense of authenticity that such acquaintance has not simply been
gleaned from books.

It is paradoxical in this respect that the end-product of his poetical
investigations should be a book. Yet clearly its contents generate
considerations that directly reflect the poet's in the reader's mind,
thus refining his power of attention to both world and word. And the
more he reads, the more he realises that in poetry the two are insep-
arable, since language is itself a formative mode of apprehension as well
as the vehicle of expression. Saint-John Perse exploits this in various
ways. Not only does he maintain that subtlety and clarity of express-

ion are imperative concomitants of subtlety and clarity of apprehension, but also he flexes the rhythms and phonic texture of his poetry in response to the impulses of his subject. He accepts as a principle that words must mean what convention (or the dictionary, embodying that convention) would have them mean. If, by additional reference to an etymological sense or to a second meaning, an ambiguity is uncovered or a new relationship revealed, Perse is quick to seize that chance. But just as he does not invent words, so he does not invent meanings for words. The poetry is generated by precision meeting precision.[4] And because Perse looks for the appropriate word, rhythm and texture, we are not surprised to see this accuracy of vision and expression continued in the very shaping and structure of his poems. The dynamic, expansive rhythms directly reflect the impulses he perceives in the rains, snows, winds and seas that permeate his work. At every level there is an attempt at a mimetic bond between form and content:

> C'est que, dans la création poétique telle que je puis la concevoir, la fonction même du poète est d'intégrer la chose qu'il évoque ou de s'y intégrer, s'identifiant à cette chose jusqu'à la devenir lui-même et s'y confondre: la vivant, la mimant, l'incarnant, en un mot, ou se l'appropriant, toujours très *activement*, jusque dans son mouvement propre et sa substance propre. D'où la nécessité de croître et de s'étendre quand le poème est vent, quand le poème est mer—comme la nécessité serait au contraire de l'extrême brieveté si le poème était la foudre, était l'éclair, était le glaive.
>
> (Pl, 921.)[5]

A few examples will illustrate some of the main points made so far. The poem 'Pluies' traces, at a narrative level, the progress of a heavy storm. It is something we have all experienced, so there is no difficulty working out the referential framework of the poem, and we can concentrate on what Perse has made of it. Glancing through the text before reading it, we see that the lines of unrhymed verse (called *versets*) start at a regular length and are grouped in threes (these groups being called *laisses*). Gradually the *versets* lengthen and the page darkens until, in Canto VII, the pattern is broken and the lines burst their bounds. We are at the height of the storm. Then the pattern is resumed as the worst of the deluge is over, and the poem ends as the last drops fall. There is a direct equivalence between the principal image, the storm, and the shape of the poem on the page. A strong visual sense is obviously at work, yet it has been translated into a readable literary

form, different from Apollinaire's *calligrammes* and similar 'visual
lyricism' in that it does not fall between the stools of two media but
thoroughly assimilates the virtues of both.[6]

A strong visual as well as analogical sense is apparent in another way
in the first line of the same poem: 'Le banyan de la pluie prend ses
assises sur la ville.' With its counterpart at the beginning of Canto VIII,
this multiple image presides over the whole text of 'Pluies'. And well it
may, for when we discover how this curious sub-tropical tree grows,
we realise why it is that, from all the trees Perse had seen on his travels
across the world, he chose this one which is unfamilar to those who
know only temperate climates. Beneath its accumulated mass of dark
foliage, in which the poet sees an image of the storm cloud, stands not
only a central trunk but, from its spreading boughs, a host of
adventitious roots linking the branches vertically with the ground. The
idea of wooden shafts of rain thrusting into the earth provides a power-
ful image both of intensity and of fixity. Reference to no other tree
would have offered such an exact image while breathing new life into
the hackneyed correlation of shafts and rain (cf. 'Il pleut des halle-
bardes').

Perse finds other ways of revifying language, sometimes using the
reader's expectations as a foil for his discoveries. Thus, in 'Neiges',
the snow takes on a silken quality in the phrase 'les choses grèges de
la neige' because the adjective is generally known only in the form
soie grège 'raw silk'. Similarly implicit in 'le ciel gemme' in *Amers*,
Invocation, 5, through its close echo of 'le sel gemme', is the reflective
crystalline quality peculiar to rock salt. The opening canto of 'Exil'
contains a striking example of the exact knowledge of a mineral being
used in a transferred epithet to disturbing and powerful effect:

L'Eté de gypse aiguise ses fers de lance dans nos plaies.

Distinguishable here are three stages in the poet's progress, any one of
which might have escaped the attention of someone less receptive and
responsive to the experience both of natural phenomena and of
language. First there is the familiarity with the particular twinning of
rhomboid crystals which gives the formation known as *gypse fer de
lance* or arrowhead gypsum. Then there is the knowledge of the name
given to this macle. And lastly there is the special use of the separated
elements of the term in the *verset*. This use is itself twofold, reflecting
awareness both of the powers of poetic language in the transference of
the epithet and of the evocative capacity of exact observation. For

the casual reader, seeing the line, will no doubt imagine a white pow-
dery substance colouring the summer day and unwisely assume there to
be no textual or textural link with what follows. But once we know
the macle's name we are likely to discover that it is not an opaque matt
white powder like gypsum in the form of plaster of Paris, but a gleaming
yellowish crystal entirely appropriate as an image of a piercingly hot
June day on the shores of the American East coast.

While the things of which Perse writes may readily be known,
either directly or from books, to anyone the world over, it is clear that
the way in which he writes of them is inextricably bound up with the
French language. He is thus at one and the same time universally com-
prehensible and ultimately untranslatable.[7] As with any poet using to
the full the particular genius of his mother tongue, the best one can
hope to do is to transpose the effect as nearly as possible by using
equivalent means. For Perse, the naming of things in his own language
is not simply a way of grasping more clearly the reality which the senses
have perceived, of defining that difficult and ever-changing relationship
between the self and the outside world, but a way of life, almost a
moral code:

> . . . la langue française [est] encore pour moi la seule patrie
> imaginable, l'asile et l'antre par excellence, l'armure et l'arme par
> excellence, le seul 'lieu géométrique' où je puisse me tenir en ce
> monde pour y rien comprendre, y rien vouloir ou renoncer.
>
> (Pl, 551)

Perse's consciousness of his deep-seated need of the French language
was no doubt heightened by his frequent absence from metropolitan
France—in the West Indies as a child, in China as a diplomat, in the
United States in exile. His love of French takes many forms and shows
in his wide vocabulary, his poetic use of etymology, his sensitivity to
the shape and sound of words, his sense of rhythm, his mastery, in fact,
of that complex phenomenon called language which we are sometimes
rashly inclined to think we have tamed by naming it. He allows it its
muscular dynamism without ever losing grip on the reins: his poetry
positively seethes with vitality.

How is such a result consciously achieved? Firstly through rhythm.
What Perse detects in the cosmic forces and seasonal cycles around and
within him is translated into the long line of the *verset*, infinitely
adaptable to the subject of its evocation. For variety a refrain line can
end each canto (as in 'Récitation à l'éloge d'une Reine', 'Amitié du

Prince' and 'Poème à l'Etrangère') or a key phrase be woven into the
texture of the whole poem ('Seigneur terrible de mon rire' in 'Pluies',
'Epouse du monde ma présence' in 'Neiges', 'Se hâter, se hâter, parole
de vivant' in *Vents*). But in general Perse relies on subtle variations and
extensions of metres with an even number of syllables, variously
grouped, and scanned not arithmetically as is traditionally the case for
French verse but in 'feet' as is the case in English and Classical prosody.
Thus a standard alexandrine would be considered not as a twelve-
syllable line but as a tetrameter, with four intonation groups. The
metronomic piano-teacher imagined by Claudel in 'Réflexions et
propositions sur le vers français' (a true reflection of many a reader's
view of French prosody and alas of many a doggerel-monger as well)
is ousted by something more supple and elastic, retaining the dignity
of prosody but not hidebound by the conventions of a bygone age.[8]

Within these varying but almost invariably urgent rhythms, how can
the words themselves, other than being repeated as refrains or ana-
phoric formulae, contribute to a sense of vitality? Other forms of
repetition are possible: a word can become a syllable of a later
word ('ris'–'irritable' in 'Eloges' IX; 'Et'–'Etranger' in 'Exil' VI), it
can be echoed through assonance or rhyme ('Face'–'grâce'–'hâte' in
'Chanson du Présomptif'; 'Guerrières, ô guerrières par la lance et le
trait jusqu'à nous aiguisées!/Danseuses, ô danseuses par la danse et
l'attrait au sol multipliées' in 'Pluies' III); allow development of a
subject through parallel rhythms (L'odeur funèbre de la rose n'assié-
gera plus les grilles du tombeau; l'heure vivante dans les palmes ne
taira plus son âme d'étrangère . . .' in *Amers*, Invocation, 1); be
juggled with for its phonetic ingredients ('ressac'–'l'accès' in 'Exil'
III; 'l'éclair salace'–'lacérées' in 'Pluies' IV; 'cabrée'–'scabreuse' in
Vents IV, 3); be juxtaposed with a morphological cousin to make us
reflect on etymology and the nature of linguistic coincidence ('Ainsi
conviée serez-vous l'hôte dont il *convient* de taire le mérite' in *Amers*,
Invocation, 4; 'le ciel plein d'*erreurs* et d'*errantes* prémisses' in 'Exil'
IV).[9]

Language is the poet's medium: one would expect close attention
to it and indeed be disappointed if there were evidence of lack of
attention creating a lack of tension. But words are expressive *of some-
thing*, and Perse is not a writer to play emptily with their sounds alone.
In a letter of 1910 to Jacques Rivière he wrote:

Je n'aurai, certes, jamais idée de dénier au poème un mystérieux
'concours' musical (s'il n'est pas préassigné): l'inconsciente utili-

sation du timbre verbal, et la distribution même ou 'composition' de toute une masse aussitôt qu'elle vit. Mais je n'admettrai jamais que le poème puisse un instant échapper à sa loi propre: qui est le thème 'intelligible'. L'art d'écrire, qui est l'art de nommer, ou plus loïntainement de désigner, n'aura jamais d'autre fonction que le mot, cette société déjà, et qui se grève encore du sens étymologique. Je ne vois là qu'un art analytique, la matière verbale la plus musicale férocement astreinte, en premier lieu ou en dernier, aux lois particulières de 'propriété'.

(Pl, 675.)

Nommer, désigner. I have already suggested what Perse most likes to name and evoke. There remain the thorny questions of how his senses respond to things before he verbalises them, whether there is evidence of existing words predisposing his perceptions in some way, and whether indeed it is legitimate at all to argue about sense-perceptions from a literary artefact.If we amass the evidence on the references to different sense impressions in the poetry, all we can reasonably extrapolate are postulates about how Perse selects and uses for poetic purposes such perception of things as he has. There is consequently a strong element of tautology in such a process, and we remain firmly within the artefact, able to make only tentative assumptions about either poet or reality. The more so as a poet's love of language makes language itself a forceful formative power over his relationship with things: if by naming we create, it is also true that the connotations and phonetic texture of the name will colour our view of what is designated.[10] How then can we speak of a poet's perception of reality without involving language? Which brings us back to the poetry, only more aware, I hope, of the limitations of any investigation into the sense-references we find there.

By tracing in the poetry the references to sensory data, we find on analysis certain patterns of which the reader is more or less conscious when he registers his impressions of the poems. If such an analysis tells us anything about Perse's apprehension of the world, it is a useful excercise even if we have to leave the realm of poetry for the uncertain science of psychology. Because of the present limitations of space, I cannot here catalogue occurrences of Perse's extraordinary visual sense, or show how taste seems to play an unusually prominent role in his perceptual range, or insist on the sensitivity of his ear both to natural sounds, to music and to the phonic qualities of words, or underline some striking olfactory images. Instead I propose to concentrate for the rest of this chapter on what appears in Perse to be the Cinderella of the senses: that of touch.

From the early poems, written when Perse was still a student, there emerges a clear picture of his sensitivity to contact, but while physical contact with creatures and things seems pleasurable, being *controlled* by the child, contact with people — invariably adults — emphasises his dependence on them and arouses either direct hostility or an ambiguous reaction stemming from his sense of nascent sexuality. The ideal seems to be a communion with one's self. Contact with things allows this: 'l'enfant . . . revient de l'école des Pères, affectueux longeant l'affection des Murs qui sentent le pain chaud . . .' ('Eloges' XIV). The brilliant and marvellous creatures of his West Indian childhood shower down in his vivid recollection of touching a certain tree: 'Et un autre [arbre] on ne peut le toucher de la main, comme on prend à témoin, sans qu'il pleuve aussitôt de ces mouches, couleurs!. . .' (IV). He straddles his first horse, rapt in admiration for a physical power which submits to his control: 'j'ai pressé des lunes à ses flancs sous mes genoux d'enfant' (II). He delights in being the centre of attraction *à distance*, touching only what he can master (rather as he controls the analogies which give such power to his imagery): 'Le vieillard même m'envierait une paire de crécelles/et de bruire par les mains comme une liane à pois . . .' (XV). In the 'Histoire du Régent', originally part of 'Eloges', admiration for power is explicitly linked to the wiping of a blade: 'Tu as vaincu! tu as vaincu! Que le sang était beau, et la main/qui du pouce et du doigt essuyait une lame!. . .'.

Even the most moderate reaction to being touched, however, can at best be called neutral: 'Je me souviens du sel, je me souviens du sel que la nourrice jaune dut essuyer à l'angle de mes yeux' ('Pour fêter une enfance' II). And in any case attention is drawn here less to the physical contact than to a substance which was to hold a constant fascination for the poet, namely salt.[11] When someone draws near, the poet remembers the child's reaction as uneasiness—genuine affection mingled with tense wariness—an expression of that ambivalent sensitivity that arises from the vulnerability of early love. The physical presence of black girls arouses feelings which potentially threaten the boy's self-control: 'et les servantes de ta mère, grandes filles luisantes, remuaient leurs jambes chaudes près de toi qui tremblais . . .' ('Pour fêter une enfance' I). Unease and affection are mingled in the following simile: 'et la présence de la voile, grande âme malaisée, la voile étrange, là, et chaleureuse révélée, comme la présence d'une joue. . .'('Eloges' IX). But the child's gauche attempt at self-protection and the assertion of independence is also expressed in the over-compensating notation of hostility:

'Quand vous aurez fini de me coiffer, j'aurai fini de vous haïr.'
(. . .)
    'Ne tirez pas si loin sur mes cheveux. C'est déjà bien assez qu'il faille qu'on me touche. Quand vous m'aurez coiffé, je vous aurai haïe'
('Eloges' XVII)

It is in communion with nature that he can escape the palpitations caused by human contact or proximity, and best of all, it seems, in contact with himself, when solitude becomes a catalyst for creative thinking. More than once in 'Eloges' the child gathers himself to himself, musing on the marvels of nature around him and keeping at bay the threat of being touched, the threat of expressing embarrassingly his incipient sexuality. He notes that 'un homme seul mettrait son nez dans le pli de son bras' (IV) and twice declares in 'Eloges' XIV: 'Pour moi, j'ai retiré mes pieds'. The cycle indeed ends with him in the same position, 'assis, dans l'amitié de [ses] genoux' (XVIII).

The very scarcity of reference to the sense of touch in all the poems written between 1920 and 1945, from *Anabase* to *Vents*,[12] suggests that Perse's sensitivity in this area had remained intact but that his capacity for self-protection had improved. The shell that masks our vulnerability is secreted as human society impinges with increasing rudeness on our developing consciousness. Where there is contact with creatures and things, there is no danger. Where there is human love which does not abuse confidence, physical contact, even at its most intimate, can be accepted and reciprocated. Otherwise Perse seems to avoid reference to touch as if, reluctant or unwilling to celebrate it, he would rather not be obliged to condemn it explicitly. A few examples from the poems of this period will indicate the tendencies, and indeed almost exhaust the references made there to touch.

A finger may be run over rows of dusty books: 'Et qu'est-ce encore, à mon doigt d'os, que tout ce talc d'usure et de sagesse, et tout cet attouchement des poudres du savoir?' (*Vents* 1, 4); a favourite dog stroked in the exiled poet's imagination: 'je flatte encore en songe, de la main, parmi tant d'êtres invisibles/ma chienne d'Europe . . .' ('Poème à l'Etrangère' III); a weapon seized: 'Saisisseur de glaives à l'aurore' ('Exil' III); the gentle brush of falling snow evoked: 'le premier affleurement de cette heure soyeuse, le premier attouchement de cette chose fragile et très futile, comme un frôlement de cils' ('Neiges' I). Various forms of distanciation from human contact are respected. On the other hand, close physical involvement is not shunned throughout *Anabase*. Overt sexual relationships expressed there, innocent of puritanical overtones, connect honey with sexuality just as do the Song of Songs and colloquial terms of affection. The desire expressed in Canto IV— 'qu'un doigt de miel longe les lèvres du prodigue'—is realised, as it were, in Canto IX, where the woman offers her mouth, 'un lieu de miel entre les roches', and asks:

> . . . ceux qui savent les sources nous diront-ils au soir sous quelles mains pressant la vigne de nos flancs nos corps s'emplissent d'une salive?

It is only much later, however, in 'Etroits sont les vaisseaux' in *Amers*, Perse's own Song of Songs, that intimate human contact becomes overwhelmingly the most prominent aspect of the poet's registration of his sense of touch. The physical detail of many of the references shows clearly that there is no inhibition concerning human contact now that any threat of being wounded is absent. Indeed the complete frankness with which Perse traces the course of a night of love is in itself an assurance that there is neither squeamishness nor prurience in his attitudes: the sexual act is part of 'le monde entier des choses' and may be praised in all its aspects when total acceptance is reciprocal.

One may trace the lovers' progress through their dialogue: 'sur la grève de mon corps, l'homme né de mer s'est allongé', declares the beloved (Pl, 327) whose face is framed by her lover's hands. The man delights in her physical proximity: 'ton visage est renversé, ta bouche est fruit à consommer' (Pl, 328). The progression is noted in her reply: '. . . Mes dents sont pures sous ta langue. Tu pèses sur mon cœur et gouvernes mes membres' (Pl, 330); 'Ta langue est dans ma bouche comme sauvagerie de mer' (Pl, 331). Her hands are allowed to explore his whole body, and touch itself becomes a direct function of praise:

> 'Ou bien libres mes bras!. . . et mes mains ont licence parmi l'attelage de tes muscles: sur tout ce haut relief du dos, sur tout ce nœud mouvant des reins, quadrige en marche de ta force comme la musculature même des eaux. Je te louerai des mains, puissance! et toi noblesse du flanc d'homme, paroi d'honneur et de fierté qui garde encore, dévêtue, comme l'empreinte de l'armure. . .'
>
> (Pl, 331)

As the climax approaches, caressing gestures give way to more violent
ones: the beloved addresses her dominating lover as a trampling stallion:
'Pour nous le dur attelage en marche sur les eaux. Qu'il nous piétine du
sabot, et nous meurtrisse du rostre, et du timon bosselé de bronze
qu'il nous heurte!. . .' (Pl, 336). Soon, evoking now a snake's animality,
she cries:

> 'Frapperas-tu, hampe divine? — Faveur du monstre, mon sursis! et
> plus stridente, l'impatience!. . . La mort à tête biseautée, l'amour
> à tête carénée, darde sa langue très fréquente.
> (. . .)
> 'Tu frapperas, promesse!—Plus prompte, ô Maître, ta réponse, et
> ton intimation plus forte! Parle plus haut, despote! et plus assidû-
> ment m'assaille: l'irritation est à son comble! Quête plus loin, Congre
> Royal, ainsi l'éclair en mer cherche la gaine du navire . . .
> 'Tu as frappé, foudre divine!. . .'

(Pl, 337)

There can be no doubt as to the crucial moment that has been reached,
the insistent repetition of the verb 'frapper' underlining the climactic
rhythm. Thereafter the references to touch are few and far between in
recognition of the fact that the lovers are no longer in one another's
arms.

While it is no doubt unwise to make any deductions about the
poet's own psychology regarding touch, we can, as it were, psycho-
analyse the poetry and see if our conclusions seem to correspond
with what we know of the man behind the words. Total contact
between two adults is restricted to those cases where it is both mean-
ingful and unlikely to be abused: then it is relished in all its sensuality.
Casual contact is shunned. Perse's view seems to be that human relation-
ships can develop more richly and at the same time leave each party
more freedom when a clear hierarchy of types of contact is main-
tained: 'la politesse n'est-elle pas encore la meilleure formule de liberté?'
(Pl, 550). Physical forms of conventional greeting within a given society
fail to be respected only by the uncouth of that society. Contact with
objects and creatures is, except in special cases involving notions of
the sacred—'D'autres saisissent dans les temples la corne peinte des
autels' ('Exil' II)—free of such a sense of conventional progression.
But as we have seen, Perse's tally of contact, even with things and
animals, is meagre. To what extent does the charge of aloofness often
levelled at Perse stem from the critic's recognition of the physical

distance the poet maintains between himself and the world about him?
To what extent is the adverse charge of the word 'aloofness' dependent
on the critic's assumptions drawn from what he knows of Perse's
biography and on his own often unrealised preference for bonhomie
over integrity? For it should not be forgotten that authenticity has
many modes, nor indeed that sincerity can never be a criterion of
literary excellence. In eschewing an appealing form of sensuality,
Perse is prepared to forfeit easy sympathy—'un poète ne peut pas
proposer sa synthèse à l'univers entier' (Pl, 577)—in order to avoid
what he sees as the prevalent myopia of our age. Remaining apart,
he increases his objectivity, as well as his freedom of action. All the
psychology of solitude, bound up with the individual will, and all the
predisposition and training of the diplomat—'le professionnel de
l'absence', wrote Claudel; the professional of politeness, we might
add—are involved in an analysis of Perse and his poetry.

If he is a 'surréaliste à distance' as Breton declared in trying to
claim another scalp for his camp, he is everything *à distance*, toeing
no party line, touching no humble forelock. Our tautological excursus
into Perse's sense of touch leads us firmly to the conclusion that
poetry depends on the poet's mastery of language and not on any
marginal differences in social attitudes or perceptual capacities
between the poet and other sensitive human beings. In writing poetry,
his involvement is with poetry alone, finding appropriate expression,
creating forms that come to be inevitable, proudly forging new relation-
ships between the world and the word that make of his poetry a total
and satisfying verbal re-enactment, in which neither the circumstances
of Perse's original perception nor the complex psychological frame-
work of that perception can or need be known. 'Le Siècle court à de
singulières défections littéraires, ou l'œuvre elle-même est éludée,
l'art en lui-même suspecté, la langue bafouée; et la stérilité s'enorgueil-
lit d'elle-même, depuis qu'à la création littéraire se substitue l'action
littéraire, à l'œuvre le manifeste, à la notion de l'homme en soi celle
du comportement social' (Pl, 559-60). The poem sails independently
on through time and space, direction given but destination unknown.
It is the product of the poet's mediation, richly expressive of his Being
in touch with reality, but as elusive in that marvellous interplay as it
is discreet about the details of its origins.

Notes

1. The abbreviation Pl followed by a page number refers throughout this chapter to Saint-John Perse, *Œuvres complètes*, Paris, Gallimard, Bibliothèque de la Pléiade, 1972.
2. See his letter to Roger Caillois, Pl, 563.
3. See Marcelle Achard-Abell, 'Heidegger et la poésie de Saint-John Perse: un rapprochement', *Revue de Métaphysique et de Morale*, LXXI, 3 (1966), pp. 292-306. Saint-John Perse admitted to me in late 1972, when he first read this article, that it had revealed a kindred spirit to him.
4. Contrast the Symbolist view as expressed in Verlaine's 'Art poétique', e.g. the line: 'Où l'Indécis au Précis se joint'.
5. Perse's inclusion of the principle of mimetic homology in his poetic practice antedates Ponge's concentration on it as a technique. For a consideration of the feature and its importance, particularly for the modern French unrhymed poem, see my '*Ut pictura poesis*: An Element of Order in the Adventure of the *poéme en prose*' in *Order and Adventure in Post-Romantic French Poetry: Essays presented to C. A. Hackett,* Oxford, Blackwell, 1973, pp. 244-56 and my *Poetry in Action*, Freetown, University of Sierra Leone, 1974.
6. For further examples, see the introduction to my edition of *Saint-John Perse: 'Exil'*, London, The Athlone Press of the University of London, 1973, pp. 15-17.
7. Alain Bosquet, in his stimulating *Saint-John Perse*, Paris, Seghers, revised and enlarged edition, 1971, pp. 101-4, confuses these two issues when judging Perse's poetry eminently translatable.
8. For more detail, see my *Saint-John Perse*, pp. 99-100.
9. For a fuller discussion and exemplification of such devices, see Roger Caillois, *Poétique de St.-John Perse*, Paris, Gallimard, revised and enlarged edition, 1972, especially the chapter entitled 'L'Ecriture'.
10. If, to students of French literature, this phenomenon is most familiar from Proust, it is also true that it forms part of the broader 'principle of linguistic relativity' formulated by Whorf and known as the Sapir-Whorf hypothesis (see *Language, Thought and Reality: Selected Writings of Benjamin Lee Whorf*, ed. J. B. Carroll, MIT, New York, Wiley; and London, Chapman and Hall, 1956, esp. pp. 212ff). Linguistic philosophers of this century have also explored the reciprocal relationship between thought and language and have sometimes given language the whip hand (e.g. Wittgenstein: 'Not to be able to name is not to know'). But earlier thinkers had noted the problem. Francis Bacon (1560/61-1626) wrote: 'Men imagine that their minds have command of language: but it often happens that language bears rule over their minds' (quoted, without source, by Stephen Potter, *Language in the Modern World*, Harmondsworth, Penguin, 1960, p. 19), and Giambattista Vico (1668-1744) explored the matter further in his *Scienza nuova*. It may well be that the concept dates back in embryo to the Indian linguist Panini who, several centuries before Christ, formulated the 'obligatory patterns' of Sanskrit (see *Language, Thought and Reality*, p. 232). The classic treatment of the subject is Ogden and Richards' *The Meaning of Meaning* (first published 1923). For a recent survey of the problem, see George Steiner, *After Babel*, Oxford University Press, 1975, esp. chap II.
11. See my *Saint-John Perse*, p. 106 and Pl, 1061.

12. An analysis of *toucher* and related words is facilitated and checked by reference to my *Word Index of the Complete Poetry and Prose of Saint-John Perse*, Durham, the Compiler, 1965; 2nd impression with supplement Southampton, the Compiler, 1967.

7 JEAN FOLLAIN: OBJECTS IN TIME

Pierre Calderon

Though sensibility and intelligence were once seen as distinct contraries, it is now accepted that they are intimately connected and that, for example, perception is an experience in which man is implicated in both body and mind. Accordingly, in this essay 'sensibility' will be taken to mean the faculty of experiencing both sensations and feelings —to which indeed Descartes, though he never failed to give priority to reason, conceded the status of thoughts. Few people indeed would now dispute the notion that sensibility and thought stand in a dialectical rather than an antagonistic relation. In this sense, the sensibility can be a channel for thought, just as thought can be a channel for the sensibility.

Though we would hardly call Jean Follain[1] the most cerebral of French poets, he is by no means the least 'intelligent' in the sense that I have indicated. In his case the first level of sensibility (the perceptual) always involves the second (the affective). Lived experience is for him a kind of first draft of the finished work: in principle, each instant of sensation can be the point of departure for the poetic process. But if the single moment is everything to him, so equally is duration. Follain's concern is above all with that which endures. He is attentive to the sensation which leaves its mark, or rather which is prolonged: in other words to the lasting *impression* which things make.

Follain's poetic process could be summarised in the following proposition which establishes that the sensation reaches the reader long *after* the event, and in an aesthetically fashioned form: 'La poésie est une affaire de mise en cave'.[2] In fact these are the words of the poet Max Jacob, spoken to the younger Follain: yet the latter has taken their lesson so much to heart that, in our present context, we could find no more appropriate motto for his work. The implications of Jacob's remark are indeed considerable: what matters most in the process of laying down wine or of writing poetry is the *tasting* of the product: if it is good, this is because it has had time to reach full maturity. There is no hiatus here: everything is perfectly continuous. Duration progresses towards the instant of transfiguration where it opens on to the eternal: 'La durée de pluie et soleil/débouche sur

---

* English version by Michael Sheringham and Roger Cardinal.

l'Eternel'.[3] The poet who exclaims 'Obsédant souvenir des contacts/
premiers!' (UT, 202) is the one who has allowed the past to mature
within him. Follain's country childhood was one of order, harmony and
secret complicity, and he is concerned to preserve its impressions in
the most emotional and complete way possible,

> lui qui eût voulu détenir un grand et à la fois très précis catalogue
> armorié de la terre, mais qu'en même temps tout fût confondu
> dans l'exquise minute.
>
> (EE, 8)

Here lies the reason for those inventories and lingering annotations
which characterise Follain's work and which have led some comment-
ators to call him a poet of the object. Max Jacob it was who, one of
the first, stated categorically that 'sa poésie est faite avec des objets'.[4]
But this time Jacob was less inspired: Follain is no more a poet of the
object pure and simple than, for example, Ponge. Rather, he is a poet
of *time*, as is clear from his insistence on compressing the diversity of
catalogued phenomena within the confines of the 'exquise minute'.
It is true that he is drawn to objects, but this is above all in so far as
they are artefacts which encapsulate human gestures across time.
What most engages his sensibility are the 'stratifications'[5] laid down
in a given object over the years of its existence.

> Il y a un jour où tout à coup j'aperçois cet objet qui, depuis dix
> ans, était sous mes yeux et qu'en réalité je n'avais jamais véritable-
> ment vu.(. . .) Tout d'un coup, ce bol oublié se rappelle à moi,
> s'impose, j'ai peur qu'il ne me tombe des mains et ne laisse plus
> sur un tapis représentant deux éléphants avec leurs tours que de
> luisants débris qu'il faudra tristement ramasser. Ce bol fut autre-
> fois lavé par des servantes caquetantes qu'entouraient des nuages et
> des vapeurs, qu'encadraient des lueurs de cuivre et d'étain. Le monde
> était neuf. (. . .) L'artisan qui l'a façonné gardait peut-être fière
> allure, doux regard (. . .)
>
> (TI, 9-10.)

It has taken a long time, ten years in fact, for this everyday object to
enter the poet's consciousness; and yet his full awareness is concern-
trated within a single moment ('tout à coup'). The object may be a
bowl of little apparent value, yet it is extraordinarily rich in terms of
the time-span it embodies. It is fragile, so much so that the poet is

scared that he may drop and smash it; and yet it has immense power to impose itself upon him as a presence heavy with a past. Pursuing his reverie, the poet traces the history of the bowl back through the times when it was washed-up by chattering maidservants in distant kitchens, to the moment of its creation by some proud and gentle craftsman. For the poet, all these layers of past experience are compressed within the one commonplace object. On the model of Ponge's *objeu*, we might here suggest that the object becomes an *obgeste*—an object which is the sum of all the gestures that have shaped its existence.

It will be appreciated that the qualities which Follain attends to are not extraneous to the object. What he takes from it, is distilled within the object, so to speak, rather than extrapolated from it. The *obgeste* concretises a span of time which is existential rather than imaginary, for there can be nothing abstract about time for Follain. The sense of time passing is always integral to his experience of the world at large. And the acuity of his sensory responses is such that, while being uniquely attuned to the fleeting instant, they have an equally astonishing capacity to endure. Let us try to hear a pin drop as he does:

> Parfois, on entendait, sur la petite table, la chute d'une épingle
> à cheveux. Puis, c'était, dans la rue, un couple se parlant sur un
> balcon, une musique derrière des rideaux. Mais, plus que tout,
> j'entendais l'épingle à cheveux tomber; je l'entends toujours.
>
> (CL, 63)

If we follow him further, we will hear, in the rattle of an old tin can kicked along a wintry road, nothing less than the music of the spheres:

La Musique des sphères

> Il suivait la route gelée
> dans sa poche sonnaient ses clefs de fer
> et sans penser, de sa botte effilée
> il buta le cylindre
> d'un vieille boîte à conserves
> qui plusieurs secondes roula son vide froid,
> chancela sur elle-même, puis s'immobilisa
> sous le ciel émaillé d'étoiles.
>
> (UT, 124)

The sensations which Follain offers here might well be termed 'meta-sensations', in the sense of perceptions which partake equally of the physical and the metaphysical. Not that this should imply any flight from the terrestrial into the angelism to which some poets tempt us. Despite his Catholic upbringing, Follain never allows the spiritual to extinguish the material. *Chants terrestres*, the title of one of his collections, situates his poetry generically while characterising its fundamental nature: 'Tout est grandement terrestre' (E, 64), the poet insists. It is through the medium of the senses that Follain apprehends everything, even including metaphysics itself, as witness the poem 'Métaphysique':

> Quand ils l'aperçoivent
> au fond des chaumières
> ses mains soutenant
> le bol à fleurs bleues
> devant ses seins tendres
> ils sentent l'ardeur
> puis tout s'évapore
> du décor fragile
> pour laisser flotter
> la seule odeur nue
> de métaphysique
>
>   (E, 21)

We may well ask which senses are involved here. The answer is simple: not the sensory responses we commonly bring to bear upon material experience, but specifically those of the poet, responses operative within the world of meta-sensation which corresponds to what Marcel Raymond has called the 'concret psychique'.[6]

Despite these subtleties, Follain's metaphysical outlook has at the same time something childlike about it. Philippe Jaccottet has rightly observed that 'au fond, Jean Follain mériterait d'être appelé "enfant et métaphysicien"; il est un des très rares poètes actuels qui touchent à l'illimité avec une sorte d'innocence, presque de nonchalance ...'.[7] What is meant here is that Follain retains something of what Baudelaire evokes in his phrase 'le vert paradis des amours enfantines', namely the child's capacity to dream of immensities. Where Follain writes that 'à tout instant, commençait en lui le monde' (CA, 17), Gaston Bachelard will speak of an archetypal reverie of space, what he terms a 'rêverie cosmique'[8] in which meta-sensation plays an

active if not determining part. But if this dream has spatial properties,
it is no less remarkable in its temporal dimension. Thus when Follain
writes

> La femme regarde sans voix
> l'étoffe qu'elle crut solide
> dilacérable
> monde pense-t-elle
> où rien ne résiste

(EI, 40)

the fabric evoked is at once that of the world *and* of time:

> Cette rêverie porte avec elle le sentiment inéluctable de l'existence,
> d'êtres et de choses prises dans la trame du temps et de l'étendue,
> et qui pourtant demeurent hors de cette trame.

(LTP, 308.)

The poet can in this way seize on any object—whether it be held in the
hand, utilised, witnessed, contemplated or illuminated by reverie — and
extract from it a sense of lived time, perceptible to the sensibility in
that it is attuned both to an immediate present and an underlying past.

We must now consider what this privileged apprehension of things
in time can bring us. It is the world itself which Follain presents, a
world which, whatever lack, surprise or evil it evinces, is fabulous,
granted that, as Bachelard says, 'Toute enfance est fabuleuse, naturel-
lement fabuleuse',[9] and that Follain is an eternal child; but fabulous
above all, if we would but heed it, in the humblest things, immense in
the infinitesimal, mighty in the apparently trivial. There is nothing that
is devoid of grace for Follain, nothing that he cannot celebrate and so
magnify, as the tin-can testifies. And if Follain writes about the world
of things, his real subject is perhaps Being itself, a Being which is
essentially concrete and profoundly immersed in time, from the eternity
of childhood to the ephemeral span of maturity. The characteristics of
Being are not difficult to establish: Being is present, 'Pourquoi ces
êtres et ces choses/plutôt que rien?' (EI, 71); Being is contingent,
'Chaque chose pourtant veillait et travaillait/pour sauver son éternité'
(E, 59); and Being implies existence, 'La vitre participe à la générale
existence' (EI, 60). In short, there is not only Being, but existence,
that is: Being-in-time. So it is that we observe that things *are* and, in
observing them, encounter their profoundly *temporal* aspect: they are,

as it were, whether simultaneously or by turns, eternal *and* ephemeral.
Eternal when the poet exclaims 'Spectacle empli à craquer d'éternité
que cette rentrée, dans une maison de pierre individualisée, d'un être
à vous lié' (EE, 53); and ephemeral when he notes that 'S'étend une
saveur d'éphémère' (EI, 36). The connection is evident when he writes
elsewhere of 'un goût très fin d'éternel' (E, 74) and is made clearer
still if we return to what I have said about tasting the product of the
'mise en cave' of the poetic process: the existence of things in time is a
process whereby they tend toward an opening on to the eternal. Bache-
lard again can help us towards a precise understanding of this process
when he formulates the paradox of 'la durée faite d'instants sans
durée.'[10] The instant is a single moment, yet one which embraces
time at large. Hence the title of Follain's collection *Tout instant*, which
implies on the one hand 'any single moment' and on the other, time as
being 'entire in the moment'. In its stark simplicity the tableau in trip-
tych entitled 'Vie' is exemplary:

> Il naît un enfant
> dans un grand paysage
> un demi-siècle après
> il n'est qu'un soldat mort
> et c'était là cet homme
> que l'on vit apparaître
> et puis poser par terre
> tout un lourd sac de pommes
> dont deux ou trois roulèrent
> bruit parmi ceux d'un monde
> où l'oiseau chantait
> sur la pierre du seuil.
>
> (T, 45)

A moment's gesture in a life-span; a life-span in a moment's gesture.
And here, as with all Follain's work, our response must be at once
literary and existential. Follain's is not an art of abstracted forms. It
is life itself which, for our delectation, the poem celebrates and eternal-
ises in its stirring.

André Dhôtel has cogently remarked that problems of language are
absent from Follain's work. We encounter no separation, no rift, no
disproportion between word and thing. Features of this kind, which are
so current in much modern poetry and philosophy, are unknown to the
poet, who sees them as relevant only to a discourse which heedlessly

severs itself from life. There is a wealth of confidence in his assertion that 'la littérature et la vie se réchauffent l'une à l'autre' (Pa, 16). In this harmonious perspective, Follain seems content to set himself apart from his contemporaries. Disarmingly, he admits the equivalence of words and things as points of departure for poetry: 'Souvent mon poème part d'un objet et souvent il part d'un mot' (CGB, 384). The symmetrical prospect of a world of things balanced by a world of words is confirmed in the story of Follain's reluctance to learn a foreign language when, as a young man, he was despatched to England by his father for that purpose: he was loath to concede that more than one word could exist to designate a single thing.[11]

For Follain, then, language is a system which functions with a reliable consistency:

> la beauté du feuillage amer
> et des oiseaux à gorge rouge
> devant les mots humains
> que gouvernait une syntaxe éprouvée
> resplendissait

(T, 21)

The jurisdiction of language is not limitless however. We note here that the beauty of natural phenomena shines forth '*devant* les mots humains', that is, outside language, prior to language. Words do not contain everything or supplant everything. At the same time, as Follain asserts elsewhere, all things 'attendent que les délivre une écriture' (DH, 17). Why should this be so if the being of things is prior to language? The answer must be: in order to be spoken and thereby to exist more fully. We must remember that for Follain there is no hiatus between life and literature. Each stimulates the other in a deep complicity whence the poem emerges:

> La genèse du poème peut naître d'un vocable usuel subitement aperçu, gorgé de tous ses sens, apparaissant sous tous ses aspects, entouré d'une sorte d'aura magnétique. Elle peut naître aussi par la vision d'un simple objet, jamais encore vu de cette façon-là, porteur de toutes ses valeurs de signes et déclenchant le poeme. L'objet ainsi vu apparaît dans sa connivence avec le reste de l'univers et situé dans cet univers.

(SP, 5)

The symmetry of this statement is extremely telling: the commonplace
word and the simple object are in identical ways 'subitement aperçu'
and 'jamais encore vu de cette façon-là'; the qualification 'gorgé de tous
ses sens, apparaissant sous tous ses aspects' and 'porteur de toutes ses
valeurs de signes' echo one another semantically with the utmost
precision; the phrases 'entouré d'une sorte d'aura magique' and 'dans
sa connivence avec le reste de l'univers' imply the same profound con-
nections within a total order. The corollary of all this is evident:

> La perception poétique des hommes et des choses vient déboucher
> sur le temps des hommes et celui des choses, et du même coup sur
> le mystère de leur écoulement.
>
> (LTP, 307)

That is, if poetic perception concerns itself with the relation of human
sensibility to the material universe, it cannot but involve consideration
of this relation in terms of their mutual evolution in time.

It is one of Follain's great strengths that he shuns ornamentation.
Dedicated to a simple task, 'de voir les choses/ telles qu'elles sont'
(UT, 103), he seeks 'l'odeur nue', 'la beauté nue', 'la vérité nue', and so
on: the naked thing, the thing itself, the thing in all its uniqueness.
There is a world of difference between what Follain calls his 'épicerie
d'enfance' and the 'magasin d'images' of which Baudelaire speaks;
between the secret relationships of things with one another which
Follain evokes, and the Baudelairean *correspondances*. For Baudelaire,
images constitute analogies and as such point to something at a distance
from themselves; the objects in Follain's *épicerie*, on the other hand,
relate to nothing outside their own realm. Follain writes:

> Je ne peux comparer rien à rien dans cet univers multiple où toutes
> choses pourtant ont entre elles des affinités mystérieuses.
>
> (SP, 6.)

The uniqueness of things is indeed a crucial motivation for Follain.
What matters is that things be shown as they are (or in certain cases,
as they were): mundane yet exemplary. This is a context in which a
poet like Ponge will turn to analogy: 'il faut, à travers les analogies,
saisir la qualité différentielle (. . .) Nommer la qualité différentielle
(. . .), voilà le but, le progrès' (GRM, 41-2). Follain however achieves
his goal without recourse to analogy, attaining the quiddity and unique-
ness of what is yet commonplace by the most direct means. It is with

the simplest words that he registers the uniqueness of the bared skin of
a woman nursing her baby:

> Le bruit que fait
> la chute d'une pomme
> l'enfant l'entendait
> en buvant le lait d'une femme
> grave et marquée
> sur sa peau hâlée
> de grains et de lignes
> d'une disposition unique
> dans l'ordre des créatures.

(T, 82)

Or again he will acclaim the singularity of the leaves on a tree:

> Pas une feuille à l'arbre
> n'est pareille à l'autre.

(DAT, 26)

At the same time it must be stressed that Follain's vision of the unique-
ness of things is intensified by a complementary vision of an underlying
continuity. Teeming singularity rests on a fundamental unity. If things
are not comparable, they are nonetheless compatible by virtue of their
'affinités mystérieuses'. Hence, when Follain spotlights the particular,
he also illuminates the universal:

> Au-delà des harmonies diffèrent
> celles de la femme qui se dénude sur un palier
> du paysage aux feuilles qui frémissent
> de la planisphère sur le mur
> de l'outil qui étincelle
> le même fonds les réunit.[12]

This 'même fonds', this common ground in which a naked woman, a
landscape, a map of the world and a tool are linked, is the darkness
which Follain calls 'la nuit de l'être' (E, 28). It is the mystery to which
all his poetry is directed. Yet this does not mean that Follain leaves us
suspended in some intangible region. For the mystery is communicated,
simply and universally, through the medium of perception:

Toutes les filles qui traversent la place de l'Opéra
celles-là qui sont subtiles et belles, celles-là qui
sont bêtes avec de si beaux yeux savent cet éternel.
C'est la connaissance de leur sang, de leur chair, de
leurs muqueuses vouées à d'allègres tombeaux. Voilà
ce que Paris nous apprend : ils sont faits pour durer
le ciel et la terre.

(Pa, 11)

Appealing though such statements of the physical certainty of the
eternal may be, the notion of the transience, the poignant irreversib-
ility of experience will as often assert itself in Follain's work:

Une petite fille s'apprête à traverser la pièce avec
un bol trop plein qu'elle tient avec une précaution
immense ; faisant mouvoir son jeune squelette, elle
va passer, elle passe, elle est passée.

(C, 95)

The passing of the girl is conjugated in time, and the passage of time
cannot be reversed. Likewise the may-bug:
Un hanneton (. . .) chemine (. . .) en ce moment qui, tous
les possibles devant se délivrer, ne reviendra plus.

(AT, 12)

It is such moments, no doubt, that have led André Dhôtel to observe
of Follain that 'il s'émeut simplement du seul fait qu'une chose ait
été'.[13] While this observation is a perceptive one, it could imply a certain
passivity or sentimentality. However, I would argue that there is an
intensity about Follain's refusal to let things vanish into oblivion
which invalidates any suggestion that his is merely a poetry of facile
nostalgia. Indeed this poet who so variously and repeatedly extols
'l'ordre merveilleux du Temps' (UT, 254) is also capable, in a poem
entitled 'Tuer le temps', of imagining a most violent revenge upon time
for what it takes away from us:

Les révoltés
s'en prennent aux horloges des tours
en fusillent les cadrans

(EI, 69)

This secret violence gives credence to and intensifies the mystery which Follain's poetry takes as its subject—a mystery which we have seen to be rooted in the ambiguous relation of the momentary and the timeless. Yet there is no reason why, given the contrasts so evident in a poet who can offer us one collection called *Usage du temps* and another called *Espaces d'instants*, we should see him as a poet of contradictions, caught between the tangible and the metaphysical, for example; or between randomness and order, fragmentation and global unity, the ephemeral and the eternal. To do so would be to fail to take into account the logic proper to poetry, which draws its very strength from such apparent contradictions. The poet must strive, like Breton, to reach the 'point de l'esprit d'où la vie et la mort, le réel et l'imaginaire, le passé et le futur, le communicable et l'incommunicable, le haut et le bas cessent d'être perçus contradictoirement'[14]—whether this point be conceived as one of dialectical resolution, as in Ponge's view, or of 'origine pure' as Claudel would have it. Follain well knew the poetic theories of his time, yet remained wary of them all, preferring to trust in his individual sensibility and refusing to be circumscribed. Yet, even if he never did so himself, I shall venture to define what the supreme point is for him: it is *the instant itself*—ever sifting time as it passes, sensitive to the breeze of eternity, alternately bearing us aloft and submerging us.

The full impetus of Follain's instant is not something accessible to theory. It is available only to a mode of feeling which can unite senses and mind, perception and intellect. The truth of poetry cannot be that of science, nor that of philosophy, nor yet of metaphysics. So that if Follain invokes 'l'odeur nue de (la) métaphysique', he is not claiming for his intuition the exactitude of the scientist's observation; nor does he see it (as the philosopher might) merely as an approximation true and adequate to reality itself only in terms of its own, independent order. Rather he sees it as having a secret depth and innocence which constitute their own guarantee of truth:

Je suis dans ce Cotentin, pays secret plein de lumières et d'ombres. Un grand silence existe propice à une vie profonde et passionnée.[15]

Lorsque la pierre du seuil rendait sa chaleur et que les hommes jetaient hors d'eux leurs manteaux, l'existence des choses apparaissait unique, multiple et innocente.

(EE II, 90)

An admirable conception, this, one which truly draws together the metaphysical and the terrestrial. The student of poetics might want to invoke the pathetic fallacy. But it is no part of Follain's ambition to revive Romantic pathos. His mode has quite other ambitions, and other credentials: those of a poet who strives towards a way of feeling which is deeper and infinitely more *captivating* than is often supposed and which allows him to maintain 'une vie profonde et passionnée'. We cannot go far astray if we read Follain's whole *art poétique* in these simple lines:

> Tout fait événement
> pour qui sait frémir

(DAT, 52)

Notes

1. I have used the following abbreviations: Pa *Paris*, Corrêa, 1935; EE *L'Epicerie d'enfance*, Corrêa, 1938. Published by Gallimard: UT *Usage du temps*, 1943 (contains *La Main chaude*, 1933; *Chants Terrestres*, 1937; *Ici-Bas*, 1941; *Transparence du monde*, 1943)); E *Exister*, 1947; CL *Chef-lieu*, 1950; T *Territoires*, 1953; TI *Tout instant*, 1957; DH *Des Heures*, 1960; AT *Appareil de la terre*, 1964; DAT *D'après tout*, 1967; EI *Espaces d'instants*, 1971. Published by Plon: CA *Jean-Marie Vianney, Curé d'Ars*, 1959. I have also quoted from the following, which contain contributions by Follain: LTP 'Le Temps du poète', in *Entretiens sur le temps*, The Hague, Mouton, 1967; SP *Sens de la poésie*, L'Arc-Création editeur, 1972 (speech given by Follain in 1967 at the Maison de la Culture de Thonon); CGB lecture given by Follain in 1970, in *Actes du Colloque Gaston Bachelard*, Union Générale d'Editions, 1974.
2. Quoted by Follain in his contribution to *L'Imagination créatrice*, ed. Roselyne Chenue, Neuchâtel, La Baconnière, 1971, p. 160 and elsewhere.
3. Poem first published in *La Nouvelle Revue française*, No. 222, June 1971, p. 59.
4. Quoted by Pierre de Boisdeffre in *Abrégé d'une histoire vivante de la littérature d'aujourd'hui*, Libraire Académique Perrin, 1969, pp. 447-8.
5. André Dhôtel, *Jean Follain*, Paris, Seghers, 1972, p. 19.
6. Marcel Raymond, *De Baudelaire au surréalisme*, Paris, Corti 1963, p. 45.
7. Philippe Jaccottet, 'Jean Follain, une perspective fabuleuse', in *L'Entretien des muses*, Paris, Gallimard, 1968, p. 138.
8. Gaston Bachelard, *La Poétique de la rêverie*, Paris, Presses universitaires de France, 1961, p. 13.
9. *Ibid.* p. 101.
10. Bachelard, *L'Intuition de l'instant*, Paris, Gonthier, 1966, p. 20.
11. Dhôtel, *op. cit.*, p. 10.
12. Poem first published in *La Nouvelle Revue française*, No. 222, June 1971, p. 58.
13. André Dhôtel, *op. cit.*, p. 12.
14. André Breton, *Manifestes du surréalisme* Paris, Gallimard 'Idées',

1963, pp. 76-7.
15.   From a letter to Lydie Chantrell quoted in her 'Portrait de Jean Follain', *La Voix des poètes*, No. 42, Summer 1971, p. 16.

8 PAUL ELUARD

Malcolm Bowie

Certain general characteristics of Paul Eluard's verse have found their place in the mythology of modern literary culture. The Eluard myth (I shall refer to it as 'Eluard' for the sake of brevity), compounded of much that the poet was and a good deal else that he was not, is so convincingly neat as an imaginative construction that it is often cherished for itself and checked only half-heartedly against the poems actually written. 'Eluard' was invented because the century made him necessary: in an age when anxiety and neurotic distraction were a dominant emotional mode, he represented joy and tranquillity; amid the oppressive clamour of mass society, his voice sounded a note of intimacy and delicate restraint; in an atmosphere of energetic verbal experiment, he was the complete possessor and master of a language; and above all he was an inveterate lyricist, surviving by some unaccountable grace of history into an era of political barbarism and world war. The imagery of 'Eluard' is appropriate to the qualities of sensibility that he is held to epitomise: wings, light, flowers, stars, water, mirrors, the female body in its particulars and its broad outlines. In the world these objects inhabit, energy is transferred in accordance with a restricted set of dynamic principles: diffusion, diffraction, reflection, immersion, interpenetration. The single most appealing and most praised feature of 'Eluard' is that the activities of the poetic mind flawlessly reflect, and are reflected in, the physical processes of the world outside it. That discontinuity between self and world which for generations of Romantic artists had been a source both of pain and of pride, and a spur to the creative power, has at last given way to willing and versatile collaboration.

In the pages which follow I shall suggest several ways in which this version of Eluard is misleadingly diagrammatic or simply wrong. I shall not seek to deny, however, that diagrams such as 'Eluard' have an important mnemonic use, nor that this one is a good deal more useful than many another: it is, for example, much less irrelevant to a reading of *Capitale de la douleur* than is the 'Dickens' of muffins, Toby jugs and the traditional English Christmas to a reading of *Bleak House*. Eluard's poems of erotic celebration are his best known. But he also wrote many poems which explore moods of doubt and anxiety; many which take suffering, war, bereavement, cruelty and social injustice as their themes; many which were inspired by political passion and have outspokenly political aims; many which are the product of a finely developed 'negative capability' and show the creative intelligence at grips with an insinuating sense of futility:

> La solitude l'absence
> Et ses coups de lumière
> Et ses balances
> N'avoir rien vu rien compris
>
> La solitude le silence
> Plus émouvant
> Au crépuscule de la peur
> Que le premier contact des larmes
>
> L'ignorance l'innocence
> La plus cachée
> La plus vivante
> Qui met la mort au monde.

$$(I, 244)^1$$

I give this list of tones and themes at the outset because, although the poems I have chosen to comment on in detail reveal certain essential characteristics of Eluard's imagination, they are too few—and my space too limited—to do justice to his astonishing range.

Eluard's poetry is richly appealing to the senses. Sense-impressions appear on the surface of many works as an insistent, baffling Brownian motion. Although large, informing patterns of imagery may emerge early in our reading of a poem, our attention is often distracted from these by a jostle of short-lived micro-sensations. The newcomer to Eluard, finding the texture of the poem so alive and so mobile, may have difficulty in deciding where to apply his imaginative effort, or how best to bring the whole thing into focus. What is strange, however, is that the objects which prompt the reader to this abundant sensory activity are often of the barest and most everyday. Eluard's chosen objects are without feature or detail; their surfaces have no roughness or variegation to engage the eye. What is more, he seldom seeks to explore their inner grain, or the minutiae of organic process.

Let us consider the following poem from *L'Amour la poésie*, for example:

Je te l'ai dit pour les nuages
Je te l'ai dit pour l'arbre de la mer
Pour chaque vague pour les oiseaux dans les feuilles
Pour les cailloux du bruit
Pour les mains familières
Pour l'oeil qui devient visage ou paysage
Et le sommeil lui rend le ciel de sa couleur
Pour toute la nuit bue
Pour la grille des routes
Pour la fenêtre ouverte pour un front découvert
Je te l'ai dit pour tes pensées pour tes paroles
Toute caresse toute confiance se survivent.

                                                          (I, 230-1)

The objects occupying the central span of the poem lend their
authority, their cumulative weight of implication, to the discreet
aphorism which is announced in the first two lines and transcribed in
the last. But in themselves these objects are void of substance. The
reader can observe them with clarity and precision, and guess at their
attributes, only by scanning the relationships into which they enter.
Each thing is enlivened and particularised by its contact with the
others and becomes a blank universal when considered alone. Many of
these relationships are minutely but firmly subversive and require us
to revise the average, practical-minded expectations of order and con-
sequence with which we confront the world. The syntax of the poem
provides conditions of exact equivalence for realms of experience
that, in the interests of clear thinking and purposeful behaving, it is
our custom to keep distinct and to think of hierarchically: the poet's
affection is such that no useful distinction remains between natural
and man-made, intimate and impersonal, physical and mental, spoken
and tacit. Certain items in Eluard's list require of us a strong effort of
intellectual adjustment. In the phrases 'les cailloux du bruit' and 'le
ciel de sa couleur', for instance, the grammatical form by which an
abstract attribute is familiarly subordinated to a concrete thing ('le
bruit des cailloux', 'la couleur de son ciel') is put to the opposite use:
we are compelled for an instant to re-think our notions of physical
causation, and envisage a world in which noise creates stones, and colour
creates the firmament. The first of these genitives ('l'arbre de la mer'),
read simply in the context of its line, is a loose bundle of meanings:
the sea's tree, the tree as occupant of sea, the sea considered as tree,
the coalescence of sea and tree, and so forth. But whatever the meaning

we may initially have chosen, the next line invites us to revise it: if we had assumed the genitive to entail, as it ordinarily does, the subordination of possession to possessor, we are now told that sea and tree are of equal status; if we had assumed the phrase to be a 'poetic' genitive by which two objects are allowed simply to blend their identities, we are now told that the sea and tree have each kept a defining characteristic intact—the one its waves, the other its leaves.

I have described these deviations from normal usage at some length because they are a strong but largely neglected source of poetic suggestion in Eluard. This fluid syntax can generate all manner of small, incidental paradoxes and give even the most transparent of his utterances a teasing complexity:

> Une femme chaque nuit
> Voyage en grand secret.

(I, 291)

This poem is a trick, a perfect ambiguity. It is a continuous sentence and, at the same time, a pair of juxtaposed noun phrases. The task of bringing its two meanings to some imaginitive reconciliation is ours, and the poet withholds all guidance. Eluard expects of his reader that he will enjoy thinking laterally, that he will rapidly adopt and discard alternative frames of reference as a poem proceeds and be prepared to seek unusual connections between usual things.

On occasion he relies heavily on the speculative prowess of his reader. The following is an extreme instance, but is in one important way typical of Eluard's method:

> Les oiseaux parfument les bois
> Les rochers leurs grands lacs nocturnes.

(I, 300)

The reader of this poem may be content to leave the objects it names hovering in a mildly countrified mental cloud—in which case the poem is trivial. Or he may try to determine the exact relations between those objects—in which case he has an embarrassing wealth of possible patterns, none having conspicuously more imaginative authority than the rest:

> i   Birds perfume the following: woods, rocks and their (the birds')
>   lakes.

ii   Birds perfume the following: woods, rocks and their (the rocks')
     lakes.
iii Birds perfume woods and rocks, which woods and rocks are
     their (the birds') lakes.
iv   Birds perfume woods and rocks, which rocks are their (the
     woods') lakes.
v   Birds perfume woods and rocks, which rocks are their (the
     birds') lakes.
vi   Birds perfume woods. Rocks perfume their (own) lakes.
vii Birds perfume woods. Rocks perfume their (the woods') lakes.
viii Birds perfume woods. Rocks perfume their (the birds') lakes.

The poem is a teeming manifold of potential relationships. It is
fascinating in its huge preponderance of implication over statement
—but otherwise scarcely at all. None of the objects has sufficient
presence or physical individuality to make relation-seeking into any-
thing more than a faintly amusing intellectual pastime. But we can
observe here in miniature a process that takes place in many of
Eluard's strongest and most original poems. The lines name physical
objects and a single physical action, but their ambiguous syntax gives
them a large abstract component. The Eluard landscape does not stay
still: we not only see things differently, but we see different things,
as fresh syntactic relationships are discovered. The object seen at
once in several contexts soon becomes a theoretical, a mentally
construed, point of intersection between a variety of possible
scenarios. We are invited to look away from the physical object in
order to discover what and where it is. The whole process of reading
these unstable texts is an oscillatory one: perceived things produce
abstract ideas, and those ideas in turn re-generate the very things we
departed from. The object becomes, in Valéry's delightful phrase,
'cause harmonique de soi-même'. Just as noise produces stones in
Eluard's world, so thoughts produce things.
    Syntax of this shifting, multi-dimensional kind is only one cause
among many of the constant ferment which takes place within an
Eluard text. In my remarks on the following poem I shall describe
several further causes, but I shall also be asking whether—and if so,
how—the poet keeps the inner multitude of relationships under control,
and so prevents his work from inducing in the reader that state of
mental panic which William Empson called 'madhouse and the whole
thing there'.

PREMIERE DU MONDE

Captive de la plaine, agonisante folle,
La lumière sur toi se cache, vois le ciel:
Il a fermé les yeux pour s'en prendre à ton rêve,
Il a fermé ta robe pour briser tes chaînes.

> Devant les roues toutes nouées
> Un éventail rit aux éclats.
> Dans les traîtres filets de l'herbe
> Les routes perdent leur reflet.

> Ne peux-tu donc prendre les vagues
> Dont les barques sont les amandes
> Dans ta paume chaude et câline
> Ou dans les boucles de ta tête?

> Ne peux-tu prendre les étoiles?
> Ecartelée, tu leur ressembles,
> Dans leur nid de feu tu demeures
> Et ton éclat s'en multiplie.

De l'aube bâillonnée un seul cri veut jaillir,
Un soleil tournoyant ruisselle sous l'écorce.
Il ira se fixer sur tes paupières closes.
O douce, quand tu dors, la nuit se mêle au jour.

                                        (I, 178-9)

The poem traces a simple contour of sexual arousal and fulfilment.
But it would be quite inappropriate to say that 'Première du monde'
is 'about' sex, if by this we meant that its diverse nature imagery is pre-
sent simply to illustrate the modes and rhythms of sexual desire. For the
large ontological theme announced in the title is forcibly restated and
developed. The phases of sexual self-discovery are timed to coincide
with those of a primordial coming-into-being. The poem depicts the
emergence of a discrete self within the spawning of phenomena: a sud-
den, threatened, intermittent awareness of an independent 'me' glim-
mers within the created order. But this birth is no one-way, progres-
sive movement. Throughout the poem clear contrasts are made
between openness and closure, liberation and repression, energy and
inertia. The striving of the emergent self towards freedom and autonomy
is checked and contested by a backward-looking impulse towards pre-
natal selflessness. This inner drama now echoes, now is echoed by, the

unceasing cosmological drama which surrounds it.

Two important features of Eluard's imagery in this poem belong
within familiar and fertile metaphorical traditions. Countless poets
have described the female body in geographical or topographical
terms, or tinged their landscapes with erotic suggestion. In *Venus and
Adonis* Shakespeare evokes his heroine in a magnificent sustained meta-
phor of this kind. Eluard would have been acquainted with comparable
inventions by Baudelaire in such poems as 'La Géante' or 'La Chevel-
ure'. Moreover the interpenetration of woman and landscape in
'Première du monde' is part of an embracing, pantheistic view of
creation at large which also has its distinguished poetic antecedents—
in the visionary works of Hugo, for example, or in Nerval's 'Vers
dorés'. Many readers of Eluard's poem will catch a reminiscence of the
closing lines from Nerval's sonnet:

> Souvent dans l'être obscur habite un Dieu caché;
> Et comme un œil naissant couvert par ses paupières,
> Un pur esprit s'accroît sous l'écorce des pierres!

But simply to recognise the images as traditional and the theme as
archetypal is not to discover the clue to a coherent reading of the
text. For Eluard does not work the theme out as a developing story or
argument, and does not appoint each image to a fixed place within an
overall scheme. In the absence of such a scheme, we have an unusually
free choice in deciding how long and how intensely any one
impression should flourish before we pass on to the next. The images
are loosely organised in accordance with an underlying emotional
rhythm: we move from pain and anguish at the start, through various
intermediate stages of puzzlement and yearning, towards a tranquil
half-resolution in the last line. Although the sleeping woman appears
at the end as a dissolver of contradictions, the instance of her power
that is specified here ('la nuit se mêle au jour') refers only obliquely
to the crucial inner divisions of self that have gone before. Many
Eluard poems end in this way—on a line which, while bringing certain
of the main issues to a clearly marked close, leaves us with a strong
residue of paradox, and a sense that reflection upon the remaining
issues could be extended indefinitely within and beyond the printed
limits of the poem.

The underlying emotional pattern is not strong enough to impose
any permanent shape upon the volatile word-by-word substance of
the text. The fluid and unpredictable exchanges which take place

between its local details give the text a remarkable recalcitrance when we seek to tighten our rational grip upon it. In the third quatrain, for example, the poet gradually sets forth an analogy between the receptive curves of the woman's body and other undulating shapes. But the five principal objects he names (*vagues, barques, amandes, paume, boucles*) appear in such quick succession, and so clearly invite comparison among themselves, whatever limiting conditions the poet may propose, that they tend to break free of the syntax and form their own instantaneous, verbless pattern of affinity. On this small scale only a minimal effort is required to bring syntax and imagery back into phase. But elsewhere it is impossible to accommodate the one to the other in anything but an approximate and provisional way. Vivid 'cosmic' images and equally vivid images of imprisonment and oppression occur at irregular intervals throughout. Although each set of images tends, by the mutual attraction of its components, to become a self-contained system, the links between the sets are casual and unsystematic. The two may appear to tug against each other, or suddenly to merge. There are abrupt shrinkages and expansions: the sky is brought down to earth and endowed with human wilfulness in the first quatrain, while in the fourth the captive projects herself with an equal and opposite movement into a luminous, interstellar region. The syntax of the poem, being for the most part composed of the simplest propositional, imperative or interrogative forms, has little power to resist the cross-currents of association that sweep back and forth in the text. Further connections are suggested by Eluard's delicately interwoven transformations of sound: *roues* → *toutes* → *routes*; *rit* → *filet* → *reflet*; *barques* → *boucles*; *douce* → *dors* → *jour*. Some of these links reinforce, and some minutely deflect, the general semantic thrust of the sentences in which they occur.

There is, therefore, a constant tension between the general discursive frames we construct in order to make the detail of the text intelligible and the capacity of the text to produce surplus meanings which none of our frames applied singly can house. The difficulties and discomforts involved in this process should not be exaggerated. For some tension of this sort is inherent in the act of reading: we need a large conjectural sense of any text in order to know how to read its particulars, and we need to keep consulting those particulars in order to know which conjectures are possible and worth pursuing. What is different about poems like 'Première du monde' is that they are constructed in such a way that the moment of perfect fit between large sense and particulars is indefinitely deferred. For Eluard this imperfection is a guarantee of creativity. Valéry's dictum 'Perfection, c'est travail' drew from Eluard and Breton in their joint *Notes sur la poésie* the counter-proposal 'Perfection, c'est paresse' (I, 482).

The reader who is accustomed to the robustness and precision of Baudelaire's images, or the piercing brilliance of Rimbaud's, or the bountiful, agglomerative energy of image-makers such as Hugo, Verhaeren or Péguy, may find the sensuous fabric of Eluard's verse thin and insubstantial. But if we take Eluard on his own terms, we can see that the recreation in words of an immediate, abrasive contact with the sensible world was not among his aims. He gives us in each poem a series of potential impressions. The fluctuating and often incompatible structures around which the text is built compel us to think and feel in the transitional realm *between* images and turn us into the inventors rather than the simple receivers of sensation. If the reader withholds his inventive power he is likely to be disappointed, and to find his imagination rewarded with no more than a pleasant, quickly forgotten ripple-and-flutter.

Until now I have been concerned mainly to show how Eluard's presentation of sense-data involves a retreat from immediacy and the creation of abstract vantage-points from which to re-approach and re-appraise those data. I have been discussing abstraction as a necessary product of Eluard's incomparably multi-focal power of vision. But it is not simply that. For abstraction also enters his texts *in propria persona*, in a wide range of conceptual terms. Such notions as *amour, liberté, tendresse, espoir, présence, haine, misère, douleur* appear repeatedly in his work. Sometimes they are closely in touch with concrete terms, and thereby regain some of their lost directness and bite, but on other occasions they are shaped into strong poetic ideas having no support at all from the perceptible world. The following poem, 'Notre mouvement', will show how imaginatively compelling such ideas can be:

Nous vivons dans l'oubli de nos métamorphoses
Le jour est paresseux mais la nuit est active
Un bol d'air à midi la nuit le filtre et l'use
La nuit ne laisse pas de poussière sur nous

Mais cet écho qui roule tout le long du jour
Cet écho hors du temps d'angoisse ou de caresses
Cet enchaînement brut des mondes insipides
Et des mondes sensibles son soleil est double

Sommes-nous près ou loin de notre conscience
Où sont nos bornes nos racines notre but

Le long plaisir pourtant de nos métamorphoses
Squelettes s'animant dans les murs pourrissants
Les rendez-vous donnés aux formes insensees
A la chair ingénieuse aux aveugles voyants

Les rendez-vous donnés par la face au profil
Par la souffrance à la santé par la lumière
A la forêt par la montagne à la vallée
Par la mine à la fleur par la perle au soleil

Nous sommes corps à corps nous sommes terre à terre
Nous naissons de partout nous sommes sans limites.

                                                    (II, 83)

The poem begins on what could easily have been a paradoxical *last*
gesture of the kind I mentioned earlier. This line has at least two
distinct meanings: 'we live in that forgetfulness which our metamor-
phoses bring' and 'we live forgetful of our metamorphoses'. At first
sight these meanings are scarcely compatible. For the one suggests:
'we are perfectly changing, have forgotten everything that is beyond
change or preceded it, everything that is constancy and identity'; and
the other: 'although we are changing, we feel ourselves to be beyond
change, to be the possessors of a constant identity'. The line is quite
without sensuous content, but derives an extraordinary suggestive
power from the presence within it of these near-opposite postulates.
The remainder of the poem may be seen as an attempt to validate this
defiant initial gesture by creating the conditions in which two such
meanings can co-exist without destroying one another. Contradictions,
paradoxes and unanswered questions accumulate in a gradually inten-
sifying list until a scene of universal reconciliation is reached in the six
lines which begin 'Les rendez-vous donnés aux formes insensées'.
Everything is compatible with everything else; all contradictions can be
resolved. So complete is this triumph over contradiction that it makes
no difference whether the members of each reconciled pair are logically
commensurate or not: they may be of separate logical kinds (*lumière :
forêt ; mine : fleur*), of the same kind, but polarised (*face : profil ;
souffrance*: *santé*), or even the bearers of a 'natural' affinity (*perle*:
soleil). The last two lines are at the same time a vindication and a

comprehensive restatement of the opening theme. But although they
mark a definitive return to the abstract world in which the poem began,
they stop far short of bland generality. In the first, the commonplace
phrases *corps à corps* and *terre à terre* enter with a splendid clinching
force: they repeat in its minimum form the grammatical pattern which
had dominated the previous list, extend the mere likeness of the last-
named couple (*perle* : *soleil*) to the point of complete identity (*corps*:
corps) and provide a touching reminder of terrestrial weight and part-
icularity before the final spreading forth into dimensionless space.
While in the second line, the very contradictoriness which the poet has
amply repudiated is shown to retain some at least of its power to
enliven and perplex. This is not an easy smoothing away of difference
and difficulty; it is inconstancy and constancy, birth and being, change
and sameness. Both the original versions of metamorphosis thus survive
into a mysterious, subdued afterlife.

The intuition that, in Walt Whitman's words, 'a vast similitude
interlocks all', provides Eluard with one of his most absorbing themes.
But whereas in 'Notre Mouvement' the principle that everything is
ultimately comparable and assimilable to everything else is articulated
in an extensive poetic structure, it often finds expression in abbreviated
form, as a maxim or as one momentary perception among others. If
we read Eluard's work at length we are reminded of the idea time and
again, and in widely different settings. Here are some examples:

Tout est comparable à tout . . .

(I, 527)

Toutes les transformations sont possibles.

(I, 104)

Mais tout est semblable
Sur la peau d'abondance.

(I, 250)

Tu es la ressemblance.

(I, 459)

Elles tranquilles et plus belles d'être semblables

(I, 1004)

Les saisons les hommes leurs astres
Tout tremblants d'être si semblables

(I, 1017)

Mille images de moi multiplient ma lumière
Mille regards pareils égalisent la chair
C'est l'oiseau c'est l'enfant c'est le roc c'est la plaine
Qui se mêlent à nous

(I, 800)

It is remarkable that an idea declared as often as this, and having in certain of its versions an unwieldy absoluteness about it, should not become a nostrum, a comforting doctrinal appurtenance, but should remain available to the poet as a spur to further innovating thought.

The idea reached its highest point of development and of usefulness as a structural device in the long poem *Poésie ininterrompue* (II, 23-44). In this work the discovery of sameness appears not only as the essential creative impetus within the life of the mind, but as an essential tendency of the 'world-process' as a whole. *Poésie ininterrompue* is Eluard's most ambitious attempt to represent the sensation of perfect continuity and an endless, abundant overspilling of vital energy. It begins and ends with suspension points, presenting itself as no more than a sample excised from a larger, unstoppable process. Eluard was outstandingly resourceful in adapting the tone and diction of his short lyrical poems to the new demands which this project made. But although the manner in which the text unfolds is immediately recognisable as Eluard's own, the poem is of a general kind familiar in French poetry of the present century. Poems as different as Valéry's *Ebauche d'un serpent*, Péguy's *Eve*, Claudel's *Cinq grandes Odes*, Saint-John Perse's *Anabase*, Cendrars' *Prose du Transsibérien* and Michaux's *Vers la Complétude* are all 'uninterrupted' in Eluard's sense. Each of them contains, of course, elements of anecdote, allegory or argument and is thereby committed to the pursuit of goals and the depiction of progress rather than simple disinterested process. But none of these poems is brought to a conclusion that fully arrests and consolidates the material that has gone before. Each poet sets in motion an imaginative dynamo, a moving portrait of creative consciousness, that the mere accomplishment of self-imposed short-term goals can do nothing to halt. At the ending of each work the poet abandons us in the interminable.

The general plan of Eluard's poem is extremely simple. The opening section contains a vision of sameness. This is followed by an extended

section in which the notion of sameness is reiterated, challenged by
difference and discrepancy, and amplified to include these challengers
within itself. The poem ends, as does 'Notre Mouvement', with a re-
statement of its dominant idea, but now seen as unconditional,
unlimited in scope and invulnerable to contradiction. It is difficult to
imagine less promising dramatic material than this totalising and equal-
ising vision of human experience. Yet Eluard creates and maintains
dramatic intensity in his poem, by presenting sameness in sharply
differentiated versions. In the long list of disembodied attributes which
begins the work, it is primeval incoherence:

> Naturelle couché debout
> Etreinte ouverte rassemblée
> Rayonnante désaccordée
> Gueuse rieuse ensorceleuse
> Etincelante ressemblante
> Sourde secrète souterraine
> Aveugle rude désastreuse
> Boisee herbeuse ensanglantée
> Sauvage obscure balbutiante
> Ensoleillée illuminée

(II, 23)

This is the sameness of a woman (or a feminine spirit, or a world-soul)
who is all things to all men and provides no opportunity for the excer-
cise of discriminating perception. By the end of the poem the battle
to make distinctions and thereby impose coherence upon the world
has been fought and all-too-completely won. Lines like the following,
read out of context, may seem naïve to the point of simple-mindedness:

> Tout se vide et se remplit
> Au rythme de l'infini
> Et disons la vérité
> La jeunesse est un trésor
> La vieillesse est un trésor
> L'océan est un trésor
> Et la terre est une mine
> L'hiver est une fourrure
> L'été une boisson fraîche
> Et l'automne un lait d'accueil

(II, 44)

But within the poem itself they have an air of exceptional seriousness and authority. For this is the final, culminating discovery of a sameness which lies beyond discrimination and to which the mind has access only when the discordant particulars of the world have been delineated and absorbed.

The verbal thread which connects these outer sections is unmatched in Eluard's work for its sustained inventiveness. The poem is a continuum, and more self-proclaimingly so than any of the comparable poems mentioned above. Throughout this middle section, the poet scans back and forth along continuities parallel to his poem and finds countless analogies for his own imaginative procedure—in human reproduction, planetary motion, seasonal change, and the growth of plants; in human aggression and the upheavals of sexual passion; in the operations of language. These examples will show with what ease and assurance all these external materials are drawn into the flow of the poem:

> Je suis ma mère et mon enfant
> En chaque point de l'éternel
> Mon teint devient plus clair mon teint devient plus sombre
> Je suis mon rayon de soleil
> Et je suis mon bonheur nocturne
>
> (II, 26)

> Et j'écris pour marquer les années et les jours
> Les heures et les hommes leur durée
> Et les parties d'un corps commun
> Qui a son matin
> Et son midi et son minuit
>
> (II, 32)

> O rire végétal ouvrant une clairière
> De gorges chantonnant interminablement
> Mains où le sang s'est effacé
> Où l'innocence est volontaire
> Gaieté gagneé tendresse du bois mort
> Chaleurs d'hiver pulpes séchées
> Fraîcheurs d'été sortant des fleurs nouvelles
> Constant amour multiplié tout nu
>
> (II, 29)

The poet is in all places and at all times; he is man and woman, past
and future, summer and winter, tenderness and violence, joy and
despair. But this is not a bragging *culte du moi*. For the poet is the
perfectly transparent meeting-place in which all identities merge and all
processes interweave. He has no personality, and no defining feature
other than his vast inclusive and assimilative power.

Within the text there are constant changes of focus. There are tiny
puckish escapades of the imagination:

> Je vois brûler l'eau pure et l'herbe du matin
> Je vais de fleur en fleur sur un corps auroral
> Midi qui dort je veux l'entourer de clameurs

(II, 42)

and expansive abstract pronouncements:

> Rien ne peut déranger l'ordre de la lumière

(II, 25)

The tone varies from grandiloquence:

> Où je suis seule et nue où je suis l'absolu
> L'être définitif
> La première femme apparue
> Le premier homme rencontré

(II, 32)

to casual jokiness:

> Ils croient qu'ils ont été . . .

> . . . la ligne de flottaison
> Sur le fleuve héraclitéen

(II, 37)

And throughout, Eluard is the complete linguistic adventurer: all
words are at hand, abstract and concrete, old and new, recondite and
everyday, delicate and coarse. These rapid textual fluctuations keep the
reader alive to difference as the drama of sameness unfolds; that
the constituents of the world should be so readily convertible one into
the next is shown to be a constant source of surprise, a miracle repeated

moment by moment in the face of randomness and fragmentation.

But a problem is posed by the very uniformity with which this *concordia discors* moves forward. The poet could murmur his litany for ever: no one moment in this infinitely stretchable sequence is appreciably closer than any other to the point of ultimate unity. Several pages before the end of the poem, therefore, Eluard introduces a change of tone and begins to prepare the way for the final paragraphs of higher revelation. The will to sameness within the self and the resistance to sameness within the world are both abruptly intensified. The refrain

> Si nous montions d'un degré

appears at irregular intervals and reminds us of the poet's urge to transcendence. But between the appearances of this line, images and statements accumulate which are much more self-contained, immobile and aggressively paradoxical than anything that has gone before. And then quite suddenly this tension between desire and circumstance vanishes: with the long-awaited phrase 'Et nous montons' all that is brutish and unstreamlined falls away, and the final liberating ascent begins:

> Et c'est très vite
> La liberté conquise
> La liberté feuille de mai
> Chauffée à blanc

> (II, 43)

Poésie ininterrompue is a brilliant poem. In it Eluard works out his largest and boldest poetic design and successfully incorporates within that design a host of clearly focused and clearly related particulars. There is no separation between the sensible and intelligible worlds: seeing, feeling, imagining and abstract thinking flow along together in ever-changing alliances. Conceptual pattern-making emerges in *Poésie ininterrompue* not as a means of retreat from the uncertainties and perils of sensory awareness, but as an enhancement of that awareness, and as a potent expression of animal vitality. Eluard seeks to re-activate the grand emotional commonplaces and to harness those underlying rhythms of the human organism from which sensations, feelings and ideas derive their peculiar shapes. This enterprise is a dangerous one and offers much scope for loose, sub-philosophical rant. Eluard has

avoided the danger by attending closely to the minute and the strange
in human experience, and by restoring to commonplaces their share of
dramatic surprise.

Furthermore *Poésie ininterrompue* presents us, and especially in
its ending, with a memorable statement of the fundamental epistem-
ological problem raised by Eluard's work at large. These are the last
lines:

> Quant au printemps c'est l'aube
> Et la bouche c'est l'aube
> Et les yeux immortels
> Ont la forme de tout
>
> Nous deux toi toute nue
> Moi tel que j'ai vécu
> Toi la source du sang
> Et moi les mains ouvertes
> Comme des yeux
>
> Nous deux nous ne vivons que pour être fidèles
> A la vie
> ·   (II, 44)

This is the moment at which identities finally and irretrievably slide
into each other: spring into dawn, hands into eyes, eyes into everything
else, woman into man, and the united couple into life itself. Or rather
this is the penultimate moment during which the merest traces of indiv-
iduality remain; in the unwriteable moment which then follows, all
substance fuses and all language becomes synonymy. The whole of the
preceding thread of the poen now appears as an exercise in the post-
ponement of identity, or in what A. J. Ayer has referred to as 'drama-
tized tautology'. At the end, tautology casts off its disguises and forms
an immovable barrier to further thinking. The problem is this: that
the swooning-away of intelligence and the surrender of discriminating
perception which provides this poem with its extraordinary dramatic
outcome are disastrous as soon as they are thought of as practical
artistic goals. The poet's mind craves after a state of perfect coal-
escence, but can remain effective within the sphere of poetic, as
distinct from mystical, activity only by resisting and deferring that
state. In Eluard's poorer poems his resistance is remarkably low; dis-
continuity is not allowed its full capacity to perplex the mind and

torment the heart; the text becomes an unchallenged and sometimes merely dainty movement from like to like. The question of the poorer poems is not an important one: a poet who wrote as many fine poems as Eluard did is perfectly entitled to his failures. What is important, however, is the atmosphere of mental risk which reigns even in his most successful works. Eluard's imagination endows the world with a new teeming energy and an exhilarating plurality of forms. Familiar distinctions and definitions are set aside, and objects are freed from their everyday settings. But for his thought to be thought at all the poet must seek for new distinctions within his unstable, recreated world. And this difficult quest is permanently threatened by the seductive and terrifying equation: anything = anything else.

My main objection to the 'Eluard' I sketched at the beginning is that the myth misrepresents the texture of Eluard's verse and understates by far the imaginative and intellectual excitement which it can provoke in the reader. To be 'Eluardian', within the terms of the myth, is to be uncommonly alert to minor nervous tremors, skilled in the expression of elementary emotion, fluently continuous in utterance—and little else. This will not do, as I hope I have shown. Eluard's verse has, to be sure, an exceptional fluidity of texture; there are few radical breaks within any one poem, and no momumental finalities; every idea, image and emotion is subject to transformation. But this constant self-adjustment of the text does not produce a smooth-moving pavement on which the reader is unthinkingly transported (although the lazy reader can, of course, create such a pavement for himself, just as the lazy listener can create an amiable tinkle from a Bach fugue). Eluard's text derives its mobility not from the mutual confirmation of image by image, but from a complex play of internal tensions, which is sustained by a sequence of paradoxes, anomalies and imaginative side-steppings. By placing discrete materials side by side and by setting up and then rapidly replacing his explanatory frameworks, the poet constantly calls upon the collaborative intelligence of his reader. The paradoxicalness and crowded multiplicity of the text make considerable demands upon our patience and ingenuity. But we are rewarded for our pains by a wonderfully strong and delicate imaginative pattern.

On several occasions I have felt obliged, in order to characterise verbal textures as precisely as possible, to speak of 'intellectual', 'emotional', and 'imaginative' elements, as if these were separable ingredients and the poem a mere mixture of them. Such divisions are particularly unfortunate in the case of Eluard, not because he refuses to recognise the existence of separate mental faculties, but because for him the poetic art is essentially the art of being between faculties, and in transition. Terminological difficulties arise, and for much the same reasons, in discussing the poet's relation to the outside world. What fascinates him is not the bird or the bush as external, tangible things on the one hand, and the bird-idea or the bush-idea as ghostly mental representations on the other, but rather the innumerable gradations which lead back and forth between the two realms. For Eluard it is the very condition of creativity that the poetic mind should invent the external world and in turn be invented by it.

Note

1.   References throughout are to the two volumes of Eluard's *Œuvres complètes*, published in the 'Bibliothèque de la Pléiade' series, ed. Lucien Scheler, Gallimard, 1968.

9 THE IMAGE OF NIGHT IN RENE CHAR'S POETRY

Nick Caistor

J'aperçois chaque jour un peu mieux que ce monde, où nous
sommes, limite ses désirs à dormir.[1]

These words were addressed by Georges Bataille to René Char, but the
writing of the latter reveals a similar attitude, and shows that he con-
centrates above all on rousing the reader of his poems from this mind-
less sleep, increasing his awareness of the situation in which he is placed,
and thus awakening a sense of sympathy and responsibility for the
world around him. This moral intention is at the centre of his poetry,
since for Char the idea of beauty immediately involves an ethical
dimension; a large part of his work, and especially the short aphor-
istic texts, seeks to define the sense and direction of this moral
perspective. What I should like to look at in this essay, however, is the
way in which these considerations inform the whole imagery of his
poems, building up a structure of implications ranging from sensual
involvement to moral import. In particular I wish to examine the use
he makes of the image of night, since it seems to me that the equiv-
alence he establishes between the alternation, in the natural world,
of day and night, and the artist's attempts to create meaning from an
initial nothingness, underpins the whole of this structure. Indeed,
it seems all the more important, given that Char is apparently con-
vinced that everybody invests the world with meaning in a manner
akin to that of the artist when he constructs his work; in fact that
we all inhabit the world as 'poets'.[2]

Whereas the moment of dawn, whose importance Char made explicit
by entitling one of his verse collections *Les Matinaux*,[3] has been
given considerable emphasis as the moment in which his poetic world
explodes into being,[4] little attention has been paid to the idea of the
night that precedes this dawn. This seems to me to falsify the
description given of the poetry, since a substantial part of it focuses
on the search that moves towards this moment: often the dawn
represents the culmination of a process begun long before, in the
darkest moments of the night.

This idea of night reveals a basic ambivalence of attitude, with a
complex of relations between the two opposite poles that the poet
re-defines with each new use of the image. Two of his collections

have the word 'night' itself in their titles: they stand at the two ends of
his production and also convey the two extremes of the sense with
which he endows night. The first is *Dehors la Nuit est gouvernée*,
originally published in 1938. Here Char is engaged in a desperate
struggle against the oppressive forces of night that threaten to sweep
him away entirely; in effect the poems are barricades thrown up to
ward off this assault. The second, which appeared in 1972, (although
the texts come both from the 1950s and from 1971), is entitled *La
Nuit talismanique*. Night is now the beneficent provider of the
opportunity for speech. We might now try to trace the steps in the
progression from the former attitude to the latter.

The poems which Char wrote as a young man in the early 1930s
are steeped in a darkness which impels the protagonist to frantic
efforts of self-protection. The dark is not simply that of the night,
but also that of the grave, of the earth at the time of an original chaos
where forms are still struggling to assume their definitive shape. The
language has all the violence of someone trying to hew an inhabitable
space for himself out of some embracing intractable matter: the poet
is fighting upwards to the light and the air. Occasionally, however,
there is a suggestion that all this obscure striving may be working to
some unexpected outcome, that the night engulfing him may reveal
itself to have been the protective cocoon for the chrysalis:

> Dans le bois on écoute bouillir le ver
> La chrysalide tournant au clair visage
> Sa délivrance naturelle
>
> ('Robusts Météores': MSM, 21)

Such optimism is rare in these texts, however, for it is not often that
these efforts to plumb the darkness (which may perhaps be identified
with the obscure levels of desire in the pre-conscious mind) meet with
any reassurance whatsoever: far more usual is the complete disorient-
ation that the following lines from *Artine* reveal:

> Un édredon en flammes précipité dans l'insondable gouffre de
> ténèbres en perpétuel mouvement.
>
> (MSM, 42)

This is the world in which the dreamer finds himself thrown, making
of sleep both a refuge and a challenge; the world also that opens before
the lovers who 'côte à côte [dorment] l'odyssée de l'amour' and leads

them deep into nocturnal regions bordering on death: 'Tard dans la nuit nous sommes allés cueillir les fruits indispensables à mes songes de mort: les figues violettes' (MSM, 61). But Char is aware of the limit-ations of these experiences, and recognises the existence of a reality beyond the world of subjective desire which remains to be challenged in the name of those 'Qui ne [confondent] pas les actes à vivre et les actes vécus/Qui [voient] la nuit au défaut de l'épaule de la dormeuse' (MSM, 81-2).

It is in the volume already cited, *Dehors la Nuit est gouvernée*, that he most openly takes up this challenge. He is soon alone facing the darkness from within the circle of his lamp, 'lampe cynique que la nuit contradictoirement interprète sur sa coque de reptile'; his only resource is that of the 'sauveur exténué ô langage', a language forged beyond the silence that the night forces on him, owing as little as possible to previous formulations, whose validity the night has totally destroyed. This new language is difficult to penetrate, as if the poet were too deeply absorbed in his combat to care about any onlooker, and the 'Postface' (DNG, 69) that closes the volume explicitly maintains a separation between this activity of the poet and the 'tâches du réveil' that confront him with the new day.

It is in fact these duties, in particular all the murderous acts of the Second World War he witnessed and on occasion performed, that bring him to a radical revaluation of the purpose of his poetry, making him far less concerned about the adequacy of language to encode the world than with making it an active force in the reality of others, a force above all to redeem something from the suffering he has found. Now night becomes precious as a possibility of respite from the destructive actions of the day:

'Venez à nous qui chancelons d'insolation, sœur sans mépris, ô nuit!'

('Feuillets d'Hypnos' 179: FEM, 134)

The night offers the poet a completely different relation to outside reality to that demanded of him during the day, when he is forced to live uniquely on the level of action, and runs the risk of being ensnared by the merely anecdotal: 'l'ennemi le plus sournois est l'actualité' he writes in *A une Sérénité crispée* (RBS, 164). Char, as his participation in the Resistance movement amply demonstrated, has never shunned action when he considered it necessary, but he has equally steadfastly upheld that the poet should remain 'l'oisif', remaining open to life in

a way that total dedication to action makes impossible. He is ready to
welcome night and its freedom, described in *La Nuit talismanique*:

> La liberté naît la nuit, n'importe où, dans un trou de mur, sur le
> passage des vents glacés.
>
>   (NT, 59)

This freedom is in no way a dissipation, nor is it any longer the escape
into a more or less private world of desire, but brings with it an increased
responsibility, since it is the poet's task to search for a relation that
will re-integrate man into the harmony which the poet senses as being
available around him. At present Char can see only disjunction between
them, which prompts him to ask plaintively:

> Combien durera ce manque de l'homme mourant au centre de la
> création parce que la création l'a congédié?
>
>   (FEM, 195)

If the rest of creation has dismissed man it can only be because he has
proved himself unworthy of it: and so it falls to the poet, Char claims,
to seek proof to the contrary. The freedom brought is this freedom of
search. Released not only from action but from the sense of sight
which imposes the specious unity of daylight on objects, the poet at
night finds himself immersed in a world open to the other senses,
more closely allied to the realm of his imagination. This gives the
feeling that the night is a palpable presence, 'l'écorce tendre de la
nuit', so enveloping that the poet may imagine himself swimming
through it (as in 'Le Visage nuptial' (FEM, 58)), or overwhelmed by
the rich profusion of the evidence revealed by touch and smell, as in
the poem 'Fenaison':

> O nuit, je n'ai rapporté de ta félicité que l'apparence parfumée
> d'ellipses d'oiseaux insaisissables! Rien n'imposait le mouvement
> que ta main de pollen qui fondait sur mon front aux moulinets
> d'une lampe d'anémone.
>
>   (FEM, 38)

Impressions so crowd in upon him here that he feels compelled to
try to transpose them into values within the world of a poem of his
own construction: whence the appearance of the 'lampe d'anémone',
the creative light of his own imagination, which in the brilliant circles

of the flower seeks to re-capture all the intoxicating movements of the night.

A triumphant affirmation such as the above is not normally available to the poet, however. As the mention of the 'vents glacés' earlier suggested, and as his first poems stressed, night first of all sweeps away all comfort. Whereas the evening brings with it peace and an impression of fulfilment, this atmosphere rarely survives the disappearance of the sun, and only in the poem 'Congé au vent' does any link between the two states seem possible: the fragrant beauty of the girl encountered on her return from flower-picking seems to him so powerful that it might even suspend for a while the ravaging wind, and perhaps offer a glimpse into the secrets of the night:

Peut-être aurez-vous la chance de distinguer sur ses lèvres la
chimère de l'humidité de la Nuit?   (FEM, 20)

Another poem, 'L'Inoffensif' (LPA, 120), is again centred on this moment of anguish when the darkness descends and brusquely separates him from the object of his love: 'Je cesse de recevoir l'hymne de ta parole'. The poem ends with a question which suggests that he must accept the loss as absolute and occupy himself with fresh discoveries for the new day. For it is above all within himself that the poet must seek the values that will be capable of withstanding the test of dawn and the inflexible judgment of mid-day, 'midi et sa flèche méritée' as he writes. The poet is the 'cendre toujours inachevée' who assures the re-transmission of a vital unity beyond the usual incoherence, and who in his solitary vigil attempts to 'essaimer la poussière'—all that remains after the foundering of the day. We might note here the distance that this attitude implies, since the poet looks for this meaning not in daily dialogues with the rest of his fellow men, but in the isolation of night, when he has the impression of sharing a privileged communion with nature without any interfering intermediary: 'Dans la nuit, le poète, le drame et la nature ne font qu'un, mais en montée et s'aspirant' ('Sur une Nuit sans ornement': LPA, 168). What in fact he is trying to achieve is an escape from normal subjectivity to the impersonal realm of art where resides 'la plénitude de ce qui n'était qu'esquisse ou déformé par les vantardises de l'individu'; at night this liberation, this capacity almost to stand outside himself, seems offered by the vast emptiness:

Illusoirement, je suis à la fois dans mon âme et hors d'elle, loin devant
la vitre et contre la vitre, saxifrage éclaté. Ma convoitise est infinie.
Rien ne m'obsède que la vie.

('Le Météore du 13 août': FEM, 203)

In this way, then, the poet becomes a more urgent, more open
recipient of all that life can propose, and although the process is one
that he undertakes alone, it will be without meaning unless it is
dedicated finally to the rest of men, if not as a present dialogue then as
a promise for the future. 'A chaque effondrement des preuves le poète
répond par une salve d'avenir' he claims in 'Partage formel' (FEM, 78):
at night, therefore, he must also use his freedom to try to capture this
future, to mould in his work what can best withstand the world of
time which will inevitably return with the daylight. And if there is a
risk of his writing succumbing to this assault of time, there can never
be any question of his refusing the challenge: for it is only in this
other world that the poetry accomplishes itself, by proffering the
freedom the poet has sought to the reader's own experience, pro-
posing to him a new and freer definition of this experience.

This journey of the poet towards the reader, whose friendship is
immediately gained by the sharing of the meaning, is admirably desc-
cribed in 'Seuil'. In this poem Char traces the progress of the poet
through the night, and his efforts to endow words with a fresh sig-
nificance, and in the final section extends a joyful welcome to those
friends whose arrival will crown the success of his struggle. The cadence
is similar to the euphoria of 'Fenaison', the happiness both of poetic
creation and the certainty that it will all have been worthwhile finding
its fullest expression in a rich musicality:

Planté dans le flagéolant petit jour, ma ceinture pleine de saisons,
je vous attends ô mes amis qui allez venir. Déjà je vous devine
derrière la noirceur de l'horizon.

(FEM, 181)

Just how he manages to find the words that will be offered in the
morning remains a mystery for Char. The nearest equivalent he can
find for the moment of inspiration is the *éclair*, the lightning flash
which reveals the world to him at night even more brightly and com-
prehensively than during the light of day. The brevity of its illumin-
ation only serves to increase the richness of what it brings, so that he
can write, 'l'éclair me dure' ('La Bibliothèque est en feu': LPA, 146).

This instant of sudden fecundation is the supreme moment of the
encounter, so vital in Char's work. In the poem 'Biens égaux' he claims
'Je n'ai retenu personne sinon l'angle fusant d'une Rencontre' (FEM,
173), and in the *bandeau* for his play *Claire* he expresses his pessimism
concerning everything the modern world has destroyed, his fear lest
'il s'apprête à descendre au centre meme de notre vie pour éteindre le
dernier foyer, celui de la Rencontre . . .' (RBS, 37). The possibilities
which such a meeting represents, the suppression of all differences
in this point of contact, are at the heart of his poetry, governing not
only the reception of his poems by the chance discovery of its reader,
but also his own conviction that there is in fact something for him to
say, guaranteed by this unheralded irruption from the outside world—
the flash of lightning, the brief passage of the meteor, both of them
close to the moment of the act of love. Frequently Char's poetry is
built around this search in the darkness—without any knowledge of
being headed in the right direction—for this point where all doubt will
be erased, and a complete affirmation of being and belonging will be
called for: either that, or silence, since the lightning 'tantôt nous
illumine et tantôt nous pourfend' ('Les Compagnons dans le jardin':
LPA, 152). This potentiality seems to him to infuse all reality, so that
even the most seemingly opposed terms can complement each other,
as do, for example, the seagull and the shark, whose communion he
manages to descry and to define as:

> Un jour de pur dans l'année, un jour qui creuse sa galerie
> merveilleuse dans l'écume de la mer, un jour qui monte aux yeux
> pour couronner midi.
>
> (FEM, 190)

The absolute represented above by the image of *midi* is the equivalent
of the flash of light in the night sky: both are the moment of complete
identity and danger towards which the whole of Char's world is in
movement. For this reason we are abruptly hoisted out of the night
in which he sees 'Le Météore du 13 août' to find ourselves once more
at the crucial instant of mid-day:

> A la seconde où tu m'apparus, mon cœur eut tout le ciel pour
> l'éclairer. Il fut midi à mon poème. Je sus que l'angoisse dormait.
>
> (FEM, 202)

Immediately, however, the darkness returns to enfold him, and once
again it is patient effort that is required of the poet if he is to bring his

creation from inception to existence, not just for himself but for everyone else. The recent poem 'Le Nu perdu' (of particular import- ance since the entire collection of poems written between 1962 and 1970 is similary entitled) stresses these two aspects necessary to ensure success, in this case seen in the perspective of the fruit-tree's renewal:

> Porteront rameaux ceux dont l'endurance sait user la nuit noueuse qui précède et suit l'éclair. Leur parole reçoit existence de fruit intermittent qui la propage en se dilacérant.

> (NP, 31)

Thus the poem emerges as the combination of endurance and inspir- ation, appearing before its reader for him to meet and understand it in an analogous fashion. For him, it is the blackness of the writing that stands out in sudden promise of meaning from the enveloping blank- ness of the white page; he must then pursue the poem's intention through the various unsuspected links that become evident (the images, the rhythm) until he too has constructed the unity which the poet initially sought.

This fundamental dynamism in Char's poetry explains why the lightning visits the nights of his poems far more frequently than does the moon. The latter neither really illuminates the objects upon which it casts its light, nor yet provides the poet with the cocooning dark that might aid him in the work of transposing objects into values. Moonlight serves only to emphasise ambiguity, to make the consequ- ences of any action unsure by robbing them of the sharp contours, of the warmth, that daylight gives them. The moon then is often associated with an unpleasant dampness (the ideal atmosphere for the nightmare described in 'L'Extravagant', FEM, 182), and as such Char rejects it with some abhorrence: 'Le regard moite de la lune m'a toujours donné la nausée' (RBS, 24). It is only in texts such as 'Chérir Thouzon', or 'Le Tout ensemble', when the moon is removed from its normal context and shines in the daytime sky, that it becomes important for the poet. In these cases it serves to remind him that, except in the rare instants of an unflawed affirmation, everything in the world around him is in a perpetual movement of transition into and out of being. In the second of the two poems mentioned above, the sight of the moon in the daytime sky underlines for him his own mood at the time, when his actions are as distant from his true feelings as the moon is from its true surroundings:

Faucille qui persévérez dans le ciel désuni
Malgré le jour et notre frénésie.
Lune qui nous franchis et côtoies notre cœur
Lui, resté dans la nuit.

(LM, 49)

If the moon fails to participate in the poet's drama during the night, there are two further sources of light which, again by virtue of the fact that they accentuate the contrast between darkness and light, are closely identified with the struggle in which he is engaged. These are the stars and the candle-flame. The former are important as points of light that punctuate the infinity of the night sky and that might otherwise overwhelm his efforts, or even lull him to sleep. Thus he says of them: 'l'étoile me rend le dard de guêpe qui s'était enfoui en elle' ('La Montée de la nuit': LPA, 189). Elsewhere he considers them as the proof that he is not working in vain:

La faveur des étoiles est de nous inviter à parler, de nous montrer que nous ne sommes pas seuls, que l'aurore a un toit et mon feu tes deux mains.

(LPA, 174)

The image of the candle-flame in an encircling darkness is a favoured one in Char's poems;[5] the light of the candle is the visible representation of man's 'lumière mentale', with all its patient probing of the threatening dark around it: 'joue contre joue avec qui la tue' ('Le Jugement d'octobre': NP, 37). This danger though is also nourishing, for in Char's work it is only by a deliberate confrontation of the forces that threaten to negate all one's values that any worthwhile assertion can be made. The recent volume *La Nuit talismanique* reproduces a painting done by the author of a candle-flame in the night, and once more the message is that of the intimate interrelation of life, beauty and risk, each fully realising itself through what might seem to be its contrary: 'La fleur est dans la flamme, la flamme est dans la tempete' (NT, 38).

This feeling he discovers, to his amazement and gratification (again he finds proof that such unlikely encounters are nonetheless central to life), to have been embodied in the work of another, more illustrious painter, the seventeenth-century French artist Georges de la Tour. Char honours him together with the Greek philosopher Heraclitus in one of the fragments of 'Partage formel' (FEM, 67), praising the way in

which he constructs a world of certainty in his art that in a certain
sense is the reverse of everyday reality, the indistinct light of events
being transformed into the irrevocable candle-flame of art. Char
salutes in these two predecessors the fact that they have:

> . . . dépensé [leurs] forces à la couronne de cette conséquence sans
> mesure de la lumière absolument impérative: l'action contre le
> réel, par tradition signifiée, simulacre et miniature.

In the first of the texts in praise of 'La Justesse de Georges de la Tour'
(NP, 73) he reiterates the idea, this time specifically locating the
venture of the artist 'dans le cercle de la bougie'. Above all, the artist
should remain faithful to this uniquely difficult pursuit, resisting 'la
tentation de remplacer les ténèbres par le jour et leur éclair nourri par
un terme inconstant'. We can judge from a poem like this the difference
between the attitude of a poet such as Valéry, who tries to explore
just how the creative imagination informs the world (this is the basis of
the chapter by Christine M. Crow in the present book); and that of
Char, whose main concern is not to question something which for him
seems necessarily to be a mystery, but to state his belief in the irreplac-
eable validity of the imaginative artist's approach to the world. This
aim is explicitly stated in the imaginary dialogue he conducts with
another painter, Georges Braque. The painter is quick to remove the
debate from the realm of ideas; the artistic process is again represented
as a night journey, whose goal is to be reached not in intellectual
hypothesising (for there is, finally, no doubt that the artist is capable
of grasping the 'nudité première' of objects) but in emotional con-
viction:

LE PEINTRE:
Les idées, vous savez. . . Si j'interviens parmi les choses, ce n'est pas,
certes, pour les appauvrir ou exagérer leur part de singularité. Je
remonte simplement à leur nuit, à leur nudité premières. Je leur
donne désir de lumière, curiosité d'ombre, avidité de construction.
Ce qui importe, c'est de fonder un amour nouveau à partir d'êtres
et d'objets jusqu'alors indifférents.

                                                              (RBS, 60)

This is how Char conceives of the artist, and of man in general, striving
to endow the world with meaning. A poignant illustration of this
attempt to find certainty in the candle-light is provided for him through

another painting by Georges de la Tour, 'Madeleine à la veilleuse'.
The poem picks out the details of the picture: the Magdalene seated
at a table on which are a whip, a wooden cross, a Bible, and the night-
light that provides the luminous source for the picture, and at whose
flame she is staring intently. One of her hands cups her chin, whilst
the other rests on a skull ('la forme dure, sans crépi de la mort', as it
becomes in the poem) balanced on her knee. Char translates her
attitude as one of a painful realisation of mortality. He wishes that
somehow he might cross the distance separating her existence of
colour and canvas from his own,[6] to ensure her immortality: indeed he
imagines that this interpenetration will one day be possible. Art is thus
held to offer a more acceptable answer for man than that offered by
religion, which in the last part of the poem is seen to be completely
inadequate:

> Un jour discrétionnaire, d'autres pourtant moins avides que moi,
> retireront votre chemise de toile, occuperont votre alcôve. Mais
> ils oublieront en partant de noyer la veilleuse et un peu d'huile se
> répandra par le poignard de la flamme sur l'impossible solution.
>
> (FEM, 215)

The claim that art can transcend time in this way and thus serve man in
general is aided, in Char's view, by the fact that it allies itself to the
night surrounding the candle-flame, yielding itself yet immediately
regaining its inviolate plenitude. The power of art, like that of the
night, can be experienced but not elucidated. Any attempt to do so
leads to falsification, Char maintains:

> La nuit se colore de rouille quand elle consent à nous entrouvir
> les grilles de ses jardins . . . Il ne fallait pas embraser le cœur de la nuit
> . . . Il fallait que l'obscur fût maître où se cisèle la rosée du matin.
>
> (LPA, 168-9)

In this way night comes to stand as a metaphor for the infinite potent-
iality Char feels to exist within man himself. The artist seizes this
capacity by the act of creating his own work in the moment of the
éclair which, like the potentiality, is outside time and definition.

  Both these absolutes must, however, submit to the different light
brought by the day. The dawn often bears the memory of the arduous
struggle that has guaranteed its existence, as the first of the texts Char
addresses to his fellow *matinaux* suggests: 'La teinte du caillot devient

la rougeur de l'aurore' ('Rougeur des matinaux': LM, 75). Often the
new day follows a night that has brought no refreshing certainty, as
is the case in the following text, 'Chérir Thouzon', which ends with
daybreak:

> Le jour tournoyait sur Thouzon. La mort n'a pas comme le lichen
> arasé l'ésperance de la neige. Dans le creux de la ville immergée, la
> corne de la lune mêlait le dernier sang et le premier limon.
>
> (NP, 16)

The poem up to this point has been a troubled self-examination,
attempting to discern the possibilities for poetic involvement left
available once the poet has accepted that 'tous les ruisseaux libres et
fous de la création avaient bien fini de ruer'—and he has been unable to
reach any conclusive answer. Then the day breaks, and shows him that
it is not just a dawn anywhere, but specifically in this place that he can
joyfully name: Thouzon; this provides him with a first reply (fidelity
to a given place and situation) to his previous doubts. This is developed
in the next sentence as the poet accepts this limited hope: here, the
change in tense and in focus seeks to incorporate the movement from
night to day within the poem itself. The moon is once more the link-
ing element in the lightening sky, showing him (with a suggestion of
the alchemical processes) the interrelation of his former doubt ('le
dernier sang') and the promise of the fresh silt ('le premier limon').
Sometimes not even this assurance offers itself and Char can be so
dubious as to insert his effort only into this narrow margin between the
two forces of night and day:

> Nous ne pouvons vivre que dans l'entrouvert, exactement sur la ligne
> hermétique de partage de l'ombre et de la lumière.
>
> ('Dans la Marche': LPA, 196)

We have seen though, how contrary to his conception of the world
this immobility is. Indeed the second half of the text quoted above
recognises this fact, and finally comes to view the onward impulsion,
even devoid of certainty, as desirable:

> Mais nous sommes irrésistiblement jetés en avant. Toute notre
> personne prête aide et vertige à cette poussée.
>
> (*ibid.*)

Much of this kind of pessimism derives from the fact that Char feels that the modern world completely ignores the opportunities night represents, and in its ignorance is incapable of acting in anything but a ruinous manner during the day. This brings the poet to a protective attitude towards all that the power of night implies, the offensive counterpart of which is to be found in texts such as the following fragment from 'Contre une Maison sèche':

> Trois cent soixante-cinq nuits sans les jours, bien massives, c'est
> ce que je souhaite aux haïsseurs de la nuit.

(NP, 121)

Everywhere around him he witnesses the negation of a harmony that he knows to have been possible from what he finds at the start of Western civilisation in the fragments of the pre-Socratic philosophers and in the traces he uncovers of the early colonists of Southern France, 'Aux Portes d'Aerea':

> L'heureux temps. Chaque cité était une grande famille que la peur
> unissait; le chant des mains à l'œuvre et la vivante nuit du ciel
> l'illuminaient.

In more recent times, Char supposes, man has rejected this side of his nature, the one that once linked him to night, to the sacred, to all that is not susceptible to rational explanation, in favour of the intellect alone. Just as Char recognises the equal, though opposed powers of day and night, so he declares his 'primordial souci' to be that of uniting 'l'intelligence avec l'ange'; he goes on to define this latter quality as:

> . . . ce qui, à l'intérieur de l'homme, tient à l'écart du compromis
> religieux, la parole du plus haut silence, la signification qui ne
> s'évalue pas . . . Ange, la bougie qui se penche au nord du cœur.

(FEM, 90)

It is only in art that Char considers this balance to be upheld, because, as we have seen, poetry and painting refuse to accept the proof of the natural world, and situate themselves somewhere beyond it in an empire of their own; they act as the go-between for this outside world and man, in order that he might not entirely become lost. In the poem 'Chanson du velours à côtes', where this debate is carried on in terms of night and day, a possibility for mediation is given in the image of the wind, which seems to me to correspond closely to this idea of the poet-mediator (as, elsewhere, the poet may be identified with the image of the tree linking two similarly opposed, interdependent forces, the earth and the sky: see, for example, 'Effacement du peuplier' (NP, 15)). The last stanza sketches these opportunities:

> Il était entre les deux un mal qui les déchirait. Le vent allait de
> l'un à l'autre; le vent ou rien, les pans de la rude étoffe et
> l'avalanche des montagnes, ou rien.
>
> (FEM, 201)

It is the task of art to ensure that something survives the encroaching darkness, to assure the continuity of 'la grappe desséchée de Dionysos— qui sait? — demain reverdissante.' Even in the depths of the Second World War Char finds confirmation for this hope, in the form of the cricket, which continues its song oblivious of all the horror and un-certainty around it. By its very refusal to be affected, it renews the determination of those lucky enough to hear:

> Il faisait nuit. Nous nous étions serrés sous le grand chêne de larmes.
> Le grillon chanta. Comment savait-il, solitaire, que la terre n'allait
> pas mourir, que nous, les enfants sans clarté, allions bientôt parler?
>
> ('Hommage et famine': FEM, 51)

Such then is the range of meaning contained in the image of night in Char's writing. Its significance has become increasingly rich through the various collections, leaving behind the merely negative sense implied in the early poems. (It may be that once an image becomes operative for a writer it ceases to have a purely negative implication: this is above all true for someone like Char, who, as we have seen, is partic-ularly conscious of the dynamic movement manifest in all things). Further, Char passes from the fact of night as a reality in the phenom-enal world, one whose attributes can be ascertained and described by an observer for whom the object remains a passive item of perception, to the idea of night as a force acting directly upon the observer at a level deeper than that of perception:

> La nuit déniaise notre passé d'homme, incline sa psyché devant le
> présent, met de l'indécision dans notre avenir.
>
> ('Sur une Nuit sans ornement': LPA, 169)

In Char's view, the poet, rather than searching the world of phenomena for a system of cause and effect that can provide a rational explanation of events, is trying to define the emotional integration of man into the chain of harmony around him: though he, too, starts from the world of matter, his main concern is with emotional conviction. The poet always works on behalf of the world, as the last line of the poem 'Le Bois de l'Epte' makes explicit: 'De chacun — ne me traitez pas durement — j'accomplissais, je le sus, les souhaits'. But his way of working remains as unfathomable as the power of night.

Notes

1.   Georges Bataille, 'Lettre à René Char sur les incompatibilités de l'écrivain' *L'Herne*, No. 15 (1971), p. 31.
2.   Martin Heidegger discusses a similar idea in the work of Hölderlin in *Approche de Hölderlin*, Paris, Gallimard, 1962; see especially pages 53-61.
3.   These abbreviations have been used for the following, most readily available, editions of Char's work: MSM *Le Marteau sans maître*, 5th printing, Corti, 1970; DNG *Dehors la Nuit est gouvernée*, 2nd edition, GLM, 1949; FEM *Fureur et mystère*, 'Poésie', Gallimard, 1967; LM *Les Matinaux*, 'Poésie', Gallimard, 1969; LPA *La Parole en archipel*, 'Poésie', Gallimard, 1969; NP *Le Nu perdu*, Gallimard, 1971; RBS *Recherche de la base et du sommet*, 'Poésie', Gallimard, 1971; NT *La Nuit talismanique*, Geneva, Skira, 1972.
4.   Jean-Pierre Richard begins his study on Char (*Onze Etudes sur la poésie moderne*, pp. 67-103) with this moment of dawn:

> Comme celle de Rimbaud, son aventure commence par l'allégresse d'un matin: en face de nous, en nous, le monde semble surgir avec l'éclat d'une neuve innocence.

The end of his article, however, shows him to have greatly modified this view, for he writes: 'je préfère à tant de matins triomphaux cette fièvre hésitante, ce trébuchement, la maladresse de cette "matinale lourdeur" '.
5.   See also the book devoted to this image by Gaston Bachelard, *La Flamme d'une chandelle*, Paris, Presses Universitaires de France, 1961.
6.   A further text that should be read with the poem is 'Une Communication?—Madeleine qui veillait' (RBS, 47-50); Char here describes his encounter, shortly after he has completed this poem, with a young prostitute named Madeleine. The chance meeting seems to him to confirm that not only may the distance between art and life be crossed, but that:

> La réalité noble ne se dérobe pas à qui la rencontre pour l'estimer et non pour l'insulter ou la faire prisonnière.

(RBS, 50)

10 FRANCIS PONGE

Ian Higgins

Bored by the flabby lyricism of much Symbolist and post-Symbolist poetry, bored by the indiscriminate welter of analogy characteristic of much modern poetry, and scornful of both, Ponge has sometimes said he would rather not be called a poet at all (cf. GRM, 40-1, 256; EPS, 57-8).[1] In both forms of poetry there is an unresisting acceptance by the poet of the elusiveness of meaning (cf. Pr, 190-1), so that the poem is 'une effusion simplement subjective' (EPS, 27). The out-pouring is not measured against the outside world before being launched into it, whereas for Ponge 'il ne s'agit pas d'arranger les choses [i.e. into either of these types of poetry] . . . il faut que les choses vous dérangent' (GRM, 257). The true use of poetry, for Ponge, is to counter the danger to which his boredom and scorn are reactions: on our use of language depends, to put it broadly, the enslavement or the liber-ation of the human mind. His aim is to 'dénoncer le langage commun, en former ou aider à en former un autre' (EPS, 16). In that this has to be done by relating language, world and man to one another, his work is indeed resistance, contestation. And, as we shall see, he has called 'poetry' the sort of text he wants to create in the pursuit of this aim. Therefore, and in so far as poetry can be defined as discourse which both *uses* language as an instrument of reference and *in so doing*—that is, through some form of suggestion, tangential to the reference—draws attention to its instrumentality, I shall call Ponge a poet and most of his texts, including many theoretic ones, poetry.

The existential importance of language is the central problem, often explicitly, in nearly all Ponge's poetry, including those texts—the majority—whose title suggests their subject is an object or creature from the non-human world. In this essay I shall look first at what Ponge says about language, both in poetic and in other texts; then at the structure of the world as it is presented in his poetry; then at the structure of the poetic texts themselves, to show how they are them-selves worlds, different from, but analogous to, the world outside them; all with a view to showing, finally, how these exhilarating celebrations of the non-human world are also celebrations of the human mind.

I

Ponge's most typical work anticipates and develops the notion of the

183

Absurd as expounded in Camus' *Mythe de Sisyphe*, which he read in manuscript in 1941. All manifestations of the absurd may be reduced to the notion of man being imprisoned in himself and at the same time exiled outside himself, unable to know whether he knows either the world or himself. All his experience is under the sign of this vicious circle or lack of self-coincidence. Now Ponge experiences this absurdity above all as 'l'infidélité des moyens d'expression, (. . .) l'impossibilité pour l'homme non seulement de s'exprimer mais d'exprimer n'importe quoi' (Pr, 181). All his work is basically a struggle to turn this inevitable failure of expression into an existential triumph, as we shall see in sections III and IV below. For in Ponge, language is seen to be the characteristic feature of man: 'la véritable sécrétion commune du mollusque homme, (. . .) la chose la plus proportionnée et condition-née à son corps, et cependant la plus différente de sa forme que l'on puisse concevoir: je veux dire la PAROLE' (PPC, 77). Addressing men, again as 'informes mollusques', he says 'vous n'avez pour demeure que la vapeur commune de votre véritable sang: les paroles. (. . .) Telles paroles, telles mœurs, ô société!' (Pr, 162-3). The striking thing about these metaphors is their combination of the most basic physicality with abstraction: perfectly proportioned to man's body, language could not be more different in form, a secretion, a substance, part of him and yet outside him, an exhalation floating round him, invisible, in other minds. In a typical piece, Ponge uses plant life to describe man. The nearest the plant can come to expression is simply to grow a bit more: 'Infernale multiplication de substance à l'occasion de chaque idée! Chaque désir de fuite m'alourdit d'un nouveau chaînon!' (PPC, 84). In contrast to man's expression, even written, every gesture 'laisse une présence, une naissance irrémédiable, *et non détachée d'eux*. (. . .) Aucun geste de leur action n'a d'effet en dehors d'eux-mêmes' (PPC, 84-5); '*L'on ne peut sortir de l'arbre par des moyens d'arbre*' (PPC, 81; cf. also 48). But the characteristic of man is the abstract gesture of language, which projects him outside himself: words may be his secretion, but they detach themselves from him and operate an abstraction even when written. 'La notion d'homme est proche de la notion d'équilibre' (Pr, 215); but it is also 'la parole et la morale' (PPC, 55). It is notable that Ponge rarely refers to language as *langage*, but as *parole*, emphasising the temporality of language as an act, something physical but immediately detached from the speaker or writer, who passes on and leaves his utterance as a 'monument', a shell which can be inhabited by others (PPC, 77).[2] The act of language in some degree realises the speaker's being in the outside world, in other minds- this is why it is a 'moral' act. For to be an individual *is* to utter: the pebble is stone at 'l'âge de la personne, de l'individu, c'est-à-dire de la parole' (PPC, 98); language is the *mode* of man's individuality, that is, of his consciousness of other phenomena, his limitation or imperfection: 'La parole n'est qu'une façon (. . .) d'avouer quelque faiblesse; de remplacer quelque vertu, pouvoir, perfection, quelque organe absent, d'exprimer sa damnation, de la compenser' (GRP, 171-2).

The characteristic potential of man is therefore to attain and preserve, through his moral-linguistic faculties, a conscious and deliberate balance between the two absolutes of his 'true' self and the 'true' outside world, including other people. Man is not fully himself unless he is *realising* his relation to the world linguistically. For Ponge, this is a fundamental need, sometimes experienced as a challenge (PPC, 89; Pr, 163) which it would be degrading not to take up (Pr, 164, 182); sometimes as a reaction against the paralysing effect the world threatens to have on him through his having to use its debased, cliché-ridden, mystificatory language (Pr, 155-6, 157, 162-4; EPS, 13-19) and sometimes as 'les muettes instances que [font les choses] qu'on les parle' (Pr, 120): man is both hostage and representative of non-human phenomena (cf. GRM, 289). But since he is both hostage and representative, his utterance of them will be 'avec mesure, mais quelle mesure: la leur propre' (Pr, 120). This notion of *measure*, both of the text and between text and world, is fundamental in Ponge, and I shall return to it in sections III and IV.

Despair at the failure of expression is certainly not absent from Ponge's work. It may lead some people to 'le suicide ontologique' (Pr, 192), since the absurd and discouraging presence of others within oneself is felt above all in trying to use words (Pr, 157). This doubt as to one's identity may be experienced as a feeling of separation from one's own thoughts (Pr, 125), and is at its most acute in any attempt to submit the world to logic (Pr, 149). Man's experience of exile or lack of self-coincidence is an experience of language. But if knowledge and logic are impossible, a despairing thirst for them is simply a perverse 'désir d'y voir trouble' (GRM, 176). There is another possible attitude to words: a clear-sighted determination to cloud their every-day meanings. If there is a necessity forcing man to adopt one posture or another, 'il est peut-être une pose possible qui consiste à dénoncer à chaque instant cette tyrannie: je ne rebondirai jamais que dans la pose du *révolutionnaire* ou du *poète*' (Pr, 159), that is, someone who practises 'l'art de *résister aux paroles*' (Pr, 157), taking the only possible way out: *'parler contre les paroles. Les entraîner avec soi dans la honte*

où elles nous conduisent de telle sorte qu'elles s'y défigurent' (Pr,
163-4). The way to remove the tragic from the absurd is 'l'expression
(. . .), la naissance (ou résurrection), *la création métalogique* (la POESIE)'
(Pr, 192-3). For Ponge, there is nothing tragic in not being able to ex-
plain 'or understand the world (logically), 'puisqu'il est en mon pouvoir
—métalogiquement—de le *refaire'* (Pr, 198) in 'un objet *fait de* l'homme
(le poème, la création métalogique) . . . descriptif . . . sans intrusion
de la terminologie scientifique ou philosophique' (Pr, 194). Although
it is impossible 'non seulement d'exprimer mais de décrire les choses'
(Pr, 182), since man exists 'dans le relatif' (Pr, 215) it is all a question
of degree: it will be possible to achieve 'dans une certaine mesure
(. . .) des succès relatifs d'expression' (Pr, 182).

Resurrection, revolution: what does this claim for poetry mean?
To speak against words and drag them down into the shame they
inflict on us is to accept and turn to account the absurdity of using
them against themselves, and the danger of not knowing the extent of
one's mastery over them, that is, what one has expressed and communi-
cated. Here, mastery would seem to be simply the disfiguring of them,
that is, breaking with usage. What is then expressed and communicated
is to some extent a matter of chance: the 'shame' is the degree to
which words themselves, or 'les autres en moi-même' (Pr, 157), still
hold the initiative. The fact that, and the way in which, the speaker
is not in complete control of what is expressed and communicated,
when set against an impossible absolute success, is precisely what
'disfigures' the word.

But this disfiguring of language, the turning to account of the
uncontrollability of language, is not tantamount to abandoning the
attempt at control. Otherwise an obvious method would be nonsense
or automatic utterance. In an enthusiastic exclamation, Ponge defines
his aim as being to 'render' the density of the world through the
semantic density of language:

O ressources infinies de l'épaisseur des choses, *rendues* par les
ressources infinies de l'épaisseur sémantique des mots!

(Pr, 176)

But although this aim is achieved 'metalogically', it is only achieved
thanks to 'une volonté sans compromission' (Pr, 118), an immense
effort at precision, which comes out explicitly in the poetry in the rep-
eated insistence on measure and in the various forms of *adéquation,*
or equivalence, of text to object, which I will be looking at in section

III. The writer's triumph is his failure to guarantee his attempted
effect: the gap between object, everyday use of the word, and his
new use of it, and the reader's creative and pleasurable hesitation
between them. This is what happens in Ponge's poetry: the effect on
the reader is a new awareness and enjoyment of the specificity not
only of objects in the world, including the text, but also, and thereby,
of the specificity and infinite potential of the human mind.

For only by changing the appearance of the world in language can
we give a jolt to our habits of thought, and it is only thanks to such
jolts that the mind can advance (cf. GRM, 199, 257). A recurrent
wish in Ponge is to escape from the 'infime manège [dans lequel]
depuis des siècles tournent les paroles, l'esprit, enfin la réalité de
l'homme' (Pr, 173; cf. TP, 258 and GRM, 254, 256-7, 295). This
manège is the vicious circle of the absurd, experienced as the
impossibility of expressing oneself without expressing at the same time
some (unknowable) thing other than oneself. Ponge emphasises that
'*l'homme subjectif* ne [peut] se saisir directement lui-même, sinon par
rapport à cette résistance que le monde lui offre, sinon par rapport à
cette résistance qu'il rencontre. Ainsi dans une espéce d'opération,
d'action' (GRM, 258). It is to the act of language that Ponge looks in
trying to escape the *manège*: 'il suffit peut-être de *nommer* quoi que ce
soit–d'une certaine manière–pour *exprimer* tout de l'homme' (GRM,
225). 'In a particular way'–but all depends on *what* way. To see what
sort of advance or escape is achieved, we must now compare the struct-
ure of the world *in* the poem with that of the world *of* the poem.

II

Look at the rain in the yard: a thin, waving curtain out in the middle,
bigger drops near the walls; the horizontal procession of drops along
the clothes-line and window-rail; the slow flow along the gutter until
at the end it drops, straight down, in a coarse skein—only to bounce
off the ground in brilliant splinters. Different movements and sounds,
a chaos of water and noise. Yet the very diversity is seen as an order:
the curtain in the middle is maybe a 'réseau', the rain is like 'un méca-
nisme compliqué (. . .), une horlogerie', it is a 'brillant appareil' (PPC,
32). Out in the country, it falls on to the complicated 'appareils' of
an 'immense laboratoire (. . .), à la fois cornues, filtres, siphons,
alambics'; their function is to temper and prolong the effect of the
rain on the soil, and the usual word for them is 'plants' (PPC, 90-1).
Indeed, the whole of nature is liable to appear as 'une montre dont
le principe est fait de roues qui tournent à de très inégales vitesses'

(PPC, 96; cf. GRP, 172). Some of the wheels, as with the stone, may be so vast that their cycle is imperceptible, and rejoins the notion of linear decay (PPC, 97), but cycle there is, from 'Le Cycle des saisons' (PPC, 48, and cf. 33-4, 45, 80-6) to the 'cyclisme perpétuel' of water under the influence of the sun (PPC, 62), and to the cultural cycle of man, the 'recommencement perpétuel de son œuvre artistique ou philosophique (. . .), ce manège' (GRM, 206; cf. 197). The cycle of the trees is indeed the tightest of *maneges*, tighter than man's: for however hard they try, 'ils ne disent que "les arbres" ' (PPC, 48), just as the millions of waves in the ebb and flow of the sea only ever utter 'une seule et brève parole' (PPC, 59).

To see nature as clockwork is to see it as manifestly obeying a law or set of laws; and the objects and creatures of Ponge's world are indeed presented as characteristic and involuntary forms of behaviour. The snail *has to* move as soon as it comes out of its shell (PPC, 51); fire *has to* move from one point to another (PPC, 47); water has the 'vice', the 'idée fixe', of a formless obedience to gravity (PPC, 61). So that even in disorder, it is possible to discern an order: the sea 'met *elle-meme* un frein a la fureur de ses flots' (PPC, 60), while on the shore the pebbles, 'perdus sans ordre', nevertheless enjoy a perfection of form which remains 'imperturbable dans le désordre des mers' (PPC, 98-100); in autumn, 'le dépouillement se fait en désordre' (PPC, 33), but is part of the cycle; the 'vomissement de vert' of the trees in spring may seem completely random, and their growth an attempt to 'se confondre les uns dans les autres', but 'en réalité, cela s'ordonne' (PPC, 48), for despite their 'monstrueux accroissement', their 'irré-médiable *excroissance*', 'il existe à chacun une borne' (PPC, 81, 84). Similarly, the leaping flames of the fire form 'une seule rampe de papillons' (PPC, 47); and the butterfly itself surely only *seems* to settle at random: 'au hasard de sa course, ou tout comme' (PPC, 56).

In this world of orderly disorder, the harder it is to discern a firm shape in an object the more sinister it seems: water is vicious; the more you explore the sea the murkier it gets (PPC, 60); the sponge has an ignoble lack of discrimination (PPC, 41) and resembles the 'ig-noble' 'lâche et froid sous-sol que l'on nomme la mie' of bread (PPC, 46). But why sinister? Because 'la raison au sein de l'uniforme danger-eusement ballotte et se raréfie: un esprit en mal de notions doit d'abord s'approvisionner d'apparences' (PPC, 58). So Ponge prefers surfaces above all: the variations of the orange's skin, 'juste assez rugueux pour accrocher dignement la lumiere', to the sponge (PPC, 42); the crust of the loaf, with its 'plans si nettement articulés', to the crumb (PPC, 46).

For 'les choses les plus simples dans la nature ne s'abordent pas sans y mettre beaucoup de formes. (. . .) C'est pourquoi l'homme (. . .) se précipite aux bords ou à l'intersection des grandes choses pour les définir', and why Ponge in his poem chooses 'Bords de mer' instead of the sea's inscrutable depths (PPC, 58-60). This is no doubt why plants, and especially trees, have a large place in Ponge's work. With the apparent randomness of their site and growth (cf. PPC, 85), their tendency to merge into one mass, the fact that they are alive but do not move, their apparent 'volonté d'expression' only ever resulting in a single word (cf. PPC, 81-2), they combine in their ambiguities the inert formlessness, the 'vice' of water—an element—with the distinctiveness of an object. They are fascinating, but also sinister, in their lack of individuality, the monotony of their expression.

It is the ambiguity of trees that guarantees them some individuality: they carry within themselves a manifest 'intersection' of qualities which makes them tolerable and enables the mind to grasp them. It is indeed the outstanding characteristic of the world in Ponge's representation of it, that it exists in this mode. The only way elements, the most generic and formless of phenomena, can be grasped is through the introduction and juxtaposition of conflicting qualities. The element is then experienced as an oscillation between these qualities, a relationship. Fire, for example, spreads 'à la fois comme une amibe et comme une girafe, bondit du col, rampe du pied' (PPC, 47): the contrasting movements introduce vertical and horizontal co-ordinates, making it possible to get the measure of the amorphous element. This is a common, if often discreet, procedure in Ponge; a clear example is the geometry of the walls, gutter, roof, clothes-line and window in 'Pluie', a firmer version of the 'network' intuitively sensed, or hoped for, in the rain (PPC, 31-2).

To render the element water, like the element earth, it is necessary to inform it, to distinguish a parcel of it: hence the choice of the glass of water (GRM, 153) and the pebble, the product of the 'effort de ce monstre informe [the water] sur le monstre également informe de la pierre' (PPC, 100). For if the mind can only envisage the sea with equanimity where it meets the land, it can only grasp the element water by considering the *obstacles* to its 'vice' and by transforming them imaginatively into unlike qualities of water: 'ce vice, qui le rend rapide, précipité ou stagnant, amorphe ou féroce, amorphe *et* féroce, féroce térébrant, par exemple; rusé, filtrant, contournant' (PPC, 62). And if the *hand* should try to grasp water, 'elle m'échappe et cependant me marque' (PPC, 62-3).

Ponge's world, then, is of orderly disorder; but order implies discontinuity, and the mind depends on it for its balance. This tension or oscillation between discrete, and usually unlike, constituents is what distinguishes objects in Ponge's representation of them. For even the individual object always tends to an unsettling elemental homogeneity in that as an object of consciousness it tends to become the sole, obsessive, object of consciousness:

> *La variété des choses est en réalité ce qui me construit.* (. . .) *Si je n'en considère qu'une*, je disparais: elle m'annihile. Et (. . .) s'il faut donc que j'existe, à partir d'elle, ce ne sera, ce ne pourra être que par une certaine création de ma part à son propos. Quelle création? *Le texte.*
>
> (GRM, 12-13)

The creation is an act of *language*, the dynamic, absurd, mode of existence of the individual, and it will protect him, through ordered discontinuity in the form of conjunction, opposition, contradiction, paradox, oxymoron, and negation, against the threat of immobility, hypnosis, 'annihilation', posed by homogeneity.

So in the ditch, the snails 'en sont un élément constitutif mais vagabond' (PPC, 52), almost indistinguishable from the earth:

> Ils en emportent, ils en mangent, ils en excrémentent. Elle les traverse. Ils la traversent. C'est une interpénétration du meilleur goût parce que pour ainsi dire ton sur ton—avec un élément passif, un élément actif, le passif baignant à la fois et nourissant l'actif— qui se déplace en même temps qu'il mange.
>
> (PPC, 51)

And the snail is saved from formlessness by its shell (PPC, 54), so that it is both vulnerable and sheltered, 'à la fois si collé au sol (. . .) et si capable de [se] décoller du sol pour rentrer en [lui-même]' (PPC, 52). In the air, the butterfly is 'une allumette volante', yet 'sa flamme n'est pas contagieuse' (PPC, 56). The 'vaste saoulerie' of the growing ferns is in fact a series of 'pulsations brèves' (PPC, 36). The fascinating ambiguity of plants lies in the hell of their only forms of address being to the eye and nose (PPC, 82); so that while 'ils ne sont qu'une volonté d'expression' or 'de formation', they cannot possibly 'se former autrement que *d'une manière*' (PPC, 82, 83).

The very earth, 'notre humble et magnifique séjour' (PPC, 93),

is seen as the product of the 'bonds pâteux' of volcanic magma and the
'lente catastrophe du refroidissement' (PPC, 92, 93-4). The tension in
these paradoxical slow-motion jumps of its evolution from state to
state is matched, in speaking of the pebble, by the periphrastic refer-
ence to rock and sand as the 'formes de son antique état' and the
'formes de son futur' (PPC, 98). The pebble fascinates, both because
it is half-way between these two states and because it is on the shore,
alternately claimed and rejected by the tide, half-way between land and
sea. The shore itself, the archetypal edge permitting the mind to envis-
age the ocean with equanimity, exists in two modes simultaneously:
'repoussée par les profondeurs quoique jusqu'à un certain point fami-
liarisée avec elles' (PPC, 58-9). In the sea, the shrimp is fascinating
because, almost invisible, half solid, half water, it seems the perfect
product of 'la confusion marine (. . .) à son comble (. . .) où les
ondulations liquides sans cesse se contredisent (. . .). Une diaphanéité
utile autant que ses bonds y ôte enfin à sa présence même immobile
sous les regards toute continuité' (PPC, 88). The mollusc is perhaps
even more ambiguous than the crustacean: it is a formless plasma,
simply contained by the shell, and yet the shell is its own secretion;
while if it has 'une énergie puissante', this is only to 'se renfermer'
(PPC, 50). When washed up on the shore, the tiny shell may appear as
'un énorme monument, en même temps colossal et précieux' (PPC,
74), and in looking at it one has an ambiguous experience of concrete
and abstract, presence and absence, which is disturbing and therefore
increases one's pleasure (cf. PPC, 75-6).

Whether the shell is empty or inhabited does not matter, it looks
the same and the effect is the same. It can 'occur to one' that it is
inhabited or one can 'add an inhabitant to it' by imagining it back
under the water (cf. PPC, 74). It comes to the same thing: each of
these inferences is an abstraction from the appearance, a notion.
This mode of 'presence' of the creature in the shell is an instance, as
regards shellfish, of the perfect proportion of the secretion or shell to
its body, and as regards man, of the 'disproportion grotesque de son
imagination et de son corps' (PPC, 76). This is brought out in the
contrast of the perfect monument of the shell and the monstrous
pyramids and cathedrals (PPC, 74, 75). As we have seen, the 'véritable
sécrétion du mollusque homme' is *la parole* , perfectly proportioned to
and yet completely different in form from his body (PPC, 77). The wish
here is that man might use his gifts 'à l'ajustement, non à la dispro-
ortion', that he might build from this secretion 'une demeure pas beau-
coup plus grosse que son corps', that 'toutes ses imaginations, ses

raisons soient là comprises' (PPC, 76). The 'presence' of the creature
here is an abstraction from an appearance, in this case a secretion/shell,
that is, an abstraction *as it were from* language; and at the same time it
is an example of a secretion/language-as-an-abstraction, manifestly
containing ('comprises') *both* the notions of shellfish in terms of
which the creature is inferred ('raisons') *and* the imaginative reference
('imaginations') of notions and inferred creature both to one another
and to man, the abstracting agent. The imagination *is* the language, both
inasmuch as language is necessary for the formulation, retention and
application of the laws or notions with reference to which imagination
operates, and because it is itself a new application of them, a new
combination or notion.

It is clear how 'un esprit en mal de notions doit d'abord s'approv-
isionner d'apparences'. The condition for appearance is discontinuity—
the edge or intersection of discrete constituents. In contemplating
anything, Ponge wants to fix its notion: 'Il s'agit de l'objet comme
notion (. . .) de l'objet dans la langue française, dans l'esprit français'
(GRM, 33). This necessitates the analytic, imaginative introduction of
limits. But this imaginative act is necessarily linguistic, and the essence
of Ponge's poetry consists not simply of synthetic notions, but of the
juxtaposition of these with the analytic introduction of limits, the
condition of the notions.

So the comparison of nature to clockwork—itself analytic—is only
possible after the inference 'par l'esprit seul' of various states of stone
from its fragmentary appearances in the world, while this activity
itself consists of a series of imaginative anthropomorphic compari-
sons and is aimed at fixing the 'notion' of stone (PPC, 92-6). So also, it
is not enough to define as 'liquid' 'ce qui préfére obéir à la pesanteur,
plutôt que maintenir sa forme, ce qui refuse toute forme pour obéir à sa
pesanteur' (PPC, 62): this notion, itself characterised by the anthro-
pomorphically presented discrete constituents of refusal and obedience,
has to be followed by the analytic anthropomorphic comparison ('idée
fixe', 'vice') and the listing of unlike attributes mentioned above.

III

Everything depends on the secretion/language. The presence of limits
—order and form, as a counter to the amorphous and elemental—in the
guise of discrete and usually unlike constituents characterises both
objects and designation in Ponge, and manifests his need to proceed
with 'précaution' (PPC, 87), with 'discrétion' (PPC, 78), with measure.
There is a sober, 'scientific' mode: the rain is 'une masse donnée de

vapeur en précipitation' (PPC, 32); from the tip of the cigarette there
falls 'selon un rythme à detérminer un nombre calculable de petites
masses de cendres' (PPC, 40); the plant has the power to 'accomplir
sa propre synthèse aux dépens seuls du milieu inorganique qui l'envi-
ronne' (PPC, 86); there are references to vectors (PPC, 79), and 'l'exha-
laison de l'acide carbonique par la fonction chlorophyllienne' (PPC, 85).
Most of the poems proceed with confident descriptive generalisations
such as are used to convey information in textbooks on botany, zoology
or geology. Most are full of the conjunctive devices that characterise
sober, precise, reflective, informative—'logical'— discourse: *et* and *mais*,
naturally, often *quoique, pourtant,* and *cependant,* and very many
conjunctive adverbs or adverbial phrases like *ainsi, d'ailleurs, de plus,
ou plutôt*—these and similar words and phrases appearing far more
often in Ponge than is usual in poetry.

Yet very often the sobriety becomes pedantry: for example, the
juice of the squeezed orange is 'accompagné de rafraîchissement, de
parfum, certes, — mais souvent aussi de la conscience amère d'une
expulsion prématurée de pépins' (PPC, 41). And the pedantry, as this
example suggests, usually becomes periphrasis, and the periphrasis
usually becomes metaphor (very often anthropomorphic). For example,
man can channel water where he likes, and yet

> ... le soleil et la lune sont jaloux de cette influence exclusive, et
> ils essayent de s'exercer sur elle lorsqu'elle se trouve offrir la prise
> de grandes étendues (. . .). Le soleil alors prélève un plus grand
> tribut. Il la force à un cyclisme perpétuel, il la traite comme un
> écureuil dans sa roue.
>
> (PPC, 62)

Even the scientific terminology works in the analogical mode: the
mass of vapour in precipitation is in fact the mainspring of the clock-
work to which the rain is compared (PPC, 32); 'le temps occupé en
vecteurs se venge toujours, par la mort' (PPC, 79)—the world defeats
the pretensions of science and philosophy to define or describe it in
categories, the text mocks those pretensions through the anthropomor-
phic metaphor, and this textual operation is itself a metaphor for the
process in the world outside the text. In fact the caution and discretion
represent an imaginative effort at uttering the objects with their own
measure (cf. Pr, 120), and always result in a tension between two modes
of discourse which are usually separate but are here associated: the infer-
ential, tending to and using definitions and laws of behaviour, and the

fantastic, analysis through the conjunction of unlikes.

This is clearest in Ponge's characteristic methods of making the text *adéquat* or equivalent to the object. The urge to do this is made explicit several times in *Le Parti pris des choses* (and very often in other works). Since the crate is made to be destroyed after use, 'Il convient (. . .) de ne s'appesantir longuement' on its fate (PPC, 38); the 'study' of the orange has been 'menée aussi rondement que possible' (PPC, 42); the very rarity of precious stones 'justement doit faire qu'on ne leur accorde que peu de mots très choisis dans un discours sur la nature équitablement composé' (PPC, 78). This form of rhetoric is one of the simplest ways in which Ponge's poetry forces the reader to give a new attention to objects, 'en dehors de leur valeur habituelle de signification' (Pr, 120). That the orange should be the object of a rhetorical study at all raises the question of what things usually are studied and how, and therefore of what faculties of judgement and expression are used in such a study.

Even where this equivalence is not mentioned explicitly, it is always apparent in practice. On the level of the word, the sound will be seen as in some way inseparable from its sense: 'A mi-chemin de la cage au cachot la langue française a cageot' (PPC, 38); 'Au contraire des escarbilles qui sont les hôtes des cendres chaudes, les escargots aiment la terre humide' (PPC, 51); there is the happy coincidence that the colour of orange juice ('ambre'—cf. PPC, 41)

> . . . mieux que le jus de citron, oblige le larynx à s'ouvrir largement pour la prononciation du mot comme pour l'ingestion du liquide, sans aucune moue appréhensive de l'avant-bouche dont il ne fait pas se hérisser les papilles.
>
> (PPC, 42)

This form of irony ensures that the reader reacts to the concrete and the referential aspects of the word in terms of one another, and helps to set up the network of associations which gives the poem its structure. It is found above all as double or multiple meaning, and often as a kind of etymological pun. Take the first sentence of 'L'Orange':

> Comme dans l'éponge il y a dans l'orange une aspiration à reprendre contenance après avoir subi l'épreuve de l'expression.
>
> (PPC, 41)

The phonetic relation of 'éponge' and 'orange', a relation of comparison

(nasal + [ʒ]) and contrast (they are different nasals), is parallel to and
brings out the *comparison and therefore contrast* between the objects
sponge and orange. Then there is the double meaning of 'aspiration'
(an 'aspiring to' something and a 'breathing in') and 'contenance'
('capacity' and 'countenance or bearing'): in each case the meaning is
only double because the words are applied anthropomorphically to
objects, so that again the relation of comparison is seen to be also
necessarily a relation of contrast. Then, the word for the squeezing of
a fruit is 'pression', not 'expression' (now archaic in this sense). 'Exp-
ression' is the noun corresponding to 'exprimer', sometimes used tech-
nically or pedantically in the sense of 'extraire, faire sortir par la
pression'. The word for to squeeze a fruit is 'presser'. Encountering
expression here, the reader is forced to consider its similarity to and
difference from *pression*: forgotten (etymological) physical connotat-
ions are reintroduced into *expression*, but at the same time the differ-
ence between concrete-abstract linguistic expression and physical
squeezing is brought out. The use of *expression*, then, firstly draws
attention to its etymology and to related words—'au niveau des
RACINES, où se confondent les choses et les formulations' (GRM, 198)
—a form of association and suggestion which is an important element
in the 'semantic density' of language (cf. EPS, 170). Secondly, in the
context as a whole, where language is so important as theme and as
motif, it recalls the potentially discountenancing *épreuve* of linguistic
expression, where so much is at stake for the individual. The physical
connotations of expression are taken up and strengthened a few lines
later, with the 'expulsion prématurée de pépins', and yet again in the
second paragraph with the change to 'oppression' (PPC, 41). Expres-
sion is seen as an ordeal imposed physically from the outside. Yet in
the final paragraph, devoted entirely to the pip, the fruit is 'une
explosion sensationnelle', within which is the pip, 'la raison d'être du
fruit' (PPC, 42): expression is only an ordeal if unresisting, 'premature',
forced into a lack of measure. The 'raison d'être du fruit' is double,
both general cause of the existence of oranges, and specific purpose of
this orange's existence; and it is in preserving the balance or measure
between these absolutes, in the resistance of consciousness (purpose)
to blind necessity (cause), that expression is happiest.

    There are scores of examples of such double or multiple meanings
and the networks of associations they generate. The effect is to set
up a rapid oscillation between the terms, a dynamic relation of one to
the other, which constitutes the reality expressed. It is a way of shaking
the reader back into self-awareness, away from the 'annihilating'

immobility of conventional attitudes to the objects involved.

Ponge also achieves density through alliteration and assonance. Sometimes this is discreet, with a measure to match that of the orange's skin (*'juste* assez rugueux pour accrocher *dignement* la lumière — my italics); for example:

> . . . l'épiderme extrêmement mince mais très pigmenté, acerbement sapide.

> (PPC, 42)

The [m]'s are first associated with the extreme thinness, because of their repetition in the first three words. Then their presence in 'mais', and then in 'pigmenté' and 'acerbement' (the third instance of the nasal [mã]), binds together the extremely *slight* skin and the extremely *full* colour, and then both with the savour. So the alliteration realises the potential *et* in the 'mais', bringing discrete constituents (small quantity/ great quantity/; mass/colour/savour) into a relationship where their similarity and difference is seen to be one and the same thing. This phonetic suggestion takes a different form, but with the same effect, in the juxtaposition of 'acerbement' and 'sapide' to suggest *acide*. And the position of these words at the end of the phonetic chain naturally generates the typically Pongian synaesthetic suggestion of the acid as a 'thin' taste. It is here that the earlier reference to the pronunciation of *ambre* opening the larynx without any 'moue appréhensive' plays a role: not only in emphasising the concreteness of the nasals, but at the end of the poem, when the pip is compared to a 'minuscule citron'. The [y]'s and [õ] do necessitate a *moue*. The pip is used here to round off the comparative-contrastive circle: not only is an orange not a lemon, its *essential quality* lies in not being like a lemon—that is, in a *difference* revealed through comparison.

A similar phonetic and referential doubleness occurs when the pip, white outside and green in the middle, is seen as presenting 'la dureté relative et la verdeur (non d'ailleurs entièrement insipide) du bois, de la branche, de la feuille'. The 'verdeur' is multiple: basically nowadays the 'vigour of the young', it has here, because it is applied to wood and leaf, and because of the earlier reference to green, the etymological sense of 'greenness of new wood', and also, through its association with lemon and orange, one of its regular senses, 'acidity of green fruit'—even though it is not here referentially applied to fruit. The 'insipide' links phonetically with the earlier 'acerbement sapide' and the suggested *acide* to reinforce the presence of this logically absent sense! This

shimmering play of comparison-contrast and presence-absence is the
same oscillation between discrete constituents as is found right from
the start of 'L'Orange' (as indeed in any of Ponge's poetic texts), where
the pip is first introduced in terms of the double physical squeezing/
linguistic expression. The pip itself is the multiple 'raison d'être du fruit':
cause of all oranges, purpose of this one, and ironic mode of existence
of the text 'L'Orange'. This creation of multiple structural relations in
the text is how Ponge realises the density, the 'thereness' of the object,
in its manifest absence.

Sometimes the alliteration and assonance are less discreet, as with
the monotonous elemental sea, which is incapable of discretion, only
ever able to utter a single word:

> Mais une seule et breve parole est confiée aux cailloux et aux
> coquillages, qui s'en montrent assez remués, et [le flot] expire en
> la proferant; et tous ceux qui le suivent expireront aussi en profé-
> rant la pareille, parfois par temps a peine un peu plus fort clamee.
>
> (PPC, 59)

The grotesque repetition of unvoiced plosives and sibilants contrasts
with the wit and erudition in the double meanings ('remués', 'expire',
'proférer') to bring out both the simple physical aspect of utterance
and its powerful abstract aspect—more powerful, by polarity, than
the pathetic ocean.

Examples of these forms of semantic density may be found through-
out Ponge's work, and the carefully wrought 'coincidence' is always so
happy as to create sets of relations in the text between phenomena
which outside the text are not usually seen as related. Hence it not
only draws attention to the necessary relation of form and content
in the text, it suggests necessary relations between text and outside
world and *in* the outside world between the phenomena linked in the
text. But the point is precisely that it does *no more* than suggest them,
so that the necessity of its structure—its measure—is not identical to
that of the object rendered, but analogous to it.

This analogical necessity of structure is the form taken by the
equivalence of text to object on all other levels as well. On the level
of the sentence, we can take two examples. First, the last sentence
of 'L'Huître', After a paragraph about the outside of the oyster, and one
about the inside, the final paragraph consists of one short sentence,
devoted to the pearl:

Parfois très rare une formule perle à leur gosier de nacre, d'où l'on
trouve aussitôt à s'orner.

(PPC, 43)

Here there is a reversal of conventional values, as in the case of the
precious stones. The pearl is small, rare and precious—and so is the
sentence. The reversal of values is obtained firstly through the contrast
with the peroration on the pearl one might conventionally have
expected, and from the relegation of the sentence to the very end.
But it is obtained also through the reversal of usage: 'rare' in appo-
sition, instead of 'rarement'; the anthropomorphic metaphor of
'gosier' — as if the pearl were some sort of opaque, soundless word
choking the oyster; and above all 'une formule perle' instead of 'une
perle se forme'. Ironically, the features which make the sentence
precious are precisely those which devalue the pearl: it is simply 'a
little shape' and a 'chemical formula', which forms like a drop. After
this, how such a thing might be decorative is anybody's guess. The
effect is, through the brilliantly ironical language, to restore to oyster
and pearl their own measure, *and* to draw attention to the moral
faculty of judgement expressed in the comparison and contrast with
convention.

A different sort of example, but equally typical, is the last sentence
of 'Bords de mer':

Ni par l'aveugle poignard des roches, ni par la plus creusante tempête
tournant des paquets de feuilles à la fois, ni par l'œil attentif de
l'homme employé avec peine et d'ailleurs sans contrôle dans un
milieu interdit aux orifices débouchés des autres sens et qu'un bras
plongé pour saisir trouble plus encore, ce livre n'a été lu.

(PPC, 60)

At least two sentences have been fused into one (and would themselves
still have been complex, witness all the subordinates), and the
order of the resulting sentence is reversed, in that the main clause is
kept right to the end. A 'muddy' sentence, with long, untidy stress-
groups, and muddied most of all by the introduction, after the refer-
ences to the other senses, of the words 'et qu'un bras plongé pour
saisir trouble plus encore', just as, outside the text, the water is muddied,
after the vain use of the other faculties, by the introduction of the arm.
The muddiness of the sentence is analogous to the muddiness of the sea.

This same sentence exemplifies another very common procedure in

Ponge. A tortuous sentence structure, keeping to the end a verb or participle which would normally come earlier, creates a tension between the normal temporality of language and the resistance to time of the sentence. The slow-motion jumps of such sentences bring out the tension between the unchanging essential qualities of the object and the turning on to it of dynamic human consciousness. They have something of the hypnotising, 'annihilating' power of the obsessive object, literally almost arresting the consciousness: but this is realised linguistically, in the association of complex rare usage and common object, so that at the same time there is an experience (as in 'L'Orange') of concrete and abstract, presence and absence, like that afforded by the imaginative, linguistic contemplation of the shell. The sea's homogeneity is respected, but the threat of 'annihilation' removed, through the discrete unlike constituents in the sentence (most obviously the metaphor of the unread book) and of the sentence—the triumph of equivalence, or in other words, the *failure to express.*

Sometimes the structure of an entire text is equivalent to the object: for example, the symmetry of 'L'Orange'; the single paragraph of 'Le Cycle des saisons', analogous to the 'flot', the 'vomissement' of the trees' talk, and the simple monotonous cycle from this to losing their leaves again (PPC, 48-9); or, in contrast, the repetitions and interminable subdivisions and additions, analogous to plant growth, in 'Faune et flore' (PPC, 80-6).

Ponge's techniques meet the conditions for success laid down in 'La Crevette':

> un petit animal qu'il importe sans doute moins de nommer d'abord que d'évoquer avec précaution, de laisser s'engager de son mouvement propre dans le conduit des circonlocutions, d'atteindre enfin par la parole au point dialectique où le situent sa forme et son milieu, sa condition muette et l'exercice de sa profession juste.
>
> (PPC, 87)

For the closer the equivalence of text to object becomes, the clearer it becomes that there is no identity of the two, that there is a *point dialectique* not only of limits defining the object, but of these and those of the minds realising them linguistically. All these forms of expression are, both in themselves and in relation to one another, different forms of the oscillation between unlikes which is the mode of existence of phenomena in Ponge. Another example of the same thing, and very important in Ponge, is description through negation, saying what is *not* the case. To say that the ferns are 'ni bois pour construction, ni stères d'allumettes' (PPC, 36), is explicitly to see their characteristic quality in dynamic suspension between the conventional representation of a fern and objects never associated with it or one another—a difference. The law—homogeneous and elemental, inasmuch as there are no exceptions—that snails always move when they come out of their shells can only be grasped through positing a contrary hypothesis, negated by the snail's behaviour: 'l'on ne conçoit pas un escargot sorti de sa coquille et ne se mouvant pas' (PPC, 51). In both cases, comparison is brought to the reflective level, in that to say what is not the case implies a conscious judgement, modulating an automatic and inevitable process into a conscious and deliberate procedure.

All these devices are forms of qualification, or relation. The abundance of conjunctions and conjunctive adverbs is the archetype: that these should be left in—conventionally speaking a lack of polish—draws attention to the act of relating. Similar devices are the 'leaving in' of statements of intent, and the insistence in the texts themselves on equivalence in expression: the essential thing is the intentional *relation* between subject and object, in terms, inevitably, of other objects.

Hence the superabundance of anthropomorphic metaphor, the archetype of all comparisons: I am aware of the world through its difference from me. The characteristics of man are 'la parole et la morale' (PPC, 55), and the human qualities attributed to objects are nearly always moral ones: the aspirations of the orange, the pride and discretion of the snails (PPC, 53), the 'variété infinie des sentiments' of the plants (PPC, 85), and so on. Such comparisons bring out particularly clearly the *difference* between man, with language as his mode of being, and the expressionless non-human world. As Ponge says, it is impossible to describe objects from *their* point of view: 'Il y a toujours du rapport à l'homme. . .Ce ne sont pas les choses qui parlent entre elles mais les hommes entre eux qui parlent des choses et l'on ne peut aucunement sortir de l'homme' (Pr, 167). Language, the very factor through which man realises the impossibility of knowing himself objectively, makes it impossible to render objects other than anthropomorphically. The secretion/language is man's; and all metaphor, anthropomorphic metaphor particularly clearly, simply accepts and turns to account the comparative-contrastive, negatory operation of all language, putting the reader face to face with his own creative capacity for language—that is, a fully (consciously) human existence, 'dans le relatif' (cf. Pr, 215).

IV

The circle of the absurd is vicious when it is unbroken: when the need
for a reassuring order, everywhere apparent in Ponge, leads to sub-
mission to an inflexible law. Then the cyclic order becomes a vicious
circle, a continuous *manège*, and so, to those treading it, it is opaque,
amorphous, elemental, as homogeneous as the monotonous drone of
flabby lyricism. For this drone is the 'ronron de l'esprit d'hier' (GRM,
256), and Ponge's hostility to it is total: 'le moindre soupçon de ronron
poétique m'avertit seulement que je rentre dans le manège, et provoque
mon coup de reins pour en sortir' (TP, 258; cf. 257, and GRM, 256-7).
This 'effusion simplement subjective' (EPS, 27) of some 'trouble de
l'âme' (Pr, 186) is as depressing as that of the muddy sea, because its
muddiness is that of a spirit which has chosen to remain faithful to a
stultifying fixed notion of man (cf. Pr, 174, GRM, 254).

To attempt the contemplation of a human essence independent of
the outside world—'purely subjective'—is to attempt to shut one's
eyes to the absurd: this absence of definition is precisely *trouble
d'âme*, the mind which 'dangereusement ballotte et se raréfie' (PPC, 58);
and it is presumably with reference to this paradox of a vicious circle
or *manège* of persistent fidelity to a fixed notion of man as fear of
the unknown but also as a source of despair, that Ponge demands of
art 'Rien de désespérant. Rien qui flatte le masochisme humain' (Pr,
186). This masochism is the 'désir de voir trouble' (GRM, 176), 'une
tendance à l'idéologie patheuse' (Pr, 186). *Patheux* is a happy coinage,
combining *pathétique* and *pâteux* to render the amorphous, 'annihil-
ating' quality of the vicious circle.

The aim is the advance of the mind (cf. Pr, 157; GRM, 257), but also
its pleasure (cf. GRM, 21). The progress and pleasure is in being dis-
turbed in one's accepted ideas (cf. GRM, 199, 257), being helped out
of the *manège*. This release is achieved in the imaginative *démesure*
through which meaning is realised: set against a grain of sand, the
shell will have some resemblance to monuments like the Pyramids,
but 'avec une signification beaucoup plus étrange que ces trop incon-
testables produits d'homme' (PPC, 74). Language in Ponge is precisely
a 'contestation', an ironic imaginative assigning of limits which results
in a refreshing disturbance, the realisation of the quality of *difference*
both of object — 'Il faut, à travers les analogies, saisir la qualitié diffé-
rentielle (. . .). Nommer la qualité différentielle (. . .), voilà le but, le
progrès' (GRM, 41-2)—and of speaker: for, like non-linguistic objects,

other writings tend to 'annihilate' him—'Il faut une création de ma part à leur propos (différence, originalité)' (GRM, 14; cf. 12-13).

In Ponge, the *démesure* is explicit in three ways: within single objects; between the conventional and the poetic-linguistic represent-ation of objects; and, in the very measure of expression, between language and the non-linguistic world. Hence the pleasure is the opposite of the unthinking 'annihilating' hypnosis produced by flabby lyricism or the indiscriminate welter of analogy. Yet the release and pleasure are afforded through—and are seen to be affordable only through—suggestion, since a relation cannot be described in phenomenal terms. It is here that Ponge's poems are poetic as opposed to informative, scientific, or explanatory. They operate metalogically, through the many forms of comparative-contrastive equivalence, through the 'caractère à la fois concret et abstrait, intérieur et extérieur du VERBE, (. . .) son épaisseur sémantique' (Pr, 201). Both the referential power and the physical presence of the word, together with the relation between the two, constitute its suggestiveness. The declared urge to equivalence, the constant thrust towards it through the manipulation of sound, multiple meaning, rhythm, syntax and textual structure, the anthropomorphism and the repeated presence of language as theme and as motif, bring out precisely the absurd ambiguity of language: to *be* the world in so far as the world is an object of consciousness, and yet to be itself a phenomenon *in* the world. It is the essential mode of man's awareness of himself as an individual lacking self-coincidence. A vital element of Ponge's poetry is that it fails, and is seen to fail, to express absolutely. This is how it embodies Ponge's belief that the essential thing is to create a text which 'works': 'c'est que pour [les poètes] enfin, qu'il signifie ou non quelque chose, le monde fonctionne. Et voilà bien après tout ce qu'on leur demande (aux œuvres comme au monde): la vie.' (GRM, 194). The successful text works, that is, analo-gously to the outside world, through the order of its manifold internal relations:

> L'épaisseur vertigineuse et l'absurdité du langage, considérées seules, sont manipulées de telle façon que, par la multiplication intérieure des rapports, les liaisons formées au niveau des racines et les signi-fications bouclées à double tour, soit créé ce fonctionnement qui seul peut rendre compte de la profondeur substantielle, de la variété et de la rigoureuse harmonie du monde.
>
> (GRP, 156)

—a density and a working like those of 'L'Orange'. So if man needs order for mental balance, this need not be a vicious circle. The order sensed in Ponge's universe is basically cyclical, and the notion of cycle, like that of order, involves the notion of discontinuity. It is in this sense that it is possible to break the vicious circle: through the imaginative, the *proper*, use of language—concrete and abstract, inside man and outside him, the fundamental mode of the absurd—to introduce the ordering voids of negatory, relational activity into the homogeneous elemental circle, and convert it into a cycle of discrete constituents, saccadic, like the apparent 'saoulerie' of the growing ferns.

There is surely no better way of accounting for the exultation, the extraordinary liberating disturbance, which Ponge's poems can provoke in the reader. They are unforgettable celebrations of the outside world: and it is precisely in being (metalogical) *celebrations* of the *outside* world—'définitions-descriptions esthétiquement et rhétoriquement adéquates' (GRM, 20), and not simple (logical) descriptions or definitions or explanations—that they are celebrations also of *man's potential* for celebration, analogy, imagination, negation, relation. They are brilliant examples of the void, the *point dialectique* of speaker, reader and outside world, where man and world properly exist.

Notes

1. The following abbreviations are used: PPC *Le Parti pris des choses*; Pr *Proêmes*, published together in one volume by Gallimard in the 'Poésie' series (Paris, 1967); GRP: *Le Grand Recueil, Pièces*; GRM *Le Grand Recueil, Méthodes* (both Paris, Gallimard, 1961); TP *Tome premier* (Paris, Gallimard, 1965); EPS *Entretiens de Francis Ponge avec Philippe Sollers* (Paris, Gallimard/Seuil, 1970).
    I take most of my examples from PPC (first published 1942) and Pr (1948). PPC is still Ponge's best-known work, and it and Pr are the most readily available. Some tendencies are more prominent in later works: for example, the explicit exploration of the phonetic and etymological associations, or even the shape, of a word, and their relation to sense; or the juxtaposition of statements of intent, exploration of associations and suggestion, and successive attempts at synthesis. These are the very stuff of the vivid and kaleidoscopic texts of *La Rage de l'expression* (in TP) and sometimes of *Le Grand Recueil*.
2. For the sake of concision, and to respect Ponge's use of *parole* rather than *langage* (and sometimes instead of *mot*), I shall refer from now on to the 'speaker', even when talking about written texts.

11 YVES BONNEFOY: THE SENSE OF THINGS

John D. Price

In this chapter I shall firstly give an account of Bonnefoy's attitude towards the material world and show how it derives more from philosophical considerations than from the poet's reactions to sensory data. I shall continue by indicating the ways in which this attitude determines the vocabulary and themes characteristic of his poetry. Finally I shall deal with the way Bonnefoy presents the material world in two collections, *Du Mouvement et de l'immobilité de Douve* and *Pierre écrite*.[1]

It is however the title of an earlier work, *Anti-Platon*, which indicates most clearly the explicitly philosophical nature of Bonnefoy's approach to the world: that is to say, he is concerned not directly with what is perceived through the five senses, but with the sense that man makes of it. Perception is not to be directly related but channelled by the poet who thereby fulfils an essentially metaphysical duty: 'le devoir de donner un sens à ce qui est' (ALP, 202). Bonnefoy's title declares his rejection of the Western tradition of idealistic philosophy symbolised by the Greek thinker, which believes in a reality and knowledge both other than and preferable to that which the senses provide. The grounds for his opposition are best expressed in a few lines from the essay 'Les Tombeaux de Ravenne':

> Parce qu'on meurt dans ce monde et pour nier le destin l'homme a bâti de concepts une demeure logique où les seuls principes qui vaillent sont de permanence et d'identité. Demeure faite de mots, mais éternelle.
>
> (TR, 22)

Bonnefoy is not hostile to the awareness that the world is not ideal, or to consequent desires for an improvement; what he regards as dangerous is that kind of idealism which considers itself a self-fulfilling and self-satisfying creation, taking an 'I think it, therefore it is' attitude to its refuge of a dream made of words, built and organised by the intellect. Above all he objects to that kind of idealism which seeks to deny the reality of death and which thereby devalues the material world as a place for man to live.

It is to combat this strain of thought, which stretches from Parmen-

ides to Hegel and beyond, and which has close formal parallels with the
Christian belief in a non-terrestrial heaven, that Bonnefoy advocates
acceptance of the material world, 'l'ici et le maintenant qu'a sacralisés
toute mort' (ALP, 195), and proposes: 'Faisons une nouvelle fois (. . .)
le pas baudelairien de l'amour des choses mortelles' (ALP, 203). The
accent in the latter quotation should be laid on 'mortelles' rather than
on 'choses': Bonnefoy does not take the part of the being of things,
examining, like Ponge, their physical attributes and using these as a
starting-point for his work, but of their *becoming*—which implies their
shortly being no longer, and losing those very attributes that the senses
perceive. The example he gives in 'Les Tombeaux de Ravenne' is
precisely that of a 'feuille brisée' (TR, 36), and in *Anti-Platon* he had
already described a consciousness 'sensible seulement à la modulation,
au passage, au frémissement de l'équilibre, à la présence affirmée dans
son éclatement déjà de toute part' (AP, 17). Bonnefoy thus seems to be
committed to a principle rather than to an object; what he is concerned
with is not the thing-in-itself, its appearance and other sensory qualities
united in a packet of perception, but the relationship that human
consciousness creates and maintains with it. Such a relationship is
essentially spiritual in nature, an attitude of mind rather than of eye,
'la foi pour orienter dans le monde mieux que la vue';[2] non-sensual,
it can only find material expression through language, in the widest,
semiotic, sense of the term.

    For Bonnefoy, of course, the expressive medium is that of words,
which, by naming, link the namer and the thing named; hence the
declaration that we find in 'Les Tombeaux de Ravenne': 'Je ne prétends
que nommer. Voici le monde sensible. Il faut que la parole, ce sixième
et ce plus haut sens, se porte à sa rencontre et en déchiffre les signes'
(TR, 32).

    Further, language permits the creation and expression of relation-
ships, not merely between consciousness and the material world, but
also, by linking them in its own structures, between the various elements
of the latter. In this way a unity can be created, and Bonnefoy describes
the aim of the poem as follows: 'Celui-ci ne prétend, en effet, qu'à
intérioriser le réel. Il recherche les liens qui unissent *en moi* les choses'
(RM, 100).

    This insistence on affirming and even creating the *unity* of the
world rather than describing its sensory qualities is, of course, meta-
physical and idealistic, as is the question that Bonnefoy poses about
unity later in the same essay: 'Que vaudrait-elle, par exemple, sans
communion ni justice?' (RM, 122-3). These, however, are aims, not

ontological assertions. Whereas Plato and the Western religious tradition in general affirm the positive existence of such a mode of being in a distant and changeless world, Bonnefoy simply considers his experience as an intuition of a possible existence in the material world.

In *L'Arrière-pays* he describes himself as 'soucieux d'une transcendance, mais aussi d'un lieu où elle aurait sa racine. [et] c'est à celui-ci, "vaine forme de la matière", que je conférerais la qualité d'absolu. . .'[3]

In other words, Bonnefoy's poetry can be seen as an attempt to reunite two worlds, the divine and the material, that the West has seen fit to keep firmly apart, considering them to be incompatible; referring to Plato's world of Forms, Bonnefoy has written: 'Que ce monde existe, j'en suis sûr: il est, dans le lierre et partout, la substantielle immortalité' (TR, 37).

In the poetry, two major strands of vocabulary and theme are thus interwoven: one taken from perception, describing or more correctly representing the physical world, and one drawn from traditional metaphysical sources, principally mythology and legend. The terms of philosophy are themselves little used; there are a few slighting references to 'les Idées' in the earlier work (eg AP, 9), but that is all.

The question I want to examine is how Bonnefoy attempts to marry these two rather conflicting areas of vocabulary and theme, while recognising and affirming the primacy of the material world. The question of whether he succeeds, and, if so, where—even if it is meaningful, given that the effect of a poem can be quite different from the intentions we are assured lay behind it, and depends on the reader as well as the poet—is not being debated, since this belongs to the realm of faith as much as to that of analysis. All that can be done here is to give some idea of the interplay between the two conflicting strands and the way in which this varies during the course of the three books under discussion.

'La parole', Bonnefoy writes, is a sixth sense, acting as a medium between consciousness and the world by virtue of its ability to name the elements of which the latter is made up. This leads us to consider first the question of Bonnefoy's poetic vocabulary: what sort of names does he use?

To name is not to describe; and we have already seen that it is not Bonnefoy's aim to write about the world's appearance, but to make sense of and unify its fundamental elements. What is required for this task, he believes, are words that convey as little about the physical

appearance of the object they name as possible, representatives of the
world rather than representations of it. Of course any word, in that it
denotes a class of objects or events, is a representative of that class
rather than a representation of a particular object in it. Some are,
however, less representational than others, since they carry less defining
information about the referent: a general word like 'tree' tells us less
about the physical qualities of the object in question (shape of leaves,
etc) than a more specific word like 'oak'. Given Bonnefoy's distrust of
physical description, of words which 'ne font que (. . .) décrire, n'ont
pour contenu qu'un *aspect*, difficilement perpétuable dans l'inté-
riorisation que la poésie se donne pour tâche d'effecteur' (RM, 104-5),
it follows that he will prefer to use these more general, less definite
words; and in 'L'Acte et le lieu de la poésie' he defines a poetic vocab-
ulary in the following way:

> Et il est vrai que dans une poésie véritable ne subsistent plus que ces
> errants du réel, ces catégories du possible, ces éléments sans passé ni
> avenir, jamais entièrement engagés dans la situation présente, tou-
> jours en avant d'elle, et prometteurs d'autre chose, que sont le vent,
> le feu, la terre, les eaux—tout ce que l'univers propose d'indéfini.
> Eléments concrets mais universels. Ici et maintenant mais de toute
> part au-delà dans le dôme et sur les parvis de notre lieu et de notre
> instant. Omniprésents, animés.
>
> (ALP, 208)

Whether Bonnefoy is correct in thinking that a poetic vocabulary must
consist of such words is an open question. What is certain is that he
has carried out this belief in his own work, where general words are
used almost to the exclusion of specific ones. The most common are:
mort, nuit, feu, eau, jour, arbre, lumière, terre. In itself this is hardly
surprising, nor is frequency of occurrence by any means the sole
criterion of importance in a vocabulary: for by virtue of its very rarity
a word used only once or twice can stand out in importance against
its context. Nevertheless it remains true that it is the common words
that provide this context, and give the work as a whole its character-
istic tone or feel. What is more important in the present case is the
almost total lack of specific words; considering the frequency of the
words *pierre* and *arbre* it is remarkable that the type of stone or tree is
so rarely specified. *Marbre* occurs a few times, there are an *érable, a
sycomore* and a *myrte* in *Pierre écrite*, an *olivier* makes an occasional
appearance, but there is little, if anything else. Even when specific

names are used the reference usually has little to do with a physical appearance or sensation. To take the example of flowers (rare items in Bonnefoy's vocabulary and hence quickly dealt with), we find that there is one instance where the physical appearance is used as an image — 'le chrysanthème de l'écume' (HRD, 178) — and one metaphoric usage to indicate the peaceful and accepted passage of time:

> Ici, et jusqu'au soir. La rose d'ombres
> Tournera sur les murs. La rose d'heures
> Défleurira sans bruit.

(HRD, 177)

Apart from these two instances, flowers are mentioned on only three occasions, once in each of the three books, and always with strong associations with death. There is the 'dahlia des morts' (MID, 120) at the end of *Douve*, the 'fleurs hautes flétries' that form the 'bouquet noir' that the poet accepts from the death-figure in 'Les Guetteurs' (HRD, 148), and finally the evocation of the Persephone myth in *Pierre écrite*, with its references to jasmin and asphodel, the flowers of the after-life:

> Et je pense à Coré l'absente; qui a pris
> Dans ses mains le cœur noir étincelant des fleurs
> Et qui tombe, buvant le noir, l'irrévélé,
> Sur le pré de lumière—et d'ombre. Je comprends
> Cette faute, la mort. Asphodèles, jasmins
> Sont de notre pays.

(PE, 74)

The lack of importance that Bonnefoy attaches to detail in describing the transitory, inessential aspects of physical appearance is further confirmed when we concentrate our study on one area of perception, that of colour. Apart from *noir* and *gris*, which can be considered as not even being colours in the first place, but degrees of the monochromatic scale of black and white, the only colour to appear at all frequently is *rouge*, with the rest nowhere. A fundamental colour such as *vert* is rarely found, and *bleu* is confined to the pages of *Pierre écrite*.

In that part of his vocabulary that represents the material world Bonnefoy thus demonstrates his lack of concern with physical appearance. In order not to draw attention away from the fundamental

subject of his poetry, which is the relationship man believes himself to
have with external reality, the material world is presented in its outlines,
as an elemental sketch; and it is a significant fact that, while *Douve*
opens on an extremely visual note:

> Je te voyais courir sur des terrasses,
> Je te voyais lutter contre le vent
>
> (MID, 45)

the object of perception—that is the animal, vegetable and mineral
world conceived as a mortal and ever-changing totality, related to the
poet's consciousness by the act of giving it a name, Douve:

> Douve, je parle en toi; et je t'enserre
> Dans l'acte de connaître et de nommer.
>
> (MID, 79)

— is in fact in the process of disappearing, of being destroyed, of dying.
It is only once Douve is dead that any real, interior communication can
begin, by means of voices; from sight we move to sound, from external
perception to internal dialogue, from the object to the relationship.

It is perhaps worth recalling briefly at this point that the vast
majority of Bonnefoy's poems have at least implicitly this dialogue
form: the distance between himself and the world is inhabited by voices
and fragments of debate that provide a discussion about the world
and man's attitude to and relationship with it. The interlocutors change:
in *Douve* it is not only the poet and Douve who speak, but also, at one
point, the sun (MID, 109) and other, unidentified voices, symbolic
figures contributing to the debate. In *Pierre écrite* the dead them-
selves bear witness, and through much of the book the poet addresses,
not a female figure, like Douve, but a fellow human being:

> O moins à contre-jour, ô mieux aimée
> Qui ne m'est plus étrangère. Nous avons grandi, je le sais,
> Dans les mêmes jardins obscurs. Nous avons bu
> La même eau difficile sous les arbres.
>
> (PE, 76)

The final aspect of Bonnefoy's poetic vocabulary that requires attention
here is the words he draws from traditional sacred sources. Two major
points can be made.

The first concerns his use of sacred vocabulary: what is retained of the meaning of such words is not its formal, that is to say physically descriptive aspect, but its functional one. Thus, in *Pierre écrite* there is a reference to 'l'ange, qui est la terre' (PE, 80); here are united the traditional messenger of the spiritual world, whose function as the mediator of the divine is retained, and the physical world itself. Similar use is made of a word such as *église*, which traditionally refers to the protected dwelling-place of the divinity. Here again the spatial, formal aspect of the word's meaning is absent from phrases such as 'le feu s'est retiré, qui était mon église' (HRD, 129) and 'la pierre l'église obscure' (HRD, 131); in the same vein *parvis* is related to 'des eaux terreuses de novembre' (MID, 120) and the 'cri de l'oiseau chancelant' (HRD, 168). We can note in all these cases a union between the spiritual function indicated by the word and the material world as described by Bonnefoy; in this way the metaphysical concern and purpose of the sacred word is retained, while its traditional, formal expression is lost.

The other point concerns the frequent allusions to mythology. Although direct reference to individual myths are made, a general motif is more commonly evoked; like the world of matter, that of mythology is presented only in outline. Our own knowledge of Arthurian legend and Greek mythology, and of Bonnefoy's interest in them, demonstrated in his essays, permits us to link these to the themes of the sword in the stone that plays so large a role in *Hier régnant désert* and of the ferry of the dead in 'Aux arbres'. However, neither is explicitly named; in the latter instance, for example, it is not Cerberus and Charon who appear, but 'les chiens, avec l'informe nautonier' (MID, 67).

We can therefore conclude this brief study of Bonnefoy's poetic vocabulary by saying that two principles seem to govern its constitution, both stemming directly from his philosophical position: there is a preference for elemental, general words, and a corresponding non-insistence on physical description.

The images which form the thematic structure of Bonnefoy's poetry are of course primarily the 'éléments concrets mais universels', such as fire, water, wind and earth, which are by no means particular to Bonnefoy, since they recur with the inevitable frequency of archetypes in myths, legends and mystical poetry throughout the world. There are also the more explicit references to myth that I touched on briefly

at the end of the preceding section. In this section I will look firstly at
Bonnefoy's use of the night image, which occurs throughout his work;
secondly I will say something about his characteristic technique of
juxtaposing and uniting elements of different themes in one and the
same image; and finally I shall make a brief analysis of an important
aspect of the thematic structure of *Hier régnant désert*.

The theme of night is drawn directly from experience of living in
the world and also has a long and honourable history in literature,
more particularly in mystical poetry. One thinks of Pseudo-Dionysus
the Areopagite and Saint John of the Cross, or, in our own century,
Pierre-Jean Jouve and René Char. (cf. the chapter on Char in this book,
which is devoted to this theme.) The prime quality of night is that it
renders the material world invisible. It is therefore a highly suitable
motif for Bonnefoy's purpose and he uses many of its possibilities.
There is the theme of night as a time of trial, loss and death, leading
to spiritual enlightenment or dawn, a theme particularly stressed in
Douve and *Hier régnant désert*. Night is thus, like death, to be
accepted:

> Demande pour tes yeux que les rompe la nuit,
> Rien ne commencera qu'au delà de ce voile

> (MID, 92)

In the same book, the traditional mystical paradox of night and
illumination is made:

> La lumière profonde a besoin pour paraître
> D'une terre rouée et craquante de nuit

> (MID, 76)

In *Hier régnant désert* the same images of loss occur as the poet
journeys through the emptiness that precedes the dawn:

> Tu as marche, tu peux marcher, plus rien ne change,
> Toujours la même nuit qui ne s'achève pas

> (HRD, 132)

Towards the end of the book, its nocturnal action is resumed in the
poem fittingly called 'L'Ordalie' (HRD, 178-9).

In *Pierre écrite* somewhat differing uses of the theme are made.
In the eponymous section, the dead come forward to bear witness.

However, in the opening sequence 'L'Eté de nuit', night is no longer seen as a time of ordeal, but one of happiness in the passing timelessness of love:

> Longtemps ce fut l'été. Une étoile immobile
> Dominait les soleils tournants. L'été de nuit
> Portait l'été de jour dans ses mains de lumiére
> Et nous nous parlons bas, en feuillage de nuit.

(PE, 16)

Nevertheless, in spite of the suitability of the night image for Bonnefoy's purpose, it is hard to believe that either his individuality or his originality can lie in the awareness and simple use of what is after all one of the most common images in literature. The lines I have quoted from *Douve* and *Hier régnant désert* do little but recall the work of other mystic poets. The part of tradition seems here to predominate over that of perception, the theme's links with external reality seem to be at their most tenuous, and if Bonnefoy's poetry consisted solely of such lines it would not be very distinguishable from that of others— or very distinguished.

What is more individual is the way in which Bonnefoy links the theme with the others that go to make up his work. The quotation from 'L'Eté de nuit' gives an example of this technique, characteristic of these three books, of uniting different themes in one image. In this case two different time-scales—the progression of the seasons, and the succession of day and night—are juxtaposed, but the entire sequence is constructed around such connections, as the ship of the earth, 'navire d'un été' (PE, 12) and 'de vivre' (PE, 13), crosses the ocean of summer and 'le feuillage des morts' (PE, 13).

In itself, such a technique is not unique to Bonnefoy; it has strong associations with Surrealism. However, Bonnefoy makes use of it in a more systematic fashion, proceeding not so much (or not solely) from a chance perceptual experience as linking themes that have a functional thematic resemblance. Thus if, in *Douve*, fire and water are combined in an image it is because, in that book, they are both seen as destructive agents of mortality.

> Ayant livré sa tête aux basses flammes
> De la mer

(MID, 69)

Et le feu vient laver sa face

(MID, 70)

By his systematic use of this technique, Bonnefoy weaves a thematic
framework, once more demonstrating his distance from perceptual
experience by his re-assembling of it, and his concern for, and belief
in, the essential unity of the material world. As he says, 'the image's
function is to recreate and multiply the ties existing among things in
order that this unity will again become universally conceivable'.[4]

In the light of this, it is not surprising that one of the most common
thematic unions should be between two of the major representatives
of the physical world: the body, and the earth, or landscape. The
opening section of *Douve* is dominated by this union, which is found,
for example, in the following lines:

Le ravin pénètre dans la bouche maintenant,
Les cinq doigts se dispersent en hasards de forêt maintenant,
La tête première coule entre les herbes maintenant,
La gorge se farde de neige et de loups maintenant

(MID, 61)

Towards the end of *Pierre écrite* another such union is made:

J'imagine souvent, au-dessus de moi,
Un visage sacrificiel, dont les rayons
Sont comme un champ de terre labourée.

(PE, 73)

Where, as in these examples, it is '[des] éléments concrets mais univer-
sels' that are linked, some connection with the material world is maint-
ained; but in *Hier régnant désert* it is elements drawn from mythology
and legend that are juxtaposed to form the thematic framework. The
book relates the poet's progress through a long night of emptiness and
trial, a movement from anguish to acceptance:

Ici l'inquiète voix consent d'aimer
La pierre simple

(HRD, 176)

It is therefore a book of passage, of ordeal and ultimate arrival, and to
express this four major themes are linked: that of the crossing to

another shore; that of the reigniting of the flame, extinguished at the beginning of the book; that of the sword in the stone; and that of the bird call. These themes are not merely juxtaposed, but also, on occasion, interwoven, as in 'La flamme qui sera le navire et le port' (HRD, 133), and the lines

> Tu entendras
> Enfin ce cri brûlant, comme une épée
> Dans la paroi rocheuse

(HRD, 168)

Thus, during the mythologically related action of *Hier régnant désert* the material world is largely absent, at least until the concluding poems, and such elements of it as are mentioned are usually drawn from mythological symbolism and integrated into the symbolic framework of the book: again, what is individual is not the simple use of such-and-such a theme, but the forging of links between themes. However, this book of transition comes between two works in which the material world plays a larger role, and it is these that we must finally examine.

In *Douve* and *Pierre écrite* the material world is presented in two very different ways. As we have already seen, the opening section of *Douve* depicts Douve in the process of autumnal destruction and in the throes of death; this completed, the action moves on to a symbolic plane, where the various voices hold their debate.

In *Pierre écrite* the material world is seen in a completely different light. Some idea of the difference can be gained from the examples already quoted of the thematic union of the body and the earth: the destruction of autumn has given way to the fullness of summer, and even if autumn is mentioned in the pages of *Pierre écrite* , it is as the season of 'mellow fruitfulness' rather than that of fallen leaves. It is late September or October rather than November. The trees, which in *Douve* bore only branches, are now laden with fruit. Other examples of the change could be cited, but a short quotation seems best to sum up the mood of the book:

> Nous n'avons plus besoin
> D'images déchirantes pour aimer.

(PE, 75)

Rather than the emphasis being on the continual destruction of the material world, which dominated *Douve*, there is in *Pierre écrite* a greater acceptance of the moment as it passes. In other words, the world seems to be viewed more immediately, in the sense that perception is no longer channelled through a mythological framework of reference. This is especially the case in the section 'Un feu va devant nous', from which the following poem is taken:

> Rayures bleues et noires.
> Un labour qui dévie vers le bas du ciel.
> Le lit, vaste et brisé comme le fleuve en crue.
> —Vois, c'est déjà le soir,
> Et le feu parle auprès de nous dans l'éternité de la sauge.
>
> (PE, 58)

This is probably the most simply descriptive poem in the book, and to that extent it is an exception; elsewhere, as we shall see, perception is associated with that concern I have termed metaphysical. Nevertheless, the mythological framework of both *Douve* and *Hier régnant désert* has lapsed. The change can be illustrated by tracing the course of one image through the three books, that of the bird.

In *Douve* it occurs only rarely, and is associated mainly with the mythological motif of the Phoenix (cf. MID, 77). However, in the course of *Hier régnant désert* the bird changes character. First, like Douve, it accepts the principle of death and becomes 'l'oiseau qui s'est dépris d'être Phénix', making 'un lent retour à la matière d'arbre' (HRD, 135). Such an action is distinctly unbirdlike, and it is clear that 'l'oiseau' is still a symbol rather than a thing of flesh, blood and feathers. Later in the same book it is seen as a guide:

> L'oiseau avait saisi
> De son chant vaste et simple et avide nos coeurs,
> Il conduisait
> Toutes voix dans la nuit où les voix se perdent
>
> (HRD, 163)

Here already, another of its attributes is its song, and from the moment of the arrival on the other shore, it is this that becomes overridingly important, allowing the bird itself to change from a symbolic figure to a simple object of perception. In *Pierre écrite* the bird-song is no longer associated with the mythological framework of which it forms

part in *Hier régnant désert,* and it too is presented simply as it passes
rather than as a sign or symbol:

> Chemins, parmi
> La matière des arbres. Dieux, parmi
> Les touffes de ce chant inlassable d'oiseaux
>
> (PE, 54)

Here it is the bird-song itself that is held to be the resting-place of the
divine. As early as 'Les Tombeaux de Ravenne' Bonnefoy makes a
similar point in his prose works, writing of the 'conjonction d'une
immortalité impossible et d'une immortalité sentie' that is to be found
in ephemeral experience, such as bird-song or 'le jeu de l'écume au
sommet de la vague' (TR, 36-7); but it is only in *Pierre écrite* that he
seems able to express it as such in his poetry.

In this book the world is presented more immediately. Nevertheless
it is not, even here, seen for itself: its appearance is not closely des-
cribed, it is still considered in terms of '[des] éléments concrets mais
universels'. That is to say, the poet's viewpoint has not changed in this
important way; and, though the view without the mythological frame-
work is clearer, his fundamental concern remains the question of man's
relationship with the world—and if this is described as it passes, in
moments of 'immortalite sentie', the passage of time is none the less
recognised by the use of the verb *vieillir*:

> Ainsi vieillit l'été. Ainsi la mort
> Encercle le bonheur de la flamme qui bouge.
>
> (PE, 56)

Sometimes Bonnefoy turns to the past, and the spiritual journeys
related in the previous books, with a reference to their thematic
structure:

> Qui ramassa le fer
> Rouillé, parmi les hautes herbes, n'oublie plus
> Qu'aux grumeaux du métal la lumière peut prendre
> Et consumer le sel du doute et de la mort.
>
> (PE, 54)

It also happens that things with no apparent connection with mythology
take on a symbolic function and play an active role. An example is that

of 'la robe rouge éclairante' (PE, 51), which does more than merely
shine:

> Le rouge de la robe illumine et disperse
> Loin, au ciel, le charroi de l'antique douleur.
>
> (PE, 53)

Recourse to literary or religious sources in an attempt to elucidate
this image is of little use, since, even if there is such a reference, it is
so fleeting and imprecise as to remain, for the reader, a matter of pure
conjecture. Even within the context of Bonnefoy's own work few
remarks can be made: it can be stated, for example, that the dress is a
regular if infrequent item in his vocabulary; 'des robes tachées' (AP, 9)
are mentioned as exemplars of material and mortal existence in *Anti-
Platon*, and Douve herself is seen wearing such a garment (MID, 53).
As far as the colour red is concerned, it has already been established
that it dominates Bonnefoy's spectrum, and this fact in itself might lead
us to expect a symbolic function which would account for the prefer-
ence of this one colour over all the others, a preference hard to
explain solely by perceptual criteria. With this in mind, we can again
find associations with material and mortal existence: there is 'le fer
rouge de l'être' (HRD, 179), and 'l'argile rouge des morts' (PE, 22).
It can therefore be argued that the two words *robe* and *rouge* are
linked for reasons of symbolism as much as of perception—not to
mention euphony.

How far such remarks add anything, by way of elucidation or
otherwise helpful commentary, to the particular image quoted, is
problematical, especially since red, through its association with fire
and heat, is anyway commonly thought of as an energetic, even
aggressive colour. Nevertheless they do show how symbolic consid-
erations influence the choice of vocabulary, so that not only is the
spectrum split up into a few elemental segments, but one of these is
selected to the virtual exclusion of the others. In this respect one can
contrast the frequency of *rouge* with that of *vert*, which, as the colour
of grass and leaves, is of more obvious perceptual relevance to the
material world, yet occurs extremely rarely.

The other senses are treated in like manner. Far from providing
information about the world in the form of sense-data, their role is
fundamentally symbolic. In a way that reverses their physical
function, they serve as vehicles for the expression and discussion of
the sense to be given the world. We have already found out that the

most common sounds in the poetry are voices, and that these carry on the spiritual debate going on within the poet's mind, rather than coming from external reality: 'Pourtant ce cri sur moi vient de moi' (MID, 83). The major exception to this rule, the bird-song, has already been dealt with, and it will be remembered that even when it is most immediately described it is linked to the divine: 'Dieux, parmi/Les touffes de ce chant inlassable d'oiseaux'. The case is the same with touch, a sense that would seem to indicate a direct contact with the world. Sometimes the act is that of a symbolic figure, as in 'Veneranda'; 'Il touche de son sang les dents de la pleureuse' (HRD, 155). Elsewhere, the subject is the poet himself, but the act described is still symbolic:

> Et il n'est plus de mort puisque mes lèvres touchent
> L'eau d'une ressemblance éparse sur la mer.
>
> (PE, 12)

In this way even the agents of perception are assigned a non-perceptual role; the physical senses, by metaphoric transfer, are transformed into the expression of a metaphysic, of a sense. What is felt, seen and heard is not so much the material world as a discussion about and an interpretation of it, an interpretation that stems from an attitude and a position that are, as we have seen, metaphysical rather than perceptual in origin; and because the vocabulary that names the elements of the material world is chosen in large part for non-perceptual reasons, it is capable of standing on its own to perform the ambivalent function of representing the world and expressing the sense attributed to it. Thus, even when the mythological strand of vocabulary and theme is absent, the expression of the concern it served to indicate can be continued.

The interplay between the two strands I mentioned at the beginning of this short study is therefore varied and continually changing. Words and themes develop, and sometimes disappear as the poet constantly rethinks the elusive triangle of himself, the word and the world, seeking to collect his words in such a way that the world perceived is at once represented and integrated into a world of meaning that embraces not only it, but also the poet, and, in the final and hoped-for event, if the permanently open end of the dialogue is taken up, the reader.

Notes

1.   The following abbreviations will be used to indicate the editions of Bonne-
     foy's work referred to in the text: AP *Anti-Platon*; MID *Du Mouvement
     et de l'immobilité de Douve*; HRD *Hier régnant désert*; TR 'Les Tombeaux
     de Ravenne'; ALP 'L'Acte et le lieu de la poésie'—all in *Du Mouvement
     et de l'immobilité de Douve suivi de Hier régnant désert* (Coll. 'Poésie')
     Paris, Gallimard, 1970; PE *Pierre écrite*, Paris, Mercure de France, 1965;
     RM *Un Rêve fait à Mantoue*, Paris, Mercure de France, 1967.
2.   Bonnefoy, 'Rome 1630: définition du baroque', *Preuves*, No. 189
     (November 1966), p. 13.
3.   Bonnefoy, *L'Arrière-pays*, Geneva, Skira, 1972, p. 45.
4.   Bonnefoy, 'The Feeling of Transcendency', *Yale French Studies*, No. 31
     (1964), p. 135.

12 JACQUES DUPIN

Roger Cardinal

When the poet confronts the surface of immediate reality, he becomes aware of an underlying level of being. It is as though his mode of perception enabled him to penetrate to the heart of things and glimpse a hidden coherence that his task will be to carry back into human language. His senses are intimately attuned to a half-muffled murmuring beneath his feet, that seems to be struggling upwards into ordered meaning: 'Entendre, ou sentir . . . ce qui gronde dans le sous-sol, sous la feuille déchirée, sous nos pas. Et voudrait s'élever,–s'écrire. Et attire l'écriture, lui injecte son intensité, son incohérence . . .' (JD, 159-60).[1] For the time being, however, this murmuring of phenomena remains absurd and unintelligible. Reality's pullulating textures are as yet unresolved into specific figures and shapes. All the poet can perceive is a 'torrent inintelligible' that has yet to fashion the 'pierre désirable' of polished, rounded meaning (EG, 194).

The poet's initial stance is therefore one of ardent attentiveness to the drifting fragments that make up the textures of the world. Scanning the restless field of phenomena, he must learn to discern the fleeting figures that hint at legibility and sense. And in the motions of particles of dust in the wind, he can already make out the first letter in reality's cipher:

L'INITIALE
Poussière fine et sèche dans le vent,
Je t'appelle, je t'appartiens.
Poussière, trait pour trait,
Que ton visage soit le mien,
Inscrutable dans le vent.

(EG, 51)

Brushed softly by a wind that gathers and disperses, shapes and erases, the minute specks of dust trace an elusive figure with which the poet senses an affinity. For he in turn is presenting his own features, the configuration of his private sensibility, to the material world; and in coming to a realisation of the way external patterns of meaning are perceived and shaped by his responses, he will acquire knowledge of the mysterious motions of his own inner being. In this sense, the poetic

220

perception promotes the intimate encounter and reciprocal illumination of self and world.

As the features of reality draw more clearly into focus before the poet's eye, the shape he next discerns is that of a woman's body which seems to sway towards him—an indistinct yet immediately desirable figure. This body, a central element in Dupin's poetry, represents an imaginary incarnation of reality as the poet perceives it. It seems appropriate that the 'figure' or hidden meaning that he seeks to decipher should be embodied in erotic form, for the poet's approach to reality is very much a passionate courtship. The woman will appear in the poetry as a material representation of the poet's subjective view of things, serving as an appealing focal image in his attempt to give articulation and substance to his apprehension of the world.

For the time being, however, given that the poet's initial perception of reality is undirected and uncertain, the apparition is a vague one. The woman is still rooted in the inchoate realm of materiality, though there are signs of meaningful contact in the making when her naked shoulder and her eyes gleam abruptly out of an enveloping darkness:

Quand le lierre de minuit eut envahi le pierre du cadran,
une épaule a jailli, un regard a brillé, suivis d'un corps
encore inséparable des collines, de l'herbe et de la nuit.

(EG, 62)

Inasmuch as perception is non-specific, the woman thus far has little recognisable shape. She merges with the nocturnal landscape. Hers is a 'corps imprononçable' (EG, 209), an inarticulate figure in that at this stage she represents nothing higher than the undifferentiated texture of an as yet scarcely intelligible reality. She remains quivering in the shadows while the poet rehearses his gestures of courtship. One of these is to address her in the most grandiose style as the goddess of all creation, 'la Déesse par excellence' (EG, 60). In such moments she is seen as a radiant source of universal being whose 'corps sans limites' (JD, 174) swells throughout space as the incorporation of a boundless, surging flow. She is 'la Diluvienne', whose 'corps, immense et léger comme un fleuve débordant ses rives' (EG, 58) is the fertile source of all life, the matrix of all forms swirling in metamorphic flux.

But as an image of reality at large, this is one of fertility without form, magma without direction. The earth has not yet become a 'lieu habitable' (EG, 133) for the poet, since the inchoate mud of genesis will need to be moulded through his own intervention if a

precise delineation of the real is to result. The lesson was given to
Dupin by the sculptor Giacometti when the poet watched him at work,
transfixed by the miracle of spontaneous birth as the figure of a woman
suddenly surged forth out of the shapeless clay:

> Giacometti dans l'atelier. Ses mains saisissent une poignée de terre,
> la montent sur une armature, la pétrissent quelques courts instants.
> Une femme debout a surgi, irréductible et vivante, comblant mon
> attente, fortifiant mon attente.
>
> (JD, 108)

Henceforth, the female presence becomes concentrated into a single
body which remains the embodiment of universal being while taking on
a clear-cut individual form. That is to say, the woman remains general-
ised, yet she is capable of manifesting herself as a particular figure so
as to become more accessible to the poet. To encounter such a creature
will be to encounter reality in a single manifestation that will then
disclose itself as a synecdochic equivalent for reality at large, the whole
crystallised in the part.

The encounter with the woman is invariably brusque, for although it
is possible to pursue her or to entice her to come near, there seems
little possibility of maintaining continuous contact with her. By this
must be understood that reality is not something to be pinned down
once and for all, but is a continuous *motion* that may only be regist-
ered in occasional moments of felicitous coincidence of mind and matter
when, graced with a kind of spontaneous second sight, the poet can
make out the glimmer of meaning below the opaque surface, 'un corps
lu avec enjouement sous les vagues' (EG, 173). When such moments
occur, the poet cannot afford to hesitate. Where there is a hint of
meaning, he must hurry to lay hold on the illumination: 'Il manque
une heure au cadran. Le temps d'accourir et de te surprendre,
déesse dégrafée . . .' (EG, 145). Furthermore, in order that each fleeting
insight should yield maximum results, it is necessary that the abrupt
apparition should be absolute: the woman must be naked, offering
her body without restraint. As the emblem of the poetic apprehension
of the real, the incarnation of reality's murmured text, she must stand
out with stark precision, outlined as a shining absolute of meaning
amid the ambient chaos and illegibility. In pursuing her, the poet will
hope that the brusque manifestation of her naked figure will instigate
a convulsive catalysation of all his unformulated intuitions about the
world. The erotic encounter equates to a flash of poetic insight,

registered as a staccato imprint of words upon a blank page: 'L'irruption
de la nudité, visible par grand vent, ne supporte que le vide et sa ponct-
uation meurtrière' (EG, 68).

Since she is the materialisation of the poet's perception of reality,
the naked woman comes to be seen as equivalent to the poem itself,
the form in which that perception is finally captured. This equivalence
is made explicit in the following lines, where the awakening of the
woman alongside the poem and the embrace that consummates their
relationship are seen as effecting an uncovering of the earth's surface.
The body of reality at large is thus denuded and illuminated by way of
a sensual and verbal fecundation.

> Une femme s'éveille dans un champ fraîchement
> retourné. Corps vivant et corpus écrit, leur
> étreinte soulève le sol. Provoque le merveilleux
> glissement de terrain dans la lumière du retour.
>
> (JD, 164)

Rather than remain the embodiment of an indistinct landscape, the
naked female form is now seen to be nothing less than the 'corps
irradiant' (JD, 156) of poetry itself, the luminous body whose 'nudité
dissolvante' (JD, 169) can institute the dissolution of the resistance that
immediate reality offers to the poet's courtship. Against that stolid
obscurity, the woman—the poem—asserts herself as a 'corps clairvoyant'
(EG, 72), a kind of magic glass through which a more profound reality
can be perceived. Thanks to the transparent medium of her body, the
world is awakened from its cold sleep and radiates anew:

> transparence têtue elle flambe
> elle environne de ses tresses
> un pays qui reprend souffle et feu
>
> (EG, 98)

The arrival at a deeper view of reality is here associated with nakedness
and with fire, for both denote the reversal of opacity into meaning,
the disclosure of a hidden truth. The physical images through which
this notion is expressed in the poetry are projected from a deep level
of the poetic sensibility, at which level the perception of the woman's
naked body seems to merge fluently into the sense of the poet's own
nakedness: the longed-for relation between self and world becomes a
denuding and a burning for him too. 'L'attente se résout en un rideau

de flammes qu'on traverse, qu'en emporte collé à la peau, comme une
nudité seconde, véridique' (EG, 142). The stress laid on nudity by the
concomitant burning of clothes, is found again in the following signally
condensed passage:

> Il n'y a qu'une femme qui me suive, et elle ne me suit pas.
> Pendant que ses habits brûlent, immense est la rosée.
>
> (EG, 68)

Emerging out of uncertainty—is she or is she not behind him?—yet
with assertive abruptness, the woman manifests herself and so releases
the world from the restriction of darkness.

Denuding and illumination are here associated not only with flames
but also with moisture, a familiar concurrence in Dupin's work. On the
one hand, the female body may manifest itself as a bursting-forth of
fire from the earth, an outburst that we may take as denoting the
eruption out of chaos of the formative energies of both nature and
language.

> par une brèche ouverte
> dans le flanc tigré de la montagne
>
> elle jaillit, l'amande du feu
>
> (EG, 129)

And on the other hand, the hidden force which lies ready to spurt
forth from beneath the hard surface of things may be water—that
other natural element conducive to change and creativity.

> Sous la roche elle se tient, secrète,
> la source qui commande
> d'anticiper sur son jaillissement
>
> (EG, 122)

The intimate interpenetration of fire and water in Dupin's imagination
becomes evident in such formulations as 'le feu de la rosée' (EG, 98) or
'un feu désaltérant' (EG, 197). (The same union of the two normally
inimical elements often occurs in André Breton's work, where it is
similarly associated with erotic desire and poetic illumination.) The
perfect marriage of the two forces is formulated in the image of a lake
hidden in the crater of a dormant volcano:

Des colonnes d'odeurs sauvages
Me hissent jusqu'à toi,
Langue rocheuse révélée
Sous la transparence d'un lac de cratère.

(EG, 94)

To mount to this high place where contraries are reconciled and illumin-
ation realised (—again we are close to Breton, whose ascent of the
volcano of Teide gave rise to ecstatic insights into the world's unity—)
is to attain to the very origins of being, to trace poetic language back to
its purest source, the place where it is most transparent, most revealing
of the earth's secrets. Through the pursuit of his relationship with
deeper reality, embodied in the figure of the unclothed woman, Dupin
has asserted his rights upon the place of profound revelation and
contact, that 'lieu où l'opacité du monde semblait s'ouvrir au ruisselle-
ment confondu de la parole, de la lumière et du sang' (EG, 134).

This last-mentioned item in the list of associations that cohere about
the notion of revelation, namely blood, serves to confirm the vitality
and fluidity already manifested (blood coursing through veins) while
opening the way to the further dimension of *violence* (blood spilt).
For in order to keep up his encounters with the real—to ensure that
the discontinuity of separate moments of insight modulates into a
fluid continuum of awareness—the poet is obliged to take progressively
more severe steps. If at first he had favoured a strategy of provocation
and pursuit, now he must intensify his mode of apprehension of the
body of the real, making the encounter much more a tactile than a
visual experience. The 'irruption de la nudité' is now forced by a
physical act. The poet grapples with the woman, wrests off her clothing,
vanquishes her resistance, even bites her white body:

Ma méditation ton manteau se consument

Pour te perdre mieux
Ou te mordre blanche.

(EG, 49)

It is as though it has become impossible to seize naked reality 'sans
l'orgasme et sans la blessure' (JD, 160). The desire to apprehend can
only increase in its intensity. So much so that the poet's passion is

exacerbated to the point of becoming a 'fureur amoureuse ou homicide' (JD, 113). For at the next stage to which his desire presses him, the poet thrusts the woman's naked body onto a sacrificial altar, her head bent back over the edge, and splits open her resistant form. In this poem from the sequence 'Saccades', the searing juxtaposition of flesh and cold stone creates an unforgettably convulsive picture:

> Ta nuque, plus bas que le pierre,
> Ton corps plus nu
> Que cette table de granit . . .
>
> Sans le tonnerre d'un seul de tes cils
> Serais-tu devenue la même
> Lisse et insaisissable ennemie
> Dans la poussière de la route
> Et la mémoire du glacier?
>
> Amours anfractueuses, revenez,
> Déchirez le corps clairvoyant.
>
> (EG, 72)

The female body seems to have become as smooth as polished granite, hard and slippery; yet the poet's tearing is as relentless as the reduction of stone to dust. Despite undertones of a strange tenderness, the woman's eyes remain firmly closed as the act of love and the illumination of the world take place with a fearful paroxysmic frenzy suggestive of natural catastrophe.

The tearing of flesh and the spilling of blood ('la table ruisselle de sang' (JD, 148)), seem to be necessary steps in the process of penetration towards the palpitating heart of being. The stone altar is the scene of a destruction, yet equally of a creation. An anvil may serve both to crush and to form, so that the woman becomes an 'étincelle entre la divagante enclume/et l'obscénité des fragments' (EG, 208), a flash of illumination amid the horror of breakage. And since the female body is the incarnation of poetry, the assault has the parallel effect of fragmenting language, sending off sparks from the anvil of expression. The act of writing has become one of fracture and ravage, a destruction aimed at triumphant renewal, as if the disfigurement of the naked body, of speech, were the only way to ensure an intensification of poetic insight:

qu'elle se montre nue dans sa parole même
.et c'est un corps de femme qui se fend

(EG, 97)

The 'parole déchiquetée' (EG, 82) and the 'corps (qui) se casse' (EG,
208) modulate into the unity of a transcendent form. The slashing of
the body of language releases obscure energies hitherto submerged:
they unite with the volatile movements of the subjectivity to fulfil the
poet's desire, fusing emotion, perception and the naked apprehension of
things through words and bringing about an orgasmic transmutation of
material reality into luminous accessibility:

```
                    cœur littéral
            boue solaire
        de l'écriture du corps
entaillé, fuse
            le dehors
            l'énergie dispersante du dehors
        à la trace volatile
le réel étant le désir, même
```

(JD, 182)

The perfect encounter of brute matter and subjective desire is under-
lined in the fusion of inchoate texture and brilliant form implicit in
the words 'boue solaire'—a phrase exactly analogous to 'corps clair-
voyant' in that it instils qualities of luminosity into a seemingly
opaque substance.

The sun is indeed another focal image in the process of disruption
and violent fracture that leads to the creation of a poem. It functions
as the factor of illumination in a triple equation: sun = wound = text.
For the tearing of the female body is equivalent to the incision of an
illuminating text that transmits a revelation through its 'plaie sans
bords,/gisement où se tord l'écheveau/de l'écriture du soleil' (JD, 169).
This 'plaie lisible' (JD, 150) is the solar text whose radiant meaning is
made manifest in the very fact of its laceration. The formulation 'le
texte dilacéré/du soleil' (EG, 179) is indeed to be taken as a definition
of the poem itself, seen as a resplendent seizure of reality achieved by
the tearing asunder of the opaque skin of the world—'et la lumière
s'éloigne de la plaie' (EG, 181).

It will now be apparent why Dupin refers to the poetic act as the
maintenance of 'la césure d'un meurtre/qu'il nous incombe de réitérer

sans retard' (EG, 174). Poetry is a ritual murder whose repetition
ensures that a caesura or wound is kept open, thus preventing reality
from relapsing into impenetrability. (In a text on Pierre Reverdy,
Dupin speaks of that poet's aim as being to 'préciser les traits d'une
blessure, la maintenir ouverte, attiser son secret' (JD, 134).) The
murder may take the form of throttling, stabbing, or, more obsessively,
beheading. Even more strikingly than the irruption of nudity, decap-
itation functions as a powerful metaphor for the instantaneous irrupt-
ion of meaning into the poem. The horrifying image of a 'tête éparpillée
sous la hache' (JD, 168) may *denote* killing and fragmentation, but
equally it *connotes* compensatory processes of fertilisation and poetic
illumination. The horrendous act elicits a sacrificial flow of blood that
enters the furrowed earth like seed: 'au fond du labour s'égoutte/le
sang supplicié' (JD, 149). This is the fluid of life that imparts fecundity
and meaning to an otherwise arid and unintelligible world. 'Le sang
coula, l'herbe devint profonde. A l'aube, en grand secret, les lèvres des
amants heurtérent une rosée illimitée' (EG, 34). The collocation blood/
seed/dew manifests a dark identification of violence and tenderness,
rape and fertility.

Throughout the poetry, the female figure, even if emergent from the
chaos of indifferentiation, never truly achieves identity as an individual
person. She remains 'innommée' (JD, 155), hers is never more than an
'identité dissoute' (JD, 185). Though we might attribute a desperate
yearning for intimacy to the lover's exclamation 'O mon amour sans
visage' (EG, 81), the murderous act he commits upon her ensures that
her individuality is never countenanced. If a smile should manifest
itself, it is smothered: it seems that if this body is to point the way to
an apprehension of the naked features of reality, it must itself be
faceless.

> Piéger le seul sourire,
> Eteindre le visage et sa suffocation
> Sous un crépi de terre calcinée.
>
> Quand même elle sombrerait toute
> Il me resterait la brèche:
> Son absence de visage et sa seule nudité.
>
> (EG, 78)

It might be surmised that the poet, in cancelling out facial features
and clothing alike, is seeking to preserve an image of a woman who is

neither an intimate nor a stranger, neither distinctly herself nor totally anonymous. This tension between contrary images is what gives her the attractive capacity to undulate between being a general incarnation of reality (the space across which poetic perception ranges) and a specific purchase on that reality (the written poem that records a particular act of perception).

It is perhaps worth stressing at this point how inappropriate it would be to think of the poet's beloved as an actual woman, or to take her execution as the literal expression of a sadistic sexuality. A purely literal interpretation of Dupin's images would entirely distort their significance. For, despite their undoubted impact on the senses, the events recorded by Dupin are in fact so many figurative expositions of what is essentially a trans-physical process—the process of creative writing whereby links are articulated between the subjectivity and the deeper reality to which the poet struggles to impart a convincing voice. This figurative dimension needs to be borne in mind even as the reader responds to the surface violence of the imagery in such passages as the following, taken from the poem 'Chapurlat'. Here, poetic activity is portrayed as a journey into a terrible labyrinth of mud, blood and excrement—an Orphic descent whereby the poet passes into the dark realm of extinction to seek a new meaning. The annihilation of the self is described as a 'second mourir', a death that transcends horror and degradation by giving access to a luminous truth:

> Aux orgues de basalte du second ravin
> le souffle manque . . .
>   il est rendu, lui,
> aux genêts, par les éclairs,
> à la charogne maternelle, par le labyrinth
> brusquement simplifié,
> avant de tomber, de fouir
> un terrain sanglant, excrémentiel,
> jusqu'à ta nudité dissolvante,
> aigre soleil
> second mourir
> vérité de sable et de vent . . .

(JD, 168-9)

Given that the poetic quest has here taken the form of a surrender to the chaos of formless being, a search for meaning at the undifferentiated levels of nature or sensibility, it is no longer necessary to stipulate whether the body described as moving below the earth is that of the woman or of the poet. If the burial of the woman can imply poetic germination, the poet's self-sacrifice can signify the same creative marriage of matter and mind: suicide is simply a variant on the 'reiterated murder' that constitutes the poetic act.

> Devant l'avidité de la terre, un immense désir de m'ouvrir
> les veines. Chaque motte de terre, l'abreuver de ma nuit . . .
> Notre amour ne compte plus ses cadavres, ses cadavres
> transparents, ses cadavres dissous dans le soleil.
>
> (EG, 164)

Once again the bleeding body is linked with earth and darkness and encouraged to focus its energies into a purifying beam of sunlight or transparent vision. The poetic process—the passage from death to renewal, from burial to fertility, from the fragmentation of perception to a sense of full participation in reality—demands the surrender of the poet's immunity. He must fully involve himself in the operations of torture, and be, like Baudelaire's 'L'Héautontimorouménos', victim as well as executioner, 'meurtrier de son objet, meurtrier de son amour, meurtrier de soi dans le même instant et avec la même innocence' (EG, 148). Just as the poem bears as the emblem of its authenticity 'le stigmate de sa terrible naissance' (JD, 111), so the poet will offer proof of his sincerity by pointing to his own scars. For Dupin, the writing of poetry is 'à la fois une pratique et une agonie' (JD, 158). In his work, meaning is what is brutally snatched out of the writhing chaos of words—sense is transfixed by dagger-like thrusts of vocabulary and syntax. This onslaught that seeks to ravage meaninglessness and to germinate significance is inseparable from a sense of strain, anguish and martyrdom. Only out of the deepest descent into the unlit caverns of being can profound insight be drawn: only by an implementation of torture and a submission to torture may poetic gains be rendered certain. Writing is a cruel commitment: 'L'acte d'écrire comme rupture, et engagement cruel de l'esprit, et du corps, dans une succession nécessaire de ruptures, de dérives, d'embrasements' (EG, 146). For if reality is to become accessible to the poet, it can only be at the price of a tireless reiteration of attacks and annihilations, which cannot but affect him too, both mentally and physically. 'Tout nous est donne, mais pour être forcé, pour être entamé, en quelque façon pour être détruit,—et nous détruire' (EG, 146). The radiant surging-forth of the body of poetry, the rendering-transparent or denuding of the surface

of things can only come as the result of thrusting painful sensations
again and again into an idiom of splintered images.

> un corps qui s'éboule, éclate
> et s'agrège autour de sa crampe
>
> à nouveau et se dresse
>
> faille du ciel effervescent

(EG, 172)

This anonymous body collapsed and convulsed, this wound incarnate,
becomes the vibrant occasion for the renascence of form out of chaos.
The fragmented particles of reality cohere around its scars, and the
world is rendered whole in a flash of solar light which thrusts concrete
sensation and abstract idea into convulsive union.

Such images of disorientation modulating into direction, of dispersed
elements reconstituted in a paroxysmic (and paradoxical) totality, of
the perception of reality as 'ce qui vient de naître d'une secousse et
qui se confond avec elle' (JD, 132), can be seen as so many enactments
of a compulsive reverie of the appropriation of external space into the
imaginary space of poetry. In spatial terms, Dupin's poetry is a territory
surveyed by a central consciousness which, moving amid indeterminate
flurries of apparently senseless signs, 'une gravitation de signes insensés'
(JD, 160), seeks to impose conditions of coherence and perspectives of
continuity, to promote a seizure of disparates in a swift 'mise à nu
(. . .) dont un espace jaillit' (EG, 148). At the outset, this space of
poetic consciousness is a vast and harsh expanse, an 'espace de la
douleur et de la chance' (JD, 160), a landscape of deserts and jagged
crags. There is little vegetation—bracken, hardy lichens, a few trees,
occasionally a dense forest. Wild creatures are few and solitary—a hawk,
a viper, an unseen boar. It is across this 'espace affamé' (EG, 69) that the
poet must trace a path and pursue his prey.

Of the elemental forces with which he must reckon, the wind is
one of the most powerful. It is initially a negative force, instigator of
the poet's 'supplice spacieux' (EG, 168), a cruel negator of meaning
'qui tonne/et tourne/autour des tempes, et bourdonne/sans signification'
(JD, 167), a suffocating movement of air that swallows meaning into
vacuity. Yet the wind can be envisaged from a totally opposite view-

point, as a positive force which, precisely because it circulates about the discrete fragments of reality, can be a factor of clarification and elucidation, an austere guarantor of the immediacy of phenomena. 'Invisible, intarissable' (JD, 164), the wind blows around things, sweeping them clear òf extraneous matter, rendering them sharp and immediately accessible to perception. In just the same way, the blank spaces about the phrases of Dupin's poems (particularly the more recent ones) are intended to sharpen and stress the particles of expression, sweeping them clear of redundancies. The connexion is made by Dupin himself, in an evocation of the 'windswept' poetry of Reverdy that might equally apply to his own:

> Car le vent brille sur les débris et les plaies. Le vent. Ou le vide
> . . . Il s'engouffre par les blancs d'une typographie ouverte et
> dentelée. Il circule à travers les intervalles d'un texte fragmenté,
> irrésolu, disjoint, dont il est le principe unificateur et comme la
> salubre énergie silencieuse. Il ruisselle parmi les images et les parcelles
> fuyantes du réel. Il en chasse les étrangetés artificielles, dissout
> l'accidentel . . .
>
> (JD, 134)

The wind is the agent of dispersal and disorientation, yet also of plenitude and meaning, 'le vent qui disperse et le vent qui rassemble' (EG, 66). It is the ambiguous force that, as we saw earlier, scatters dust yet equally shapes it into meaningful figures; it is the invisible agency that circulates between the disjointed images of a poem, binding them into a significant statement.

Wind cannot exist without space in which to move, and similarly poetic perception can only function where there is room for manoeuvre. One of the most awkward paradoxes the poet needs to grasp in his endeavour to appropriate and to articulate 'une réalité plus profonde' (EG, 134) is that the deeper reality lies not so much *out of reach* as *too close to be reached*. The body of the real in fact lies so near as to be invisible: 'Invisible, elle occupe tout l'espace et cependant elle marche à mes côtés' (EG, 137). As long as the poet peers at reality from close to, he will see nothing. He must learn to maintain a certain *distance*. This was another lesson that Dupin drew from Giacometti's example. The sculptor's brusque, merciless handling of clay ('cette rude et injurieuse caresse' (JD, 109)), meant that the figure he moulded never actually achieved definitive polish. Seen from close to, the material disintegrated, and became 'une masse déformée et crispée, boursouflée et atrocement distendue' (JD, 111). Only by stepping back from sensory proximity was it possible to take in the sculpture as a meaningful form, to reinstate the equilibrium of its conception and establish a proper relationship with it. The lesson was applicable to the poetic perception of reality at large. Witnessed from close to, phenomena revert to a non-patterned materiality and become murky and unintelligible. Only distance renders the world truly visible, truly legible. Accurate poetic perception therefore consists in a posture of alienation: a painful deferment of contact is the pre-requisite of lucid apprehension. It is as though consciousness, as a mode of superior awareness of what lies beyond it, needs to hold back from the immediacy of specific sensory contact in order the better to grasp reality as a total pattern. The caesura the poet seeks to sustain in the gesture of writing is nothing less than the gap between outer and inner reality. Only by affirming their difference can the poet preserve a 'pacte fragile' (EG, 135) between the vitality of natural events and the abstract dimension of thought.

The implication of this posture of separateness from things is not that the world's multiple aspects are distilled into a purely abstract concept. On the contrary, the farther away from things the poet stands, the more deeply he can perceive and understand them. The movement of withdrawal becomes a paradoxical advance towards deeper intimacy. Admittedly the relation of perceiving subject to perceived object is supremely fragile, and may last for only a moment, yet in that moment, distance is annulled, that which is far-off is made as accessible as if it were near, in a marvellous reconciliation of the strange and the familiar. In short, an intuition of limitless space is generated at the finite centre of perception: perspectives converge in a mighty revelation of the real, at once unsubmissive in its alien, non-human complexity, and magically acquiescent to the poet's ordering consciousness. This is what Dupin means when he says of the poet, 'il fait corps avec la distance qui le sépare de son objet' (EG, 148): the gap between consciousness and its object needs to be drawn into consciousness as *itself* a fact of consciousness—a kind of negative sensation—which then promotes a superior form of apprehension, a synthesis of external space and mental space, of perceived reality and imagination.

One method Dupin uses to represent this insistence on and abolition of distance is to silhouette close-up figures against a far-off background. A bleak horizon-line is humanised by being crossed by the tremulous curl of smoke from a fisherman's fire (EG, 103); or a woman's finger-nail is juxtaposed with the surface of the ocean in a striking conjunction of the close-up and the infinite (EG, 64). In this way, empty distance is transformed into accessible plenitude. In one poem, the female body is set against the horizon in such a way that figure and ground, single woman and generalised landscape merge into a perfect whole:

> Cette silhouette désormais, à chaque instant comme redessinée
> par son ombre dansante, s'apprête à sortir du jardin par une
> porte dérobée. Un bras levé devant les yeux, la paume ouverte
> contre le dehors effrayant, son geste fait scintiller la ligne
> des montagnes au-delà de la cime des arbres.
>
> (EG, 149)

As ever, woman is visualised in a manner calculated to divert attention from her individuality. She is seen only in silhouette, her face withheld from view. Her gesture of withdrawal from the alien world outside the garden is envisaged as a magical means of bringing that very distance within reach. Her outline seems to draw into proximity both the trees in the middle-distance and the mountains on the horizon, as though her pose were the spelling-out of the initial letter that projects legibility on to the rest of the world.

A further means of assimilating space to human proportions is to measure it out. The crossing of space and the counting of steps become a further metaphor for poetic appropriation. 'La traversée qui nous scande, la trajectoire qui nous mesure' (EG, 190) are a measuring of the proportions of the world and of the self, and an establishment of relations between the two. That is, in projecting the human rhythm of walking on to non-human space, the poet hopes to bring about a marvellous conjunction of physical and of mental space, experiencing 'l'émerveillement comme à la frontière d'un territoire excessif/après l'incorporation de la marche à l'étendue' (EG, 197). The shape of a poem such as 'La Ligne de rupture', a sequence of self-contained statements that Dupin lays out as discrete steps in a progression towards meaning, reflects this notion of apprehension through measured movement. Elsewhere the articulation of space is manifested in the image of ploughed fields: the ploughshare of consciousness cuts into the indeterminate texture of earth to imprint humanising patterns upon it.

But, as we have seen, the characteristic rhythms of Dupin's poetry are scarcely those of patient perspective and laboured progression. His work is more distinctively a reiteration of abrupt gestures of laceration and ravage, the movements of a subjectivity whose breakthrough to deeper reality cannot be propelled by long-winded methods

alone. Tentative exploration makes little headway, and the poetry
therefore becomes one of disruption and cleavage that grapples with
space in violent fits and starts. Dupin's is a writing that is relentlessly
sharp and impulsive: 'L'intense écriture s'aiguise,/scrupuleuse, haîssant
l'échec' (JD, 173). And the landscape against which this aggressive
writing measures itself is determined by a sensibility that would seem
to prefer resistant as against docile forms. Yet, paradoxically again,
at the very same time as this solidity is invoked, the poetic process
demands that it be revoked; so that, in the last analysis, the poetic
landscape is to be seen as both rugged *and* acquiescent. Not only are
its rocks solid and immutable, but they are also prone to spontaneous
erosion. 'La roche qui se délite est la sœur du ciel qui se fend' (EG, 53):
the impassive sky and the impenetrable rock alike may split open at
any moment. Exploring an obscure universe seemingly closed off from
human understanding, the poet keeps on stumbling upon places where
opacity is repealed by the naked torch of poetic language as it pierces
through the fissure in the inscrutable wall of reality:

Ouverte en peu de mots,
comme par un remous, dans quelque mur,
une embrasure, pas meme une fênetre

pour maintenir à bout de bras
cette contrée de nuit où le chemin se perd,

à bout de forces une parole nue

                                                                   (EG, 118)

This illuminating breach in an impenetrable wall is an established
surrealist metaphor for the break-through to a deeper reality. In Dupin's
poems, the revelation is often provoked by eruptive images that evoke
the colossal energies unleashed by primeval cataclysms; yet he can also
draw maximum benefit from a minimal fissure, since even the slightest
embrasure in the smooth wall gives promise of penetration and insight.
The term *embrasure* denotes a slit in a fortified wall, and thus carries
the suggestion of a vigorous attack on external space as well as of a
more docile passage of light into the darkness outside. In this sense,
both maximal and minimal breakage are extremes of the one process
of subverting normality, and are not exclusive. The phrase 'un saccage/
d'absolu et de brindilles' (JD, 185) intimates that Dupin's poetic on-
slaught is directed towards disrupting-and-apprehending both the

absolute unity of things and the multiplicity of phenomena, in a movement that reconciles the yawning immensity of space with the tiniest fragments scattered therein. The correlation of spatial extremes— near and far, microcosm and macrocosm, subjective space and alien space'—is perfectly crystallised in the following lines from the poem 'Le Prisonnier', where a branch passing through a break in the prisoner's wall gives him hope of breaking out of the finite restrictions of ordinary consciousness and of achieving contact with distant space and the starry sky of a kind of 'absolute' consciousness. It is as though by passing through the narrowest gap he seizes reality at its very 'point de rupture' (JD, 121), and gains a purchase on a second, more meaningful space which normally lies beyond his reach and which now reaches out to him:

> Par une brèche dans le mur,
> La rosée d'une seule branche
> Me rendra tout l'espace vivant,
>
> Etoiles,
> Si vous tirez à l'autre bout.

(EG, 48)

In this felicitous enactment of the passage from a restricted to an unbounded consciousness, the image of the dew-laden branch gives special force to the notion of imaginative perception as being a projection outwards from within the closed space of the mind. For Dupin, dew is the medium of universal transparency. Composed as it is of a myriad droplets of water—'une goutte d'eau/innombrable/et la même' (EG, 201)—yet capable of imbuing surfaces near and far with a unified translucency, it is a perfect token of the appropriation of space and the purification of vision. A kind of deluge in miniature, dew materialises as if by magic out of the chaos of night, manifesting the purity and limitless freshness of a reality revived by the poetic word. Dupin's 'offrande de rosée au soleil, dehors, sur chaque ronce' (EG, 134) is, like Rimbaud's revelation of a world re-born in the poem 'Après le déluge', an affirmation of the potential of poetry to realise a transfiguration of reality through 'l'illumination fixe de quelques mots inespérément accordés' (EG, 134).

When the poet succeeds in grasping reality at its point of rupture,

the poetic illumination will be all the more intense if it emerges
suddenly from an ambient obscurity. Dupin likes to depict the poet
as a somnambulist who stumbles uncertainly, his lamp guttering out,
across a nocturnal terrain of deep grasses or sandy expanses where
paths are obliterated. He feels himself to be propelled by an injunction
he cannot define yet which he cannot contest. He may not pause to
take stock of the ground he traverses, yet he accepts the restriction on
sight with good cheer, working his way through a dark labyrinth in
expectation of eventually crossing 'la limite fractionnée que la perte de
la vue transgresse' (EG, 192)—that absolute limit of obscurity beyond
which blindness paradoxically modulates into a strange and compelling
lucidity. Reality lies outstretched in the darkness, its body veiled by an
'afflux d'obscurité' (JD, 164) which is now disclosed as being tantamout
to the 'nudité seconde, véridique' (EG, 142) of poetic insight. This
approach to darkness runs parallel to the poet's approach to words.
Dupin's night-writing is a 'sommeil plus mobile' (EG, 131), a descent
into the subterranean depths of language whereby 'terre et nuit
emplissent la bouche' (JD, 165). Yet this submergence in words as in an
unintelligible substance does not entail the suffocation of all sense in
the poetry. Rather, true poetic meaning is that which can only be
unearthed through such a prospection of obscurity. 'Il m'est interdit
de m'arrêter pour voir. Comme si j'étais condamné (. . .) à donner à
voir ce que je ne vois pas, ce qu'il m'est interdit de voir. Et que le
langage en se déployant heurte et découvre'(EG, 139). Here the poet's
somnambulist advance is described as an exploration without fore-
knowledge, the tracking of a prey whose nature remains a mystery
until after the capture. The poet's blindness does not therefore mean an
extinction of sight, but a faith in second sight—a seeing which thrives
on darkness.

In the poem 'Forêt seconde', the idea of catching the prey of reality
is expounded in terms of an alchemical transmutation whereby density
and obscurity turn into radiant transparency: 'la forêt (. . .) accueillerait
le vent, s'ouvrirait à la rude et radieuse alchimie de la seconde nuit'
(EG, 43). Dupin's usage of the term *second* here and elsewhere ('nudité
seconde', 'second mourir', 'prison seconde', etc.) denotes a pitch of
intensity conducive to startling transformations that entirely reverse
the established situation. Thus the phrase *seconde nuit* carries the
sense of an extreme of obscurity that prompts an illumination more
profound than would be possible by daylight: night as the realm of
impenetrable darkness modulates into a 'second' or intensified night
wherein appearances are rendered luminous and intelligible. 'Tant que

ma parole est obscure il respire' (EG, 120) claims Dupin, confident that the best way to subvert opacity and lack of meaning, is to allow language its full freedom of initiative. It is as though the deeper import of things can be revealed if language first mimics their apparently haphazard idiom. Obscurity and careless utterance lead to a reversal of the negative situation—to sense, and an ordering of space: 'Et le paysage s'ordonne autour d'un mot lancé à la légére, et qui reviendra chargé d'ombre' (EG, 67). In this way, the acceptance of a provisional obscurity is the poet's means to attain an eventual clarity. The subliminal murmur of things and of undirected language is no longer vacuous babbling but creative fermentation. Reality's text may at the outset be one of 'foisonnante et meurtrière illisibilité' (EG, 159), but this illegibility is not absolute. Rather it is an 'illisibilité clignotante' (EG, 190)—a meaninglessness which generates dazzling flashes of perfect lucidity and form.

A complementary example of Dupin's concern to 'inverser les termes' (EG, 139) is his evocation of the silent message that lies at the heart of audible speech. Just as obscurity secretes light, so words contain a core of silence that is pregnant with meaning: 'Le silence qui reflue dans la parole donne à son agonie des armes et comme une fraîcheur désespérée. (. . .) Distincte du mouvement des lèvres grises, la parole silencieusement irradie . . .' (EG, 147). Silence—the idiom of so many inscrutable objects in the world—is seen as the luminous axis on which rotates the nocturnal being of reality:

> Cela qui dans la parole scintille et se tait,
> La nuit roule sur cet essieu

(EG, 93)

This axis or pivot is perhaps the key image in the poet's work, for his most typical poetic climaxes manifest themselves as pivotal moments wherein a situation of negativity tilts soundlessly into its opposite. The ultimate 'point de rupture' of reality is that 'axe du renversement du réel' (JD, 163) upon which the poet centres his energies, pressing death into a more profound life, turning descent into ascent, forging new structures out of collapse. In this way, the dulled ploughshare thrusting into inert matter may suddenly be transformed into a medium of delirious illumination: 'Ivre, ayant renversé ta charrue, tu as pris le soc pour un astré, et la terre t'a donné raison' (EG, 55). Out of darkness comes a flash of total light that regenerates what had seemed inert and entirely reverses the negative character of disintegration:

Dans ce pays la foudre fait germer la pierre.

Sur les pitons qui commandent les gorges
Des tours ruinées se dressent
Comme autant de torches mentales actives

(EG, 18)

The stylistic corollary of this poetic operation of reversal is the use of
paradox or of oxymoron, as in such phrases as 'divorce fécond' (EG,
135), 'récolte incendiée' (EG, 69), 'ombres transparentes' (EG, 142)
and 'rupture compacte' (JD, 132). Poetic truth for Dupin seems indeed
to be precisely a matter of expressing compressed contradictions, all of
which may be seen as variants on the central paradox—that reality can
only be apprehended at the moment when it most resists, in the same
way that Giacometti's woman was brought near only through a conv-
ulsive affirmation of her distance: 'elle avance sur moi et recule, dans le
même instant' (JD, 110). Putting his trust in paradox as a means of
discovery, the poet advances confidently into the night of uncertainty—
'le poete marche à sa perte entière, d'un pied sûr' (EG, 135)—secure in
the expectation that his downfall into chaos will be reversed into a
triumphant grasp on meaning. 'Où tu sombres, la profondeur n'est
plus' (EG, 17) becomes his defiant watchword. Disintegration is his
springboard to an intuition of unity.

Jacques Dupin's characteristic tone thus manages to combine confus-
ion and confidence, his harsh voice—'vertigineuse, gutturale' (EG, 87)—
to express a secret tenderness. The poet's style of ambiguity and
wracked complexity is something the reader must acknowledge not
as a capricious assault on his attention, but as an index of the intensity
and authenticity of Dupin's endeavour to make an accurate statement
of his relationship with reality. No poetry can be other than thorny
and obscure when it tries to snare meanings that lie beyond the normal
frontier of human intelligibility. Dupin's poems are an attempt to
transliterate into figures of accessible speech, those figures that lie
half-buried amid the fragmentation of material experience. In trans-
lating the enigma of the non-human world into poetry, the poet still
feels bound to respect the character of that primary text in all its
'hermétique fraîcheur' (EG, 189), so as to preserve the authentic
mystery and richness of the native idiom of things.

The poems that emerge from this process are mobile, undirected
structures that the poet hopes will veer with the current of the real
to release continually modified patterns of meaning flowing within

lack of meaning. For Dupin, insight derives from a constantly re-defined relationship with an elusive reality, a 'fuyante relation' (JD, 181) that can never be immobilised—else it would cease to be. The desire to articulate his experience of the world therefore demands tactics mimetic of this restless, discontinuous motion. If the poet is to capture the prey of reality without killing it—if, as it were, he is to intermittently define the world while still honouring its resistance to final definition— he must never quite spring the noose of his poetic trap. For if it closes, he will forfeit the very life he hopes to snare: 'Le piège est ouvert. Est l'ouverture même' (EG, 140). Writing thus becomes a hit-and-miss affair, a gathering-and-relinquishing, a desperate groping in the shadows. Any record of the body of the real must make allowance for its shifting postures and for the fluctuation between indeterminacy and precision attendant upon any perception of the world, by somehow zigzagging between confusion and insecurity on the one hand and clarity and fixity on the other. And whenever the poet's efforts *are* rewarded, it is never quite in a manner that cool forethought could have anticipated.

> En effet tous les mots nous abusent. Mais il arrive que
> la chaîne discontinue de ce qu'ils projettent et ce qu'ils
> retiennent, laisse surgir le corps ruisselant et le visage
> éclairé d'une réalité tout autre que celle qu'on avait
> pursuivie et piégée dans la nuit.
>
> (EG, 165)

The deeper reality in the shadows will always diverge from our pre-established definitions, for reality is not something we can hope to know in advance of our direct experience of it. This is why Dupin's poetry must be obscure and impulsive, for such are the motions of his quivering prey.

Note

1.   Quotations are from two sources: EG *L'Embrasure précédé de Gravir et suivi de La Ligne de rupture et de l'Onglée*, 'Poèsie', Paris, Gallimard, 1971 (*Gravir*, 1963, and *L'Embrasure*, 1969, being Dupin's two major collections to date); and JD *Jacques Dupin*, 'Poètes d'aujourd'hui', Paris, Seghers, 1974 (a selection which complements EG by gathering up several recent poems and examples drawn from Dupin's writings on poets and artists, such as the *Textes pour une approche* on Alberto Giacometti).

BIBLIOGRAPHY

This Bibliography does not attempt to list each poet's works exhaustively, but gives a selection of important texts, wherever possible in accessible editions. Prose works are listed in several cases where they seem of particular interest to the reader of the poetry. It will be noted that the Gallimard 'Poésie' series provides excellent coverage in an economical format of all the poets studied in this book. All but Bonnefoy are featured in the Seghers 'Poètes d'aujourd'hui' series, whose volumes comprise an extended critical essay, together with selections, illustrations, bibliography, etc. The volumes in the Gallimard 'Bibliothèque de la Pléiade' series give maximum coverage of the work of the poet concerned, and contain full bibliographical information on both works and criticism.

The critical works listed are, in general, those which correspond most closely to the concerns of this book.

Unless otherwise stated, the place of publication is Paris.

GUILLAUME APOLLINAIRE (1880-1918)

A. Works

Alcools, 'Poésie', Gallimard, 1966.
Alcools, ed. A. E. Pilkington, Oxford, Blackwell, 1970.
Calligrammes, 'Poésie', Gallimard, 1966.
Œuvres poétiques, ed. Marcel Adéma & Michel Décaudin, 'Bibliothèque de la Pléiade', Gallimard, 1956.
Le Guetteur mélancolique, suivi de Poèmes retrouvés, 'Poésie', Gallimard, 1970.
Poèmes à Lou, précédé de Il y a, 'Poésie', Gallimard, 1969.

B. Criticism

Claude Bonnefoy, *Apollinaire*, Editions universitaires, 1969.
Jean Burgos, 'Pour une approche de l'univers imaginaire d'Apollinaire' *La Revue des Lettres modernes*, Nos. 276-9 (1971), pp. 35-67.
Marie-Jeanne Durry, *Guillaume Apollinaire: Alcools*, 3 vols., Société d'édition d'enseignement supérieur, 1956-64.
Roger Little, *Apollinaire*, 'Athlone French Poets', London, The Athlone Press, 1976.

S. I. Lockerbie, 'Le Rôle de l'imagination dans *Calligrammes*', *La Revue des lettres modernes*, Nos. 146-9 (1966), pp. 6-22; & Nos. 166-9 (1967), pp. 85-105.

Philippe Renaud, *Lecture d'Apollinaire*, Lausanne, Editions L'Age d'homme, 1969.

YVES BONNEFOY (1923-   )

A. Works

i. Poetry

Du Mouvement et de l'immobilité de Douve, suivi de Hier régnant désert, 'Poésie', Gallimard, 1970.

Pierre écrite, Mercure de France, 1965.

ii. Prose

L'Arrière-pays, Geneva, Skira, 1972.

'The Feeling of Transcendency', *Yale French Studies*, No. 31 (1964), pp. 135-7.

L'Improbable, Mercure de France, 1959.

Un Rêve fait à Mantoue, Mercure de France, 1967.

Rimbaud par lui-même, Editions du Seuil, 1961.

B. Criticism

Walter Albert, 'Yves Bonnefoy and the Architecture of Poetry', *Modern Language Notes*, LXXXII, No. 5 (1967), pp. 590-603.

Béatrice Arndt, *La Quête poétique d'Yves Bonnefoy*, Zurich, Juris Verlag, 1970.

Jean-Pierre Attal, 'La Quête d'Yves Bonnefoy', in *L'Image métaphysique et autres essais*, Gallimard, 1969.

Claude Estaban, 'L'Echo d'une demeure', *Nouvelle Revue française*, No. 225 (September 1971), pp. 19-34.

Jean-Pierre Richard, 'Yves Bonnefoy', in *Onze Etudes sur la poésie moderne,* Editions du Seuil, 1964.

ANDRE BRETON (1896-1966)

A. Works

i. Poetry

Clair de terre, précédé de Mont de piété, suivi de Le Revolver à

cheveux blancs et de l'Air de l'eau, 'Poésie', Gallimard, 1966.
Signe ascendant, suivi de Fata Morgana, Les Etats généraux, Constellations, etc., 'Poésie', Gallimard, 1968.
Poèmes, Gallimard, 1948.
Poésie et autre, Le Club du meilleur livre, 1960.

ii. *Prose*

L'Amour fou, Gallimard, 1937.
Arcane 17, '10-18', Union générale d'éditions, 1965.
Full details of Breton's writings may be found in Michael Sheringham, *André Breton: a Bibliography*, London, Grant & Cutler, 1972.

B. Criticism

André Breton 1896-1966 et le mouvement surréaliste', issue of *La Nouvelle Revue française*, No. 172 (April 1967).
Philippe Audoin, *Breton*, Gallimard, 1970.
Roger Cardinal, 'André Breton: the surrealist sensibility', *Mosaic*, I, No. 2 (January 1968), pp. 112-36.
Michel Deguy, 'Sur moi une influence tardive', *La Quinzaine littéraire*, No. 114 (March 1971), p. 18.
Marc Eigeldinger (ed.), *André Breton: Essais recueillis par Marc Eigeldinger*, Neuchâtel, La Baconnière, 1970.

RENE CHAR (1907-   )

A. Works

Fureur et mystère, 'Poésie', Gallimard, 1967.
Les Matinaux, suivi de La Parole en archipel, 'Poésie', Gallimard, 1969.
La Nuit talismanique, Geneva, Skira, 1972.
Recherche de la base et du sommet, 'Poésie', Gallimard, 1972.

B. Criticism

Les Cahiers de l'Herne: René Char, Editions de l'Herne, 1971.
'René Char', issue of *L'Arc*, No. 22 (Summer 1963).
'Hommage à René Char', issue of *Liberté*, No. 58 (July-August 1968).
René Ménard, 'Cinq essais pour interpréter René Char', in *La Condition poétique*, Gallimard, 1959.
Georges Mounin, *La Communication poétique, précédé de Avez-*

vous lu Char?, Gallimard, 1969.

Jean-Pierre Richard, 'Réne Char', in *Onze Etudes sur la poésie moderne*, Editions du Seuil, 1964.

JACQUES DUPIN (1927-   )

A. Works

'Choix de textes', in George Raillard, *Jacques Dupin*, 'Poètes d'aujourd'hui', Seghers, 1974.

L'Embrasure, précédé de Gravir, et suivi de La Ligne de rupture et de L'Onglée, 'Poésie', Gallimard, 1971.

B. Criticism

Pierre Chappuis, 'Jaillissement et mensonge du poème', *Critique*, XXVII, No. 289 (June 1971), pp. 520-31.

Georges Raillard, 'L'Injonction maîtresse de Jacques Dupin', in *Jacques Dupin*, 'Poètes d'aujourd'hui', Seghers, 1974.

Jean-Pierre Richard, 'Jacques Dupin', in *Onze Etudes sur la poésie moderne*, Editions du Seuil, 1964.

PAUL ELUARD (1895-1952)

A. Works

Capitale de la douleur, suivi de L'Amour la poésie, 'Poésie', Gallimard, 1966.

Le Livre ouvert, 'Poésie', Gallimard, 1974.

Œuvres complètes, ed. Lucien Scheler, 2 vols., 'Bibliothéque de la Pléiade', Gallimard, 1968

Poésies 1913-1926, 'Poésie', Gallimard, 1971.

Poésie ininterrompue, 'Poésie', Gallimard, 1969.

La Vie immédiate, suivi de La Rose publique, Les Yeux fertiles, etc., 'Poésie', Gallimard, 1967.

B. Criticism

Raymond Jean, *Eluard par lui-même*, Editions du Seuil, 1968.

Gaëtan Picon, 'Tradition et découverte chez Paul Eluard', in *L'Usage de la lecture*, Vol. I, Mercure de France, 1960.

Georges Poulet, 'Eluard', in *Le Point de départ*, Plon, 1964.

Jean-Pierre Richard, 'Paul Eluard' in *Onze Etudes sur la poésie moderne*, Editions du Seuil, 1964.

JEAN FOLLAIN (1903-1971)

A. Works

Appareil de la terre, Gallimard, 1964.
Canisy, Gallimard, 1942.
Chef-lieu, Gallimard, 1950.
L'Epicerie d'enfance, Correa, 1938.
Espaces d'instants, Gallimard, 1971.
Exister, suivi de Territoires, 'Poésie', Gallimard, 1969.
Tout instant, Gallimard, 1957.

B. Criticism

André Dhôtel, *Jean Follain*, 'Poètes d'aujourd'hui', Seghers, 1956.
'Jean Follain', issue of *Nouvelle Revue française*, No. 222 (June 1971).
Philippe Jaccottet, 'Une Perspective fabuleuse', in *L'Entretien des muses*, Gallimard, 1968.
'Portrait de Jean Follain', issue of *La Voix des poètes*, No. 42 (Summer 1971).

SAINT-JOHN PERSE (1887-1975)

A. Works

Amers, suivi de Oiseaux et de Poésie, 'Poésie', Gallimard, 1970.
Eloges, suivi de la Gloire des rois, Anabase, Exil, 'Poésie', Gallimard, 1967.
Exil, ed. Roger Little, 'Athlone French Poets', London, The Athlone Press, 1973.
Œuvres complètes, 'Bibliothèque de la Pléiade', Gallimard, 1972.
Vents, suivi de Chronique, 'Poésie', Gallimard, 1968.
Full details of Perse's writings may be found in Roger Little, *Saint-John Perse: a Bibliography*, London, Grant & Cutler, 1971.

B. Criticism

Alain Bosquet, *Saint-John Perse*, 'Poètes d'aujourd'hui', Seghers, 1971.
Roger Caillois, *Poétique de St.-John Perse*, Gallimard, 1972.
Albert Henry, *'Amers' de Saint-John Perse: une poésie du mouve-*

ment, Neuchâtel, La Baconnière, 1963.

Arthur J. Knodel, *Saint-John Perse: a Study of his Poetry*, Edinburgh, Edinburgh University Press, 1966.

Roger Little, *Saint-John Perse*, 'Athlone French Poets', London, The Athlone Press, 1973.

Jean-Pierre Richard, 'Saint-John Perse', in *Onze Etudes sur la poésie moderne*, Editions du Seuil, 1964.

FRANCIS PONGE (1899-   )

A. Works

Entretiens de Francis Ponge avec Philippe Sollers, Gallimard/ Editions du Seuil, 1970.

La Fabrique du pré, Geneva, Skira, 1971.

Le Grand Recueil, 3 vols.: I. *Lyres*, II. *Méthodes*, III. *Pièces*, Gallimard, 1961.

Méthodes, 'Idées', Gallimard, 1971.

Le Parti pris des choses, suivi de Proêmes, etc., 'Poésie', Gallimard, 1967.

Pièces, 'Poésie', Gallimard, 1971.

Le Savon, Gallimard, 1967.

Tome premier, Gallimard, 1965.

B. Criticism

Albert Camus 'Lettre au sujet du *Parti pris*', *Nouvelle Revue française*, No. 45 (September 1956), pp. 386-92.

Henri Maldiney, *Le Legs des choses dans l'œuvre poétique de Francis Ponge*, Lausanne, Editions L'Age d'Homme, 1974.

Jean-Pierre Richard, 'Francis Ponge', in *Onze Etudes sur la poésie moderne*, Editions du Seuil, 1964.

Jean-Paul Sartre, 'L'Homme et les choses', in *Situations*, Vol. I, Gallimard, 1947.

Marcel Spada, *Francis Ponge*, 'Poètes d'aujourd'hui', Seghers, 1974.

Jean Thibaudeau, *Ponge* (with selected texts), Gallimard, 1967.

PIERRE REVERDY (1889-1960)

A. Works

i. Poetry

Flaques de verre, Flammarion, 1972.
Main d'oeuvre, Mercure de France, 1949.
Plupart du temps, 2 vols., 'Poésie', Gallimard, 1969.
Sources du vent, précédé de La Balle au bond, 'Poésie',
    Gallimard, 1971.

ii. Prose

Cette Emotion appélee poésie: écrits sur la poésie (1932-1960),
    Flammarion, 1974.
En Vrac, Monaco, Editions du Rocher, 1956.
Le Gant de crin, Flammarion, 1968.
Le Livre de mon bord, Mercure de France, 1948.
Full details of Reverdy's writings may be found in Michael Bishop,
Pierre Reverdy: a Bibliography, London, Grant & Cutler, 1976.

B. Criticism

Peter Brunner, *Pierre Reverdy: De la Solitude au mystère*, Zurich,
    Juris Verlag, 1966.
Gaëtan Picon, 'Poétique et poésie de Pierre Reverdy', in *L'Usage
    de la lecture*, Vol. I, Mercure de France, 1960.
'Pierre Reverdy', issue of *Mercure de France*, No. 344 (January
    1962).
Jean-Pierre Richard, 'Pierre Reverdy', in *Onze Etudes sur la poésie
    moderne*, Editions du Seuil, 1964.
Anthony Rizzuto, *Style and Theme in Reverdy's 'Les Ardoises du
    toit'*, Alabama University Press, 1971.
Jean Rousselot and Michell Manoll, *Pierre Reverdy*, 'Poètes d'au-
    jourd'hui', Seghers, 1951.

JULES SUPERVIELLE (1884-1960)

A. Works

i. Poetry

La Fable du monde, Gallimard, 1938.
Le Forçat innocent, suivi de Les Armes inconnues

'Poésie', Gallimard, 1969.
Gravitations, précédé de Débarcadères, 'Poésie', Gallimard, 1966.
Naissances, Gallimard, 1952.
Oublieuse mémoire, Gallimard, 1949.

ii. Prose

Boire à la source: Confidences, Gallimard, 1952.
L'Enfant de la haute mer, Livre de poche, 1966.
Premiers pas de l'univers, Gallimard, 1950.

B. Criticism

Etiemble, *Jules Supervielle* (with selected texts), Gallimard, 1960.
Tatiana W. Greene, *Jules Supervielle,* Geneva, Droz/Paris, Minard, 1958.
J. A. Hiddleston, *L'Univers de Jules Supervielle,* Corti, 1965.
Claude Roy, *Jules Supervielle,* 'Poètes d'aujourd'hui', Seghers, 1949.
Christian Sénéchal, *Jules Supervielle, Poète de l'univers intérieur,* Les Presses du Hibou, 1939.
Robert Vivier, *Lire Supervielle,* Corti, 1971.

PAUL VALERY (1871-1945)

A. Works

La Jeune Parque, etc., 'Poésie', Gallimard, 1974.
Œuvres, ed. Jean Hytier, 2 vols., 'Bibliothèque de la Pléiade', Gallimard, 1957 and 1960.
Poésies (Album de vers anciens, Charmes, etc.), 'Poésie', Gallimard, 1966.

B. Criticism

Lucienne Julien Cain, 'Valery et l'utilisation du monde sensible', in *Trois Essais sur Paul Valéry,* Gallimard, 1958.
Christine M. Crow, *Paul Valéry: Consciousness and Nature,* Cambridge, Cambridge University Press, 1972.
Jacques Duchesne-Guillemin, *Etudes pour un Paul Valéry,* La Baconnière, Neuchâtel, 1964.
Jean Hytier, *La Poétique de Valéry,* Armand Colin, 1953.
James Lawler, *Lecture de Valéry: une étude de 'Charmes',* Presses Universitaires de France, 1963.
P.-O. Walzer, *La Poésie de Valéry,* Geneva, Cailler, 1953; and Geneva, Slatkine Reprints, 1966.

GENERAL WORKS

A. Anthologies

Jean-Louis Bédouin, *La Poésie surréaliste*, Seghers, 1964.

Georges-Emmanuel Clancier, *De Rimbaud au surréalisme: panorama critique*, Seghers, 1959.

Wallace Fowlie (ed.), *Mid-Century French Poets*, New York, Grove Press, 1955.

C. A. Hackett (ed.), *Anthology of Modern French Poetry*, Oxford, Blackwell, 1964; *New French Poetry: an anthology*, Oxford, Blackwell, 1973.

Anthony Hartley (ed.), *The Penguin Book of French Verse IV: the Twentieth Century*, Harmondsworth, Penguin Books, 1959.

Graham D. Martin (ed.), *Anthology of Contemporary French Poetry*, Edinburgh, Edinburgh University Press, 1972.

J. H. Matthews (ed.), *French Surrealist Poetry*, London, University of London Press, 1966.

Jean Paris (ed.), *Anthologie de la poésie nouvelle*, Monaco, Editions du Rocher, 1956.

B. Criticism

Marc Alyn, *La Nouvelle Poésie française*, Les Hautes Plaines de Mane, Robert Morel, 1968.

Gaston Bachelard, *L'Eau et les rêves*, Corti, 1942; *L'Air et les songes*, Corti, 1943; *La Terre et les rêveries de la volonté*, Corti, 1948; *La Terre et les rêveries du repos*, Corti, 1948; *La Poétique de l'espace*, Presses universitaires de France, 1957; *La Poétique de la rêverie*, Presses universitaires de France, 1961.

Anna Balakian, *Surrealism: the Road to the Absolute*, London, George Allen & Unwin, 1970.

E. M. Beaumont *et al.*, *Order and Adventure in Post-Romantic French Poetry*, Oxford, Blackwell, 1973.

Albert Béguin, *Poésie de la présence*, Editions du Seuil, 1957.

Yvon Belaval, *Poèmes d'aujourd'hui: essais critiques*, Gallimard, 1964.

Serge Brindeau *et al.*, *La Poésie contemporaine de langue française depuis 1945: études critiques*, Editions Saint-Germain des Prés, 1973.

Roger Caillois, *Art poétique*, Gallimard, 1958.

Mary Ann Caws, *The Poetry of Dada and Surrealism*, Princeton, N.J., Princeton University Press, 1970.

Georges-Emmanuel Clancier, *La Poésie et ses environs*, Gallimard, 1973.

Jean Cohen, *Structure du language poétique*, Flammarion, 1966.

Hugo Friedrich, *Die Struktur der modernen Lyrik*, Hamburg, Row'holt Verlag, 1956.

Jacques Garelli, *La Gravitation poétique*, Mercure de France, 1966.

Robert Gibson, *Modern French Poets on Poetry*, Cambridge, Cambridge University Press, 1961.

Edouard Glissant, *L'Intention poétique*, Editions du Seuil, 1969.

Leon-Gabriel Gros, *Poètes contemporains*, Cahiers du sud, 1951.

Michael Hamburger, *The Truth of Poetry*, Harmondsworth, Penguin Books, 1972.

Jean Hytier, *Le Plaisir poétique*, Presses universitaires de France, 1923.

Philippe Jaccottet, *L'Entretien des muses*, Gallimard, 1968.

Aron Kibedi-Varga, *Les Constantes du poème*, Den Haag, 1963.

James R. Lawler, *The Language of French Symbolism*, Princeton, N.J., Princeton University Press, 1969.

Henri Meschonnic, *Pour la poétique*, 3 vols., Gallimard, 1970-3.

Jules Monnerot, *La Poésie moderne et le sacré*, Gallimard, 1945.

Jean Onimus, *La Connaissance poétique*, Desclée de Brouwer, 1966.

Gaëtan Picon, *L'Usage de la lecture*, 2 vols., Mercure de France, 1960.

Georges Poulet, *Le Point de départ*, Plon, 1964.

Marcel Raymond, *De Baudelaire au surréalisme*, Corti, 1963.

Jean-Pierre Richard, *Poésie et profondeur*, Editions du Seuil, 1955; *Onze Etudes sur la poésie moderne*, Editions du Seuil, 1964.

Jean Rousselot, *Présences contemporaines: rencontres sur les chemins de la poésie*, Nouvelles Editions Debresse, 1958.

Ferdinand Simonis, *Nachsurrealistische Lyrik im zeitgenössischen Frankreich*, Heidelberg, Carl Winter, 1974.

Jean Starobinski, *La Relation critique*, Gallimard, 1970.

Claude Vigée, *Révolte et louanges*, Corti, 1962.

Jean Voellmy, *Aspects du silence dans la poésie moderne*, Zurich, Altorfer, 1952.

Bernard Weinberg, *The Limits of Symbolism*, Chicago, University of Chicago Press, 1966.

NOTES ON CONTRIBUTORS

DAVID BERRY is Lecturer in the Department of French at the University of Leeds. His publications include articles on Apollinaire, and a monograph on Diderot (1974). He is currently preparing a study of Apollinaire's poetry.

MICHAEL BISHOP is Lecturer in French at Dalhousie University, Nova Scotia, Canada. He is the author of essays on Stendhal, Reverdy and Jean-Pierre Burgart, and of a Bibliography of Reverdy (1976). He is currently preparing studies of the work of Reverdy, Denis Roche and other modern French poets.

MALCOLM BOWIE is Professor of French at Queen Mary College, London. He is the author of *Henri Michaux: a study of his literary works* (1973), and of *Mallarmé and the Art of being Difficult* (forthcoming). He is at present working in a study of Mallarmé.

NICK CAISTOR was until recently *lecteur* at the University of Besancon, and is writing a thesis on *Humanism in the Poetry of René Char*.

PIERRE CALDERON is French *lecteur* in the Filozofski Facultet, University of Zagreb, Yugoslavia. He recently completed his *maîtrise d'esthétique littéraire* with a dissertation on *L'Image chez Follain* and is now preparing a doctoral thesis on Follain's poetics.

ROGER CARDINAL lectures in French at the University of Kent at Canterbury. He is the author of *Surrealism: permanent revelation* (with Robert Stuart Short, 1970), and of books on Art Brut and the German Romantics. He is at present working on a book about the poetic imagination.

CHRISTINE M. CROW is Lecturer in French at the University of St Andrews. She has published several pieces on Valery, including a study of his conception of the creative mind, *Paul Valéry: Consciousness and Nature* (1972). She is currently preparing a book about his poetry.

IAN HIGGINS lectures in French at the University of St Andrews. He has published articles on Prévost and Verhaeren, and edited the volume has published articles on Prévost and Verhaeren, and edited the volume *Literature and the Plastic Arts 1880-1930* (1973). He is at present working on a monograph on Ponge and on an edition of *Le Parti pris des choses*.

ROGER LITTLE is Lecturer in French at the University of Southampton. His publications in Saint-John Perse include a *Word Index* (1965), a *Bibliography* (1971), a monograph (1973) and an annotated edition of *Exil* (1973), as well as numerous articles on and translations of the poetry. Other publications include articles on Rimbaud and a book on Apollinaire (1976). He is currently working on the *poème en prose* in general.

GRAHAM D. MARTIN is Lecturer in French at the University of Edinburgh. He has written on, and translated from, French poetry in numerous publications, including an annotated edition of Valéry's *Le Cimetière marin* (1971), an *Anthology of Contemporary French Poetry* (1972) and a translation of Louise Labé's *Sonnets* (with Peter Sharratt, 1973). He has also published translations of poems from the Chinese in *Love and Protest* (with John Scott, 1972). His book *Language, Truth and Poetry* (1975) is an investigation of the status of poetic language as a medium of truth.

JOHN D. PRICE has published articles on Rimbaud and Perse, and wrote his doctoral thesis on *Le Chemin du seuil: une analyse thématique de la poésie de Valéry, Jouve, Frénaud, Bonnefoy et Saint-John Perse*.

MICHAEL SHERINGHAM teaches French at the University of Kent. He has compiled a Bibliography of André Breton (1972), and is now engaged on a study of Breton's prose-works and articles on Michel Deguy and Sartre's views on modern poetry.